در این وقت یاری ده ای بی نیاز
که بی چاره مایم تو چاره ساز

Help me now, O all-sufficient One;
Needy am I, You are my shield and sun.

(A Persian Poem)

"Yea, let none that wait on Thee be ashamed." (Psalm 25:3)

THE UPPER HAND

GOD'S SOVEREIGNTY IN AFGHAN CAPTIVITY

JOEL DEHART

1994

Contact addresses: P.O. Box 1778   C/o D.M. De Hart
                   Islamabad   17-W.Cloverdale Ave.
                   PAKISTAN   Pine Hill, NJ 08021
                                         U.S.A.

Cover : design by Marie Dalton Lehmann
         front photograph by Nasrullah
         carpet photograph by Randy Salway

This orange and black striped carpet was woven in Sang-i Masha, Jaghori, Afghanistan by professional male carpet weavers. These carpets are called *gilims*. Most homes I visited during my six and a half months in the eastern part of Ghazni Province had carpets like these.

Inside cover by Sarah DeHart Raiter
Inside back cover by Mark Morris

PanGraphics (Pvt) Ltd., Islamabad

Contents

FOREWORD

Born in Pakistan in 1957, Joel DeHart, as far as nationality and heredity is concerned, is American. Yet having lived nearly all of his life in Pakistan, Joel has become not the ordinary American aid worker living overseas. In fact, Joel is often presumed to be Pakistani because of the way he lives, walks, talks, eats, sleeps, acts, dresses, and more than anything, because of the way that he relates to people. One could easily make a case that Joel is more Asian than American.

Joel is an English as a Second Language teacher in Islamabad, Pakistan, where he has worked since 1987. As a Christian layman working for World Relief, Joel serves his organization and God well. Joel doesn't just do his job, he loves his students--laying his life down for them, pouring his soul into theirs, sharing even his own self. Scripture talks about this kind of love, as exemplified by the self-sacrificial act of Jesus Christ's death on the cross:

"Greater love has no one than this,
that he lay down his life for his friends." John 15:13 (NIV)

The events that are recorded in this book depict merely one example of Joel's undying commitment to live an exemplary Christian life and to approach difficulties with peace, with perseverance, and with love. While serving as a translator in Afghanistan for a Texas veterinarian, Dr. William Lewis, Joel along with Dr. Lewis was taken hostage on the final day of their animal health training seminar. This book was drawn from Joel's personal journal which he penned while in captivity on scraps of paper and minuscule tablets.

"Mister Joel" (Joel DeHart) and "Doctar Saib" (Dr. William Lewis), as they are affectionately known in the central mountains of Afghanistan, became known throughout the region as persons of outstanding godly character. For many of their captors and friends, Joel and Doc were some of the first Christians whom they had met. A folklore about these two men spread for miles around as stories were told of their unwarranted captivity by rogue Mujahideen commanders.

During the six months in captivity, rumors as well as eye-witness accounts were spreading rampantly about Joel and Dr. Lewis. One day a villager from the north of Afghanistan came to me and reported some of the stories that were spreading throughout the country. He told me that everyone is saying Mr. Joel and Doc were being unjustly held as prisoners. "Mr. Joel and Doc are godly men. Everyone knows this. These two men only wanted to help poor villagers," he said. "In spite of their poor treatment, Mr. Joel is helping to bring in the harvest for his captor. He is even teaching the captor's children English." Thus the living witness of two faithful Christian laymen spread throughout a country barely exposed to Christianity.

Similar stories spread rapidly about family members of the captors who appeared at local "pharmacies" with prescriptions scribbled by Doc. In fact, Dr. Lewis was reported to have saved the life of one of the women in his captor's family. Dr. Lewis himself would become critically ill before his eventual release after three months of captivity.

The service of Dr. Lewis and Joel DeHart during their captivity is indelibly etched into Afghan history. The tragic, yet by God's hand triumphant, events of those six months spread over what seemed to be two lifetimes for most of us. The hostage incident and the eventual release of these two friends shaped my own personal spiritual development like no other single event in my Christian pilgrimage.

As a person responsible for facilitating their journey, I was devastated by my utter helplessness in the midst of their unfortunate detainment. I couldn't help but blame myself. Yet throughout the entirety of those long six months, God gave me the assurance that he would somehow prevail through it all. Never before had I experienced such complete dependence upon God's sustaining grace for such a prolonged period of time.

Realism told us that at any point we might receive the dreaded phone call indicating the news that we feared most--they were dead. At other times we imagined that the hostage crisis might continue for many years. But

God intervened and answered the prayers of thousands upon thousands of saints, some of whom prayed without ceasing.

In my own private devotions during those six months, I clung for dear life to I Corinthians 10:13, one of the first verses I memorized as a young adult.

"No temptation has seized you, except what is common to man. And God is faithful; he will not let you be tempted beyond what you can bear. But when you are tempted, he will also provide a way out so that you can stand up under it." (NIV)

Many of us hung on to God's promises from His Word as we wrote letters to Joel and Doc, sent care packages, negotiated with their captors, held prayer meetings, and at times simply survived.

As family and friends, we too often concentrated on our own pain and struggle--our own grief and loss. All the while, Doc was deteriorating physically and Joel was locked in a room, the key to which was held by his dear friends, the children-prison guards. Too often we selfishly asked the wrong questions of God.

Joel and Doc's captivity forced me to fall back on some advice received from a dear professor who shared with me how to deal with adversity.

Don't be afraid to ask, "Why, Lord?" But don't stop at this first question. Instead, we must allow God to **convert the question** *in our hearts from "Why, Lord?" to "Lord, how will you use this difficulty in my life? How do you want me to grow?"*

Many of us who walked through this crisis with Joel and Dr. Lewis have seen God convert the question in our own lives. As one reads Joel's account of those 180 days of captivity, one can't help but see God's hand at work in circumstances, through Joel's and other lives, and by direct intervention.

As we try to ask, "Why did it all happen?" we are forced to look at Joel's words and say,

God has the upper hand,
No matter what the plans of man.

iii

He rules and reigns above,
And does His will.

Truly the question, "Why, Lord?" has been converted in my own heart to, "Lord, why were you so gracious and merciful?"

If nothing else, this book is one man's expression of God's sovereignty. God demonstrated His sovereignty to Joel from the depths of a flea-infested home prison to the heights of the snowy mountain-top military base. As you read the pages of his journal, Joel would insist that you look not to the man of Joel DeHart, but that you would see Joel's sovereign Lord.

For He certainly is Lord!

Mark Morris

PREFACE

My reason for writing details of my time as a hostage in Afghanistan is to tell of God's goodness to me. Like David in Psalm 142:7, I made a promise to God:

"Set me free from my distress;
then in the assembly of your people I will praise you
because of your goodness to me."

God did great things for me and I want to tell others.

To those people who worked for my release--whether interceding before the throne of almighty God, or doing any practical thing which might lead to a solution--I'm grateful to you. I owe you my side of the story.

Finally, I want to share things I learned of language, culture, and a closer walk with God to any who may benefit.

The account of my six months as a captive is in the form of a journal with entries for each day. I was able to keep a diary all the time I was there.

I have also included some notes from the *"Hostage Log"* that Mark Morris kept in Pakistan as he and others worked for my freedom. These notes appear in boxes at the end of the corresponding day in my journal.

The journal account is followed by an epilogue, and then **"Writings from Patu"**. This appendix consists of things I wrote while I was at the soldier's base in Patu.

I have changed some names in the story. I have written **Persian** or
Hazaragi words in italics in a simplified kind of transliteration.

I have really appreciated help from Mark Morris, Rose Cardenas, Brent
Jones, Amina Corley, Mike Raiter, Barbara Rasmussen and Marie Lehmann
in putting this book together.

Joel DeHart
May, 1994
Islamabad, Pakistan

INTRODUCTION

Dr. Bill Lewis and I left Quetta, Pakistan, on June 20, 1991 heading for Afghanistan. Our assignment was to train a team of animal vaccinators and begin a program to vaccinate all the sheep, goats, and cows in the district of Jaghori in the Ghazni province of central Afghanistan. We were scheduled to return after two or possibly three weeks. We would be staying in the district capital of Sang-i Masha (Trigger Rock) and working in the surrounding area. The eventual goal was to have the team, over a period of many months, vaccinate all the animals in the scattered regions of this district.

Our host, traveling companion, and the Animal Health Project Field Coordinator was Engineer Abdul Kabir Shahi. He spoke English quite well. He had studied engineering in Czechoslovakia. Several months earlier he had taken the Global Partners representative in Pakistan on a successful fact-finding tour of the same district. Our liking for Engineer Kabir and his family grew over the weeks that we traveled, worked, and lived with him.

Global Partners is an aid organization registered in England. Desiring to help out in some way the suffering people in Afghanistan, they began doing research on the situation there. They became concerned with the plight of the people who occupy the most remote areas of the country including the central region of Afghanistan, known as the *Hazarajat*. This area is largely inhabited by the *Hazara* people, a group of three to five million people who have a long history of oppression by the other peoples of the area. There are several reasons for this oppressive treatment. Firstly, from a religious standpoint, the Hazara are **Shia** Muslims while the majority of Afghans are **Sunnis**. Secondly, from a social standpoint, the Hazaras are a distinct people group with their own dialect, **Hazaragi**. Historically they have performed many of the menial services for the nation's population. Economically they are poor largely due to the shortage of arable land in the mountainous region where they live. Furthermore, the Hazara people are probably descendants of the Mongols of Central Asia. Memories of the atrocities of Mongol armies discourage amiable relations with other people groups.

Dr. Bill Lewis is a veterinarian who recently retired after over 30 years of practice in Texas. He was the designer, trainer and organizer of the Animal Health Project under the supervision of Global Partners. I was accompanying Dr. Bill as a translator and facilitator.

Before our capture, we were able to start a program that we felt could continue successfully after we left. We had trained ten vaccinators. Of these we had selected one man to be assistant coordinator, one to receive para-medical training, and others for various positions. We enjoyed traveling around the countryside in the role of aid workers. Almost everyone we met seemed friendly and appreciative. We felt privileged to visit this beautiful area and be of some help to truly needy people. We felt that we could leave with a heightened understanding that would be useful for future assistance.

Then, suddenly, the whole picture changed! In seconds we turned from relief workers into hostages.

At first, we felt that our captivity spelled the ruin of everything we had worked for in our project--and maybe even the whole effort of Global Partners to alleviate suffering in Afghanistan. But later on in captivity, and now from the vantage point of freedom, we began to see that this experience opened up many new opportunities. Something was lost, but much was gained. I was able to keep a diary during my captivity. I am using this as a basis for this journal to give a record of day-to-day events, observations, and feelings.

MAPS

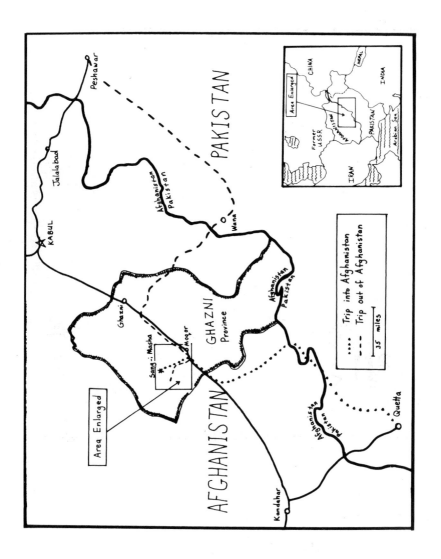

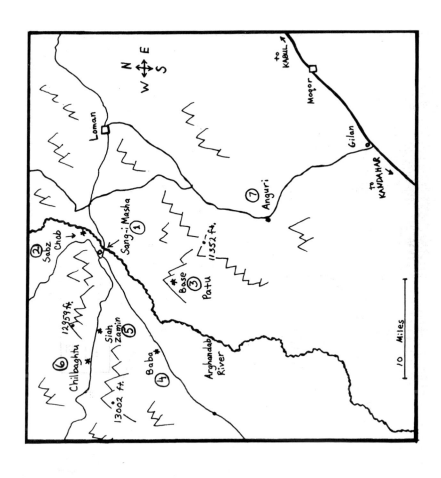

JAGHORI Area of Ghazni Province

1. JOURNAL

A. Kidnapped!　　　(Sabz Chob and on)

July 6-24, 1991

Saturday, July 6

We had been living in Engineer Kabir's mud "castle" in Sang-i Masha for the past two weeks as we conducted our training program. Alim, the friend who brought me home late last night from a wedding in upper Sabz Chob, slept in the guest room with Doc and me. He was working on fixing the puncture in his motorcycle tire as I left the house for my morning meditations in a field.

Breakfast featured the usual bread and tea. Doc often supplemented his breakfast surreptitiously with pork sausages in small cans that he had brought along!

As usual we gathered our equipment together and went out to meet the students/vaccinators by the hired jeep at 8 a.m. None of them was supposed to know it, but this would be our last day with the team. We had purposely not disclosed the day of our departure to anyone.

Wahid, the assistant coordinator, had lined us up to work today in lower Sabz Chob. We had covered the upper part of the valley the day before. It took us about half an hour by jeep to get to the place where we started vaccinating.

THE UPPER HAND

We had a nice morning break in front of one home with an especial abundance of mulberry trees. The mulberry season was just beginning. Locals typically shake branches above huge sheets connected to poles on both ends. Then they collect these ripe mulberries and rinse them in the clear cool water flowing by in channels coming from underground *karezes*, tunnels dug horizontally into hill sides to inner water sources. Then it's time for a "belly full of mulberries"--which traditionally must be followed by a drink of buttermilk for strength and good digestion!

Locals benefited another way from the mulberry trees. In hot weather they would put freshly-picked mulberry leaves under their hats, saying this helped them feel cooler. I didn't notice much difference!

Back to Engineer Kabir's home for lunch. Students and trainers always ate together. Often after the stew and tea we would enjoy short siestas before getting back to work. Each day was beautiful--cloudless, warm in the day, but cool at night. There had been no rain for months, but an especially heavy snowfall the past winter had made for plenty of water and good harvests.

I waited a long time by a stream with most of the students while Doc and several others covered an area. On Doc's return we were called to visit what turned out to be a dying cow. If we had been called earlier, we might have saved its life. This particular home was a beautiful and ancient fortress. A little boy and girl with blue eyes watched us intently. I took their picture.

We went back to the jeep to load up supplies. It was about 4 p.m. There was only a little time before we would be heading home. I was already thinking of the bazaar trip I had planned to pick up some souvenirs before our departure the following day.

A racing engine drew my attention and I looked up to see a jeep of armed men top the hill to the north of us. "They're soldiers", a student told me. I tried not to stare since I didn't want to draw their attention. But they headed straight for us. The jeep screeched to a halt and the seven armed men jumped out. Five men cocked their kalashnikovs. One had a "rocket".

"*Shor na khor!* Don't move!" one of them shouted.

2

Kidnapped!

Everyone was obviously surprised and scared. None of our students was armed. There was nothing they could do. Latif of Tailoom, the ruffian of the soldier group, gave me a whack on the neck.

"Hurry up! Get into our jeep!" he yelled.

Several soldiers had pulled Doc to their jeep. Others were busy gathering all of our equipment. For some reason they forced two of the students into the jeep with us, but after we took off and traveled some distance, they stopped, cuffed the boys several times and told them to get out.

We continued at breakneck speed. The soldiers kept looking back. Haidari, whom I later discovered was Commander Wasim's body guard and representative in this group of Hizb-i Islami soldiers, was on his walkie talkie shouting exultantly, "Mission successful! Mission successful! We got the two foreigners and are now on our way back."

Soon the soldiers noticed that our jeep was on their tail with the driver and students.

"If that jeep comes any closer, we'll blast it with a rocket," shouted Haidari.

It turned out that our rented jeep couldn't match the speed of the newer model Russian jeep we were in now. Our captors could make good their getaway.

We rode by some shops in a part of the Sang-i Masha bazaar. I recognized some people and saw them looking at us. Then we passed Qala-i Rais, the home of Engineer Kabir's brother-in-law. A group of our friends was standing outside. Doc waved at them and was immediately struck from behind by another soldier. We crossed the bridge over the Arghundab River and turned off on the less-traveled Patu road, heading south-west. From here on it was new territory for us.

After about a half hour, everyone noticeably relaxed. Rough Latif took Doc's and my watches and Doc's glasses. We could hear the boys in the back fishing through all our supplies and my day pack--which contained most of my money. Arif, sitting up front, offered us cigarettes. Then he said, "Which one of you speaks Persian?" I said I did and we talked a little.

3

THE UPPER HAND

The driver stopped at a stream to pour cool water over the steaming radiator. Haidari wanted to give us a body search. He took Doc's penknife and pen. He took my camera (and later was asking me questions about just how it worked). "What's in your other pocket?" "Money," I replied. "I'm sure you need that, too." But he said, "No. You can keep that."

The jeep was still going fast as we bumped along the rough dirt road. On one downhill stretch too much speed made it careen wildly to stay on the mountain track. Doc and I didn't know what was happening or why. We prayed together in the jeep and encouraged each other that God was in control. In the two weeks we had been in Afghanistan we had not been around armed groups. We had seen people with guns here and there but we felt distanced from the fighting groups. After all, we had just come to help poor people. Politics and the local factions had seldom entered our thoughts or discussions.

Arif asked, "Are you okay? Is there anything you need?"

I said, "You took Doc's glasses. He really needs them to see."

After some discussion and persuasion, Latif was finally forced to give up one of his prizes. We thanked them.

After riding for about an hour and a half, we drove off the road, down a hill, and parked by a small group of houses. The supplies were quickly taken into a house and the jeep was covered with a tarp. It was time to walk--and the soldiers told us we were only going a short distance. This little settlement was called Dodal.

We walked for a good two hours. Doc was tired after the many climbs and descents. We followed a small valley and then crossed a rocky plateau. Soldiers along the way had let us stop frequently to catch our breath. Once they gave us a handful of dried fruit. The conversation was also instructive. "How many dollars did you bring with you and where are they?" "What is your project budget?" "Was there any money in your bag?" "We are just taking you to protect you from another group who wants to kidnap and harm you. Don't worry."

It was dusk as we approached a lone home and were told to turn into the guest room. This long basement was carpeted with the typical red and orange striped wool *gilams*, rugs.

4

Kidnapped!

I was angry inside. I was used to being treated as a respected guest, but now I was forced to obey anything these men with guns said. What were these guys doing to us? They should be ashamed of their actions! Doc, however, didn't evidence these emotions. Whenever they did something for him, he would say a loud "thank you" in English, or *tashakur*, the Persian equivalent. Tea soon appeared. The soldiers were obviously tired, too. They hung their guns up and chatted among themselves.

After some time supper appeared. It was my second and Doc's first experience of eating the favorite Hazara dish called *qurti*. I quite enjoyed the broken bread soaked in buttermilk. There was a depression in the middle of the contents for hot, melted butter. One such large bowl is supposed to serve four or five people. Thin, dry bread, about one and a half feet in diameter, was also served. This dry bread was to break up into small pieces and then dip into the butter or it was used to scoop up some of the soaked bread from the bowl. Doc didn't take to this as much as I did.

The men arranged bedding on the floor after tea. We went outside for a visit to the wide open bathroom before settling down. A soldier with his kalashnikov accompanied us.

Much excitement was aroused when a poisonous spider, called a *ghondal*, appeared in the brush that made up the ceiling. The men didn't have time to hit it before it ran off to another hiding place.

Doc went right to sleep. I slept fitfully. My heart was pounding as I tried to trust in God, but kept thinking and worrying about what might happen.

I later found out that our seven captors were each from a different place. They were also from two different political parties--Akhund Salim's *Hizb-i Islami* (Islamic Party, hereafter referred to as "HIA"), and Wasim's *Nahzat-i Islami* (Islamic Organization).

Sunday, July 7

We were up with the soldiers at the first light of dawn. They did their ablutions and said their morning prayers. Then tea and bread appeared. Soon after, they motioned that we were going. On with our shoes and off

THE UPPER HAND

to the next unknown destination. The next hour was a steep climb. We rested frequently. We were glad the soldiers weren't in a hurry and Doc commented about how good it was that we had been walking a lot in the last two weeks to get in shape.

We stopped at a spring for a cool, refreshing drink. Then we arrived at the top of the mountain to the sound of several big guns. We saw three small stone-and-mud buildings--and several large guns. This was the *paigah*, the Hizb-i Islami military "base", one of several in the district. The guns were fired to welcome us, and, as we found out later, to impress us that they really worked!

Several armed soldiers quickly gathered around and greetings were exchanged. We were ushered into the "office". Tea and thick bread soon appeared. After some more discussion, all seven soldiers who had taken us left. Clearly we were now in the charge of the commander of the base. This man was known as "Doctor" because he had worked for years as a dispenser in a drug store in Kabul. His legs had been badly deformed by polio in his childhood. Indeed, we were amazed that he could get around as well as he did.

The office was a room where about ten men could sleep. It had two windows with glass panes. There were nails on most of the poplar rafters to hang guns or *shajoors*, a kind of bandoleer for holding up to four kalashnikov bullet cases. On one wall was a large picture of the Hizb-i Islami leader, Engineer Gulbuddin Hikmatyar. He seemed to watch everything seriously! Beside him there was a Persian couplet written in large, colored letters. It read:

The tulips in this field are still covered in blood,
Don't put down your shield because the war is still on.

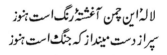

6

Kidnapped!

Doctor turned out to be a gracious and cheery host. He went out of his way to ensure our comfort in these primitive surroundings. After a rest, he had a soldier bring fresh mulberries for us. When we finished this treat, it was lunch time. Rice cooked with vegetable oil followed by tea.

In the afternoon two soldiers accompanied us on a walk over to an abandoned farm with many loaded mulberry trees. We snacked on mulberries and talked. The soldiers told of their rough experiences while working in Iran. They told of the neglect of their region, and how they had received no aid from anyone.

One of the first verses that Doc grabbed a hold of after our capture was Philippians 4:6 and 7.

> *"Be careful for nothing; but in every thing by prayer and supplication with thanksgiving let your requests be made known unto God.*
> *And the peace of God, which passeth all understanding, shall keep your hearts and minds through Christ Jesus."*

We did make our requests known to God, and we did experience a special peace from Him. I don't think it was a coincidence that I had just finished teaching Philippians in Islamabad.

We walked back to the base and sat on the roof of the main building and watched as Doctor and one of the boys worked at cleaning the big guns. Time was dragging. As evening approached, we ate supper on the roof. Once again it was rice cooked with vegetable oil followed by tea. Doctor had spoons brought for us although everyone else just ate with their hands.

The night was quite chilly. The base owned two quilts. Doctor had these brought for Doc and me, and he arranged our "beds" there on the roof with the other soldiers. The stars shone brilliantly in the dark sky above us.

Doctor assured us today that he was on our side. A terrible wrong had been done. He would see that we were released soon--preferably peacefully,

THE UPPER HAND

but if that didn't work, then he would get us out secretly. There was some discussion about us today over the walkie talkies at the usual prearranged times for keeping in contact with commanders in other areas.

Monday, July 8

As usual, we were up at dawn with the soldiers. Shortly after, tea and bread were served. We walked down the partially constructed jeep road with Doctor and Khaliqdad, a foul-mouthed local sub-commander. Together they discussed how they would work to free us. They told us not to tell anyone else of this discussion.

As we walked up the trail, I remember singing Isaiah 40:31.

"But they that wait upon the Lord shall renew their strength;
they shall mount up with wings as eagles;
they shall run, and not be weary;
and they shall walk and not faint."

Many times we knew renewed strength when our own had gone.

After some rest back at the office, Doctor informed us that, if we wanted, we could go down to the river valley below and enjoy some good food and an excursion that day. Doc wasn't keen on the thought of climbing all the way back up! But he was game for an outing and something to keep our minds occupied. We took the base's donkey along since Doctor assured us that it could carry Doc Lewis up the mountain on the way back!

The five of us took off--Doctor, with his pronounced limp, Khaliqdad, a soldier, and the two of us. Our three guards were armed with kalashnikovs and Doctor had at least one hand grenade in his vest.

A steep descent brought us to the river level. Doctor led us immediately to the home of **Numainda**, the title of a man of some means. He ordered lunch and soon pillows and rugs were placed out in the open under loaded apricot trees. The setting was idyllic. It wasn't long before I was up the trees enjoying a feast of apricots! Doc ate some, too, and discovered that the acid that had bothered his stomach with apricots in the US didn't affect him here.

Kidnapped!

Tea appeared. Then an omelette, bread, and fresh mulberries. Soon we were ready to move on down the river. We arrived at a crossing place. The bridge had been washed away. The current was strong but the locals seemed to have no problem. Nevertheless it was decided that Doc should cross on the donkey. Fateful decision! The donkey had no sooner come to knee-deep water when he faced the current broadside and was swept over. The audience let out howls of laughter! Doc was thoroughly drenched--but remained his cheerful self. When we reached the other side, we walked to a nearby house where Doc put on some borrowed clothes and hung his wet fatigues and shirt out to dry. His little notebook had been soaked but the writing was still legible.

After a nap and more fresh mulberries, we walked on down the valley to a nice place to swim! I joined some kids who were swimming there--then had a bath with a borrowed bar of soap. We had tea at another home before walking along farther to the place where we began our ascent.

Doctor encouraged Doc Lewis to ride the donkey. But Doc felt he was too heavy. The trail, too, proved to be very steep. We made it back to the base after nightfall. We were just in time for rice and bread with the gang. We were delighted to find out that in our absence, a messenger had come from Engineer Kabir's house bringing us toothbrushes, toothpaste, soap, and a change of clothes each!

Tuesday, July 9

After breakfast Doc and I caught up on some more sleep. This time proved to be good for meditation and prayer as well. I began a habit of daily praying for each family member, each co-worker back in Islamabad, and each church member.

I looked at some Persian books that Rasooli had brought for me. Rasooli was the man immediately responsible for the affairs of the base. Later I would come to see him as a true friend. But now he was just another of our captors. He had sprained his ankle so had it wrapped up in a poultice of egg, salt, and goat hair.

9

THE UPPER HAND

We were taken to another spring for baths. The water was cold, but it felt so good to be clean! I washed my clothes and stretched them on a sunny rock to dry while I climbed a tree and snacked on mulberries.

Doctor had bought some eggs especially for us and we had an omelette lunch. After another rest we went with some soldiers again to the "park", my name for the abandoned farm. On the way I climbed a rocky crag with Rasooli. He told stories of the fighting that had gone on in these hills as the combined enemy parties had time and again tried to conquer the base and wipe out the Hizb-i Islami party. They hadn't been able to do it.

I consider myself a good rock climber--but I was scared to follow Rasooli, with his bad ankle, up to the highest point! He told me how a lion used to live in the rocky crevices, but when soldiers inhabited the area, it left for quieter places. Bears also had lived there, he said.

As we sat in the park, several men approached us from the direction of the base. Our guards were excited. It must be someone important, I thought. It was Mamur Ahmad, a brave and famous local commander, they informed me. He had long hair and an authoritative manner. He sat down with us and began discussing our "problem". He talked about how he would try to help and said that he would send us a message the next day. I asked him about his education and he said that he had studied in Kabul and then worked as a meteorologist for the government before the Soviet invasion.

Mamur Ahmad left us with a new hope.

One of the first songs that came to mind in these first days was, "*He giveth more grace.*" What a comfort these words were!

> "*He giveth more grace when the burdens grow greater,*
> *He sendeth more strength when the labors increase;*
> *To added affliction He addeth His mercy,*
> *To multiplied trials, His multiplied peace.*
>> *His love has no limit;*
>> *His grace has no measure,*
>> *His power has no boundary known unto men;*
>> *For out of His infinite riches in Jesus,*
>> *He giveth, and giveth, and giveth again!*

Kidnapped!

When we have exhausted our store of endurance,
When our strength has failed ere the day is half done,
When we reach the end of our hoarded resources,
Our Father's full giving is only begun. "

Back to the base for supper. Guess what we had? Yes! Rice and bread. A new group of soldiers had just arrived so it made about 20 of us in all.

In my time at the base I had become friends with the old cook. He was the only salaried worker at the base--with a salary of about 100,000 Afghanis ($100) a year. He had spent many years in Pakistan so spoke a mixture of Urdu and Panjabi well. I called him *chacha*, or "Uncle". One of the reasons for our friendship was that he was the only one really busy doing things. The soldiers would spend most of their time chatting and gossiping!

As usual, Doc and I ended the day with prayer together. I was somewhat discouraged since I had specifically prayed that this day would be the day of our release.

Wednesday, July 10

After breakfast we went to the nearby spring. Following a rest, a boy of 18 appeared and we chatted for a while about English, which he really wanted to learn. Doc and I went out to the farther spring to snack on mulberries and kill time. Doc told me about his veterinary business. We were back at the base by 11:30 and the others were already eating lunch. We waited for a special fare: omelette and bread.

After a couple of hours, Doctor appeared and informed us that he had talked to Rasooli and had permission to take us to his home where we could get better food and care until we were freed. We left with a soldier who turned out to be likable and gregarious. On the way he told us of how he had worked in Iran for six months and, on his return, all his savings were stolen by Pashtun bandits who often prey on Hazaras on their way in or out of the Hazarajat.

THE UPPER HAND

We must have walked for three hours. Doc was exhausted. We arrived around six at a huge house which was still under construction. We had tea there as we rested in the shade of the thick walls. Kids brought small poplar branches for us to use to keep the flies away.

Doctor ushered us to his nearby home where we sat to meet some of the neighbors and eat apricots. One of the elders there had served in the Pakistan army for many years and knew Urdu along with a smattering of English. What a wonderful feeling of relief when attention was turned to some men approaching and I recognized Alim, the son of the *tahweeldar*, store keeper, who had brought me back from the wedding a few days ago. He brought us another parcel of clothes and some cooked chicken and cake from Engineer Kabir. He also brought the message that Engineer Kabir would probably come the next day to secretly meet with us. I felt almost as good as if we had been freed!

The warm and happy feeling was reinforced when we were taken to a large home in that village, where a feast was prepared. It seemed like all the leaders of the community were invited. I thought the celebration and honor were for us--but later learned that the occasion was the return from Iran of one of the men in the family.

Doc and I were given seats of honor. I sat next to Alim. The atmosphere was friendly and many of the men were expressing sorrow that we had been taken captive when we had come for the best interests of the people. I wrote a note in front of everyone for Alim to take to Engineer Kabir. I wrote that we wanted to see him very much.

When the meal and tea were over, we were led back to the big, unfinished house where we would spend the night.

Thursday, July 11

We rose early and said good-bye to Alim, who was heading back to Sang-i Masha on his motorcycle. Breakfast tea was supplemented by the goodies that Engineer Kabir had sent. I climbed the nearby rocky hill for my morning meditations--feeling almost free now.

Kidnapped!

We wiled away many hours talking to Ali Daryab and Muhammad Ali, boys who were curious and kind. It was nice to be able to explain some aspects of the Good News.

The architect and builder of the house we were now staying in was Juma Khan. He and his sons (15 and 10 years old) had been building this edifice for the last couple years and now it was nearing completion. The walls were about two and a half feet thick. The first four feet were made of stone--to withstand the melting snow of winter. On top of this were the thick *paksa* mud walls. *Paksa* walls are different from mud brick walls. Mud is mixed to just the right consistency and plopped down in the proper place. This kind of construction takes longer--since only about one and a half feet can be added per day due to the softness of the mud. But these walls are more durable than mud brick walls. Natives claim that they will withstand fire from rockets and heavy guns.

The rooms on the first story had dome roofs made of thin mud bricks stacked against each other in arches. Juma Khan explained that this method was fairly new in Jaghori--but it was more economical than using poplar beams. Furthermore, rooms with dome roofs contained the heat better in the winter. The roof of the second story used the common poplar cross beams on which brush was stacked, then grass, then mud, and, finally, mud plaster mixed with salt for a hard, rain-resistant finish.

The downstairs rooms were for animals, with one for the family in the winter. The second story, with spaces for big windows to catch the breeze, was for summer living and guests.

Most of Juma Khan's wheat was ready to harvest--so he was busy with his sickle most of the day. I looked around the fields that were newly cultivated. Crops could be grown here because of the *karez*, horizontal well, that he had dug many feet back into the hillside. Gunpowder from shells and bombs that hadn't exploded was in plentiful supply in Afghanistan. This was used to blast tunnels in the rock for the *karezes*. The trickle of water collected at night in an *ahoor*, irrigation pond, which the farmer would open up at different times and channel into different fields.

Juma Khan had planted mostly wheat, but then there were some cherry seedlings, poplars, as well as mulberry, almond, peach and apricot trees.

13

THE UPPER HAND

Doc and I were outside in the late afternoon when Engineer Kabir and Sufi (a respected elder from Sang-i Masha) arrived. There was an air of secrecy as they discussed things for a long time with the locals out of our earshot. Finally, we were summoned to join them for tea in Juma Khan's house. They looked tired and worried. They were very apologetic about what had happened. Their coming was a relief to us and we expected them to be confident and have good news for us. But this was not the case. They spoke of the complexity of the situation and said that they hoped to work something out in a couple of days. Sufi noticed that Doc's watch was gone. Sufi insisted on giving his valued "Seiko 5" watch to Doc.

Without warning our tea party was rudely interrupted. Latif of Tailoom, the ruffian of several days ago, suddenly burst into the room, gun in hand and scarf wrapped around his head.

"Come on! Get moving!" he bellowed.

We were all in shock. My heart sank. Engineer and Sufi said nothing. We moved to get our tooth paste, soap, and a few other things. Doctor made a costly mistake. He cocked his gun. Later he was punished for being on our side. All he could do was tell Latif, "Treat them well."

Another soldier was outside. We were hustled along quickly past a few homes, across the stream, up to the road where a jeep was waiting. It was dusk and the men in the jeep were in a hurry. As we took off, a man with long hair sitting next to the driver looked around at us and asked if we were okay.

"I think he's a nice man," I remarked to Doc.

Little did I realize then that this was Akhund Salim, the local Hizb-i Islami commander, and our co-captor. I was to get to know him much better later.

We only traveled a short distance when the jeep stopped. I recognized Tahir, our host from last night, as he gave a warm greeting to Akhund Salim. Doc and I wondered whether our dinner last night was somehow connected with our re-capture today.

At the top of the pass on the way out of Patu we picked up another soldier. Apparently he had been dropped off there for security. Then, a little later, this soldier and Akhund Salim got out at a village and we continued on. The road was rough and we traveled for several hours. The jeep had

Kidnapped!

obviously overheated. On one upgrade, the jeep stalled and wouldn't start. The driver and the others fiddled with the ignition wires for some time, and finally the engine roared to life.

The road wasn't familiar. We were hungry and thirsty--but more than that, discouraged and let down. We pulled up to the big doors of a fortified house. It was at least three hours after nightfall. Soon we were let inside and guided up to a richly carpeted and decorated guest room. The soldiers were tired and stretched out. Hot milk and bread appeared, and then an argument began. The soldiers tried to convince the house owners to keep us for a few days until our future was decided. The hosts stubbornly refused again and again. Finally, young Latif had an idea and left for about an hour. When he returned, he told us to go. Another home had agreed to take us.

We walked about 15 minutes in the dark. I asked if we could stop to go to the bathroom. That was no problem. When we were finished, Latif searched me and Doc again, taking the rest of my money and the watch that Doc had just received from Sufi. I was incensed.

When we entered the smaller house, we had to wait while the sleeping women and children and supplies were emptied out of the room that would be ours. Our new hosts turned out to be an elderly couple with four sons: Jalal, Khudadad, Dadmurad, and Zahoor. The father was traditionally and respectfully referred to as Atee Jalal, the father of Jalal, his oldest son. (It is more respectful to call an older man "Father of ___" his oldest son, than by his real name. If a man has only daughters, he may be called the father of his oldest daughter.) The settlement was known as Safed Sang, White Stone, in the Baba valley.

Pleasantries were exchanged. The soldiers explained to our hosts that we would only be there for a few days. As they sat around talking, I made a request.

"You have taken us hostage," I remarked. "But you are Muslims. Why do you steal our things, too? Please give me back my money."

Latif just laughed. "It's only enough to buy a few cigarettes," he said.

I had been counting on a sense of justice and a fear of God in someone else in the group to put pressure on Latif to release the money. But no one seemed to care. I was filled with helpless rage. Somehow I got into a

15

THE UPPER HAND

discussion of love as the essential characteristic of a Christian. I talked for quite some length about Christianity with these men. Dadmurad, better known by his chosen name, "Ahmadi", expressed the most interest.

The soldiers refused offers to stay. After they had left, the brothers brought in sleeping mats for us. The last thing they said to us was, "This room has fleas. There's some flea powder on the shelf if you need it."

Friday, July 12

All day we were locked inside this room. It was about 10 feet by 20 feet. There was one small window through which we could look out on to the area in front of the house and into the apricot and mulberry tree garden. Our hosts told us that we could only look out of the windows from a distance. No one should be able to see our faces.

This confinement was new and difficult. I mixed naps with reading a Persian book and pacing around the room. Doc and I spent time talking. And we would pray together whenever either one suggested it. This valley was hotter than the other places we had been. Hence flies were in abundance. It was really too hot to rest with a sheet over my whole body--but the sweat was worth the relief from pesky flies. We looked forward to dusk when the buzzing would die down and the flies would either leave or settle on the ceiling.

There was a kind of poem hanging on the wall that grabbed my attention.

LEARN FROM ALI PURE AND SINCERE ACTIONS

1. The biggest sin is fear.
2. The best relaxation is work.
3. The worst evil is hopelessness.
4. The highest valor is patience.
5. The best teacher is experience.
6. The biggest secret is death.
7. The greatest honor is faith.

Kidnapped!

> 8. The biggest profit is a virtuous son.
> 9. The greatest gift is forgiveness.
> 10. The greatest wealth is self-confidence.

We had a simple lunch around two. Father and sons were working hard on building another house some distance away. They were involved in a land dispute and it was imperative that they build this home in a matter of days.

In the afternoon unexpected relief came in the form of patients! They had heard that there was a doctor in the house. (Of course, these people must have been from the inner circle of the family's relatives and friends.) There were stomach, eye, allergy, and other problems. Human contact helped time pass and helped us forget our own sorrows. Doc was always glad to see patients and felt that it was important to help people when he could.

After dark one of the sons took us outside for a short walk and a bathroom visit. During the day if we needed to use the facilities we would knock on our door. Someone would open it and we would wrap ourselves in a shawl and go either to the garden or to the outhouse.

We had a supper of rice and tea by lantern light--then retired.

Saturday, July 13

We had a good sleep--but then slept quite a lot during the day. We managed to go out to the bathroom about five times today.

We had mulberries and then rice and spinach for lunch.

Ahmadi was home most of the day. We only found out that night that it was because his wife was in labor with a firstborn! Anyway, he was in our room for some time and we had further discussions about the West and our faith. Some patients appeared after lunch. When the other men returned from work, we had some more discussions. We were beginning to know this family as real people.

17

THE UPPER HAND

Sunday, July 14

We didn't sleep too well last night. Fleas were bothering me. Also, there was lots of noise and activity outside. Finally at 1 or 2 a.m., Ahmadi's wife gave birth to a healthy little girl.

Afghans love injections. Almost everyone knows how to give them. And the syringe is usually a plastic, disposable type which is "re-sterilized" in hot water before the next use. Before the birth, Ahmadi had brought several ampules to show Doc--asking what they were and when to use them. He had purchased them from the local medicine seller, "doctor". Doc didn't encourage the use of any of them.

The family was gravely concerned today because the placenta had not come out. They wanted to do more injections but Doc kept encouraging them to give the new mother nourishing food and let her move around. They came to us frequently for advice, and we could see them weighing what we said with their traditional knowledge and the instructions of the older ladies! Doc was never asked to take a look at the new mother.

In the morning I had a good time of meditation and prayer. I thought of God's people meeting in different places. We had no Bible or written material with us except for my little pocket notebook (which I had begun to use as a diary).

We had *qurti* , bread soaked in buttermilk, for lunch. Doc had difficulty stomaching it.

Later I noticed the jeep driver and some other soldiers outside the house. I tried to peep cautiously--but the driver later told me that he had seen me in the window! We felt a mixture of excitement and fear. We hoped their presence might mean something good for us.

Our patients this afternoon turned out to be the father and mother of Latif--the soldier who stole my money and Doc's watch. They were the parents of Ahmadi's wife! We felt we had an opportunity to follow Christ in returning good for evil.

We went out for a short walk after dark. We are learning to be content and God is helping us in our thoughts. That night the men told us of a meeting in Sang-i Masha about our situation. They said that an amount of money was being demanded. Khudadad, the second oldest brother who

18

Kidnapped!

functioned as the Hizb-i Islami sub-commander of Baba, told us that they expected to hear something soon about our release. "If we don't hear anything in three days, I will go to Sang-i Masha myself and find out how things are," he said.

Monday, July 15

As usual I began the morning with stretching exercises, push-ups, running in place, etc. We went out to wash up in the nearby *karez* and use the bathroom. The sugar was gone, so it was unsweetened tea and bread for breakfast. We realized that sugar was a luxury for most of the people in the area.

Outside in front of the house nine men gathered this morning for a meeting. I listened carefully but couldn't make out any of the conversation. The men told us later that we'd be released tonight. Commander Khudadad, who had studied martial arts while working in Iran for many years, came in and talked with us for a while. He spoke of what he called the "hopeless" situation in his country. "You wouldn't believe the things I've seen in the fighting here," he said. "I've seen men killed like flies--and no one asks 'Why?'" Doc prescribed something for his stomach problems.

Jalal, the oldest brother, brought his wife for a medical exam. Doc wondered how often there were real physical problems, and how often there was just the need for attention.

We had apricots in the morning--and then spinach and rice for lunch. I'm feeling restless. After a long nap I walked quickly around the room many times. I began singing songs and found this a good diversion.

I spent a lot of time at the window as the sun was setting and the family prepared for supper. Several headed off with large sheets with poles to collect mulberries. The men came back from the building project with muddy feet.

Arif, Jalal's oldest son, seems to be about 12. He has had no schooling and he is the family shepherd. Most shepherd boys take the sheep and goats of several families, receiving some kind of payment for their service. We noticed that Arif would leave right after breakfast with the flock and then come back at noon to be home for a couple of hours in the hottest part of the day. Then he would take off again and be back by dark.

Arif became our friend. He sat with us sometimes and we taught him some key words in English like "teapot". Months later his father reported that he still remembers them!

We had a late supper of bread in broth with two pieces of chicken! We realized later that a chicken had been killed especially to feed to the new mother. We talked with Ahmadi later and he reported that his wife was okay.

Hostage Log

This is the first statement from the "Hostage Log" that was kept in Pakistan during the entire crisis. Some parts are included in boxes like this on the day that they were originally written.

Mark and Cindy Morris and their three girls had been away at a conference in Indonesia for about two weeks. They asked Olga Nava to stay in their home and receive any phone calls if Dr. Lewis and Joel returned early. The Morris' planned to return today, the day that Dr. Lewis and Joel were also due back.

Around 9 a.m. Olga received a call at the Morris home from a Canadian friend in Quetta. He first asked for Mark, then for Dr. Lewis and Joel. He said that in a meeting the night before, two Afghan men came to tell him that two Americans had been taken as hostages in Afghanistan. They were quite sure the men were Dr. Lewis and Joel. He requested Mark to call him as soon as Mark arrived. An hour and a half later a phone call came from the American embassy asking many questions.

The Morris' arrived from Bangkok to Islamabad at 1:45 p.m. Mark had had jaw/neck surgery the previous week. They were glad to be home and everyone was happy to see them. Mark asked about news from Dr. Bill and Joel. Olga asked to see them privately because she had some serious news. Mark knew something was wrong and took Cindy by the hand into the

---

bedroom. Olga told them of the calls. Mark raised his hand to his head and said, "Why couldn't it have happened to me?"

Mark went to the phone immediately.

"We went to work immediately to contact the families. Joel's parents and Bill's family were aware within three and one hour respectively from the time it was confirmed that we had a genuine hostage crisis.

A friend reported that a vehicle was leaving Quetta now that would pick the two Americans up in two days. I stressed: no money and no deals. All agreed that this was the best and only safe approach in the long and short term.

Phone calls came all day. After the last one (1 a.m.), I went to bed."

Initial Statement:

"Two American volunteers who were working with Global Partners are rumored to have been detained by an Afghan commander in that country. We cannot confirm the validity of these rumors at this time. The two Americans were involved in a humanitarian agriculture-veterinary project in a needy area of Afghanistan.

Multiple sources indicate that the detainees are being held for no reason other than monetary gain. Twenty million Afghanis (Afghan currency) are being demanded by the captors. This equals $20,000. Local sources are optimistic that the Americans will be released unconditionally and returned home safely."

Tuesday, July 16

I was bothered by fleas again last night. I wonder why they don't bother Doc! The men had left and so breakfast was brought to us by a sister. Slowly the family is getting less scared of us! In fact, even the mother would come in now and then to talk to us. Her natural sensitivity made me feel so good. It wasn't right, she said, that we should be kept locked up like this.

The morning in our "cell" went s-l-o-w. I'm discouraged. We made one morning excursion, one in the afternoon, and one in the evening. We had a late lunch of *qurti*. Doc didn't eat much. Thankfully we were brought some *toots*, mulberries, later, along with apricots. No patients came. We walked around the room hundreds of times.

As dusk settles, I lie down and God's spirit ministers to me through Scriptures and songs I remember. In my afternoon nap I had dreamed of Mom and my family. God encouraged me. Now I prayed for the right attitude toward my captors. I acknowledged my sin of bitterness and unbelief.

Before supper Jalal and then his father came for visits. We are encouraged by their care. The family had been concerned that Doc wasn't eating much, so tonight they made an omelette for us--much to Doc's pleasure.

I remember thinking, "We've been prisoners for ten days now. Surely that's enough punishment for any crime we might have done!"

The embassy recommends a statement not be made.

The office in the US has formed a task force to deal with the crisis called Crisis Management Team (CMT).

Susanna Brown, wife of the local Protestant church pastor, called and offered to be a point of contact for the DeHart family. This is a big assistance to me, since I have tried unsuccessfully tonight to get through to Phil DeHart, Joel's youngest brother, and was preparing to try to get through to Sarah DeHart Raiter, Joel's sister.

Every report we have received from every source has been encouraging. We are guardedly optimistic. If we receive a negative word, however, I am prepared to travel by appropriate means (e.g. with Mujahideen convoy) into the area if necessary to bring out bodies, to discern the actual scenario of events, or to arrange travel for other representatives into the area.

I will need to plan trips to Peshawar and Quetta soon. At the present, however, I am certainly most needed here in Islamabad.

Wednesday, July 17

I slept well after using flea powder around my wrists, ankles, and neck. I think that scared them away! I was bold enough to quickly wash my feet and hair at the *karez* when I went out for the morning bathroom trip. I returned for some time of meditation on what I remembered of Philippians before a late breakfast. Just before leaving Islamabad I had finished teaching this book. Many of its verses were fresh in my mind.

After I spent some time in prayer and walking around the room, Ahmadi brought his uncle in for a check up. He had problems swallowing. This was a good diversion. Doc and I had a good discussion about Southern Baptist churches.

I happened to be looking out of the window when the soldiers came at dusk. My heart started beating wildly. I didn't want to be around those soldiers again. I didn't want another change. We had just become used to these people and this situation. I told Doc that we should gather our possessions.

Soon the men were up in our room. As we prepared to leave, Jalal spoke to us. "We have tried to treat you well. You have learned our names. Please don't tell anyone else." We gladly agreed. They let us eat some rice quickly and then we took off by foot to the jeep which was parked near the walled home we had gone to several days ago. Five soldiers were with us this time in the jeep. More rough roads. Two of the soldiers took scarves off their heads and wrapped them around our heads. It was dark, but they didn't want anybody suspecting that we were in the jeep.

We traveled several hours then got out of the jeep and waited for a while. The jeep returned and we went on. Soon I recognized the road we had come to. It was the road we had traveled on with our vaccinator's team to Chilbaghtu. The man who seemed to be giving orders (later we discovered he was Nadir, Akhund Salman's brother) told the driver to speed up as we went through the village of Jaudri. It seemed about midnight when we pulled off the main road into a little group of houses. The driver hopped out and beat on a huge wooden door. It soon opened and we were all ushered in. This would be our home for the next six days.

Doc and I were taken into an inner room. The roof was low. Again there was one window--looking out into a small courtyard. The room was smaller than at Safed Sang, but the redeeming factor was that the air was

THE UPPER HAND

much cooler. Here we slept comfortably with quilts. We were tired and fell asleep quickly.

> Many friends in Islamabad gathered at the Morris' house this morning for intercession and sharing of ideas. The group came up with names of additional contacts who will be approached.

Thursday, July 18

We slept well and enjoyed the coolness. After a breakfast of tea and yesterday's bread, Nadir came in and asked if we were okay. He searched us before leaving. The driver, known as "*Khalifa*", master, left with the other men and said he'd be back by noon. This was his home, we learned.

We were left to enjoy our new room! We were locked in, but we could open or close the window of glass panes. We could have stepped out this way into the courtyard, but we were more interested in building trust. We watched as Khalifa's wife walked back and forth occasionally. They were newly married and had no children. A servant girl helped with the chores. This little girl might have been embarrassed if she knew that sometimes we were watching her as she took her nap or picked mulberries and cherries from the small trees in the courtyard!

We discovered a wonderful thing about our room. If we closed the window we could kill all the flies in the room and rest in PEACE! There were less flies, too, because of the cooler air. So this morning I had a good rest and time of meditation. The song, *May The Mind Of Christ My Savior*, was much in my thoughts. It was helpful to counteract the resentment I felt.

We had lunch soon: rice, bread, tea--and onion sprouts! Afterwards, Khalifa took me out for a bath in a secluded part of an irrigation canal. Sure felt good to be clean again! The water was bracing. As we left the house, Khalifa told me, "Roll down your sleeves. And if anyone greets you, answer in good Persian."

Doc had his bath inside the courtyard while we were gone. He used solar heated water. The bucket of water had been left in the sun all morning for this purpose.

24

Kidnapped!

The view outside was strikingly beautiful. We both felt great with the little bit more freedom we had. But the afternoon was boring. It seemed like a long time before the rice and bread supper was served. We had to wait until Khalifa returned from another excursion. He let us walk in the courtyard in the dark. Later we heard some firing and our host told us stories of the increase of armed robberies in the area. It was all the work of the *Shola*, the Chinese Communists, he said.

We went to sleep thankful that our situation had improved somewhat and that our host seemed to be trying to be kind to us.

A very good lunch meeting with Joel's parents, Don and Garnett DeHart. They had a few questions. They were very complimentary of the way that Global Partners is handling the entire process. They made the statement, "We don't hold you responsible." They also commented about the fact that Joel did not enter into this trip lightly. He spent much time deliberating about the trip beforehand. He had consulted with them and others.

Thoughts on the aftermath of a pending release: the top priority is that Joel's ongoing work should not be jeopardized further.

The embassy emphasized the fact that only one hostage (a Frenchman) has been killed in Afghanistan in the last couple of years. There should be no press leaks. All US funded projects are halted.

My boss agreed to call me every three hours. He insisted that I get some rest for the long haul--well taken.

Friday, July 19

Our host appeared late. We were eager to go outside and use the facilities. Since the latrine (*kinar aao* in the local dialect--meaning "beside the water") was outside the big courtyard gate, Khalifa would always look out to make sure no one was in sight before giving us the go ahead.

The bathroom in Engineer Kabir's "castle" in Sang-i Masha had been only slightly more sophisticated. In one of the corner towers there was a room with a simple hole in the floor. It must have been 15 feet above

THE UPPER HAND

ground level--from where the refuse was periodically collected. Here the latrine was about the size of an outhouse. But it wasn't a "pit" latrine. Rather you would climb several steps to enter and there was a door about two feet by two feet at ground level from which the excrement would be taken in rubber donkey bags at intervals to spread on the fields as fertilizer. Often there was some kind of curtain on the door. Or else, the door would face the side of a hill or some cover. Dirt clods or water served as the common equivalent for toilet paper. There were usually some flies buzzing around, but not as many as I would have expected.

People in homes that did not have a latrine would simply use the nearest secluded spot. In the commander's home where I stayed later, the latrine was really just for guests--or sometimes the men of the house. Other people used the rocky hillside.

Our lunch was milk and bread. Since Khalifa was away, we felt awkward asking the lady of the house if we could go out and use the latrine. Fortunately our room opened into a little store room. From there a door led to the *tabila*, barn. We relieved ourselves here out of desperation. Later we enjoyed pacing back and forth here, although the roof was low and sooty. There was not much chance of escape as the windows at either end of the barn were only about one foot in diameter.

Hazara homes usually have a long "barn" at the back of the house. This makes it easy to care for animals in the cold and snow of winters. Often the hearth or kitchen is here too--so that the chimney can go horizontally (at a slight angle) under the main room of the house to provide central heating whenever food is cooked! On top of the kitchen and barn is usually the "hay mow" where cultivated grasses and mountain plants are kept dry as fodder to last through the winter.

Khalifa returned sometime after lunch and let me wash Doc's clothes. It had been 11 days since we had changed, and the clothes showed it! Again I used solar heated water. Khalifa found a spare pair of tambans, trousers, for Doc to wear. They looked pretty funny as they didn't make it down to his ankles!

We were thankful for a chance to walk a little and eat a snack--boiled *mashong*, mini peas. Then it was back in our room. I spent some time reading the Quran which was on a shelf above the door. This volume had a short concordance, so I found it interesting to look up some verses on God's view of injustice and falsehood.

Supper was delicious. Cooked greens and bread. After our usual time of prayer together, we hit the sack.

It is speculated that the release will coincide with the Muslim holiday of **Muharram**.

My wife, Cindy, and I are beginning to pace ourselves for the long-haul. We have made room for some long-term guests. We are setting up some extra work space. Cindy's primary job right now is to keep the family's needs met. She is enabling me to be an absent father until this thing passes.

Logistics: Let's continue to keep this as quiet as we can. This event must be the most difficult thing that I have ever faced, yet no one in either Cindy's nor my family knows about it. Our children don't even know. Thus far, we've done a good job at keeping the lid on this.

Saturday, July 20 --My brother, Jonathan's, birthday--and the second week anniversary of our captivity

This morning's breakfast featured milk and bread. Khalifa had left for Sang-i Masha, or so he told us, and the day turned out to be quite long. We made many trips to the barn just for variety. I walked around the room many times and sang hymns. Often Doc and I would walk together. I entertained him by singing and he entertained me by telling stories! I spent more time with the Quran and an English textbook printed in Iran. Khalifa had taken this for us from a neighbor.

Khalifa returned in the evening with guests. There was a lot of bustle as supper was prepared for all of us. Doc and I ate alone. After some time we were called in to join the guests in the guest room. It turned out to be a serious and very upsetting dialogue for me. Akhund Salim did most of the talking. (We still didn't realize that he was Akhund Salim! I thought he

THE UPPER HAND

might be the spokesman for the Akhund. Akhund is a religious title for a leader--similar to mulla or "pastor".)

After pouring us some tea, the Akhund began with this question:

"Why do you think you have been taken captive?"

"As far as I know," I replied, "Akhund Salim and Wasim are powerful men who do not fear God. They have kidnapped us to try to get a ransom even though we have come to serve the poor people of this area."

This got Akhund Salim started. He is a man in his late thirties. He wears his hair long and, on trips, wraps it in a scarf, which, like elastic leggings, has become a symbol of a *nizami*, soldier--or *mujahid* (religious title for one who fights in a holy war--*jihad*), which they like to use to refer to themselves. I object to using *mujahid* (plural, *mujahideen*) because there is only infighting going on now and the soldiers are far from godly in their actions.

"You are very sly men," the Akhund began. "We think you are CIA spies. You have not come here to help--rather to exploit us and help those who are against our Islamic revolution. Furthermore, you are cooperating with the Chinese Communists. Engineer Kabir and his crowd are Communists and enemies of the people. They stand for the very principles that we've been fighting against for these 12 years. Not only that, but you have not helped us and the truly poor. Your efforts have been directed to the people in Sang-i Masha--where people always benefit the most from foreign aid. All projects start there and never make it out to our area--Patu, Baba, and Chilbaghtu."

(I think this was one of just three times I was accused of connections with the CIA. This was not a serious possibility in the minds of the local people.)

The Akhund had charisma and a way with words. I tried to give a direct and rational answer. Later I realized how useless this was. The Akhund was putting up a smoke screen to disguise his real motive. He was speaking more to the group around him than to us. Thus nothing we said would make any difference. I was wasting my time.

"We have no connection with the CIA," I said. "And we are not working with Communists. You say Engineer Kabir is a bad man and an enemy of the people. But to us, he is the best Muslim we have seen here.

28

Kidnapped!

God is merciful and just. Those who follow him should have the same characteristics. Our project planned to cover every area of the Jaghori District. We have only been training students so far. We have only been in operation two weeks--not enough time to cover the whole district. We decided to do the training in Sang-i Masha just because it is logistically simpler. Our tractor and trailer haven't come yet. We wanted to spend most of our time vaccinating, not traveling. But, as a gesture of our intentions, we made a day trip to Chilbaghtu-i Waqi and vaccinated animals there."

I found out later that while we were on that trip to Chilbaghtu, we had vaccinated all the animals in the Akhund's own house!

The Akhund negated my answer. Then he asked, "What is your project budget?"

I translated this to Doc and we replied that we didn't know.

The Akhund laughed and said we were obviously lying. How could we not know?

"There's no way you can ever be free without paying us money--and a lot of it. This will be your contribution to the Islamic revolution. We need your help. You have put out a lot of money to help our enemies. Now you will help us.

If you don't come through with money, you may not see your families for a long, long time. We have been treating you like guests. We may have to start treating you like regular prisoners. Also, we may decide to sell you to the Communist regime in Kabul. Then you would be in much hotter water. Finally, who knows? You could even die.

So, how much money can you put up?"

My heart sank. Lower than ever before. I translated this to Doc. And, before I could think, or we could discuss the issue, he responded, "Tell him that I can borrow $10,000 from my bank. I'm willing to pay that if I will be released immediately."

I translated this back to the Akhund. And I added that I could come up with $5000. The Akhund then said that the money would have to be brought in and given to him. Then he would guarantee our safe passage

29

back to Quetta. We said that we could only give him the money when we were free and back in Pakistan.

We left things that way for the night, saying that we would talk again in the morning. That night was the most difficult night of my life. Doc and I prayed together--but the tension and fear wouldn't let me sleep. I kept praying and trying to trust God. But my heart kept beating violently and fearful thoughts assailed me. Finally and mercifully, I fell asleep.

> A friendly commander who recently came from Jaghori said that Engineer Kabir had met the hostages in a secret meeting. They are definitely in Baba. He thought the hostages would come in five or six days.

Sunday, July 21

After breakfast the Akhund came into our room and we discussed conditions again for getting the money to him.

"You must bring the money here," he said. "Nothing else is acceptable." But he didn't press the issue then. Before he left, he asked if we needed anything. We asked him to bring some flea powder, books, and Doc's personal medicine from Sang-i Masha. He said he would do this for us.

Our morning was relaxed. I caught up on sleep--and God's peace seemed to flood my heart in a way I can't explain. We walked around the room many times.

Knowing it was Sunday, Doc and I decided to have a worship service together. We both contributed in songs, prayer, and sharing some verses from the Bible. This was to be our last Sunday together in Afghanistan.

I remember listening to the water rush in from the irrigation channel to water the garden in the courtyard. I thought of God's abundant mercies to me and started to sing "Channels only":

Kidnapped!

"How I praise Thee, precious Savior,
That Thy love laid hold of me;
Thou hast saved and cleansed and filled me
That I might Thy channel be.
Channels only, blessed Master
But with all thy wondrous power
Flowing through us Thou canst use us
Every day, and every hour."
Etc.

It was here also that *"May the mind of Christ"* challenged me to have a godly attitude towards my captor and those around me, no matter what my circumstances. I sang it many times later when struggling with bitterness and anger.

"May the mind of Christ, my Savior,
Live in me from day to day,
By His love and power controlling
All I do and say.

May the love of Jesus fill me
As the waters fill the sea
Him exalting, self abasing
This is victory."
Etc.

Lunch was served about 3 p.m. It was **nan tar**, dried bread crumbs in fresh buttermilk. Doc and I quite enjoyed this meal. We were given two spoons with each meal.

Towards dusk Khalifa let us out in the courtyard to walk. We met another boy from the village who Khalifa had brought into confidence. The boy mentioned that when Khalifa had borrowed an English book from him earlier, he had become suspicious. His name was Rajab Ali. Though only

31

THE UPPER HAND

about 16, he had a gun and was on guard duty that night against the "robbers".

An official in Washington informed our representative that kidnappings in Afghanistan have been quite common over the past decade and usually work themselves out in a fairly routine manner. The average tenure for a forced detainment is about three to four weeks.

The official confirmed the involvement of Hizb-i Islami (HIA) in the kidnapping. This party is known as one of the most religiously conservative, and xenophobic parties. It is one of the best disciplined and organized factions. The US has virtually no clout with its leader, Gulbuddin Hikmatyar. The kidnapping, however, was likely the action of a petty local commander, so might be resolved independently of Hikmatyar. Westerners need to understand that "detaining guests" is a time-honored tradition in Afghanistan.

One of the worst things that could happen in the negotiating process would be a sudden release of the story to the Western media.

A visitor commented, "It's good to be with Mark. He looks well although he's been averaging five hours sleep per night for the past couple of weeks. Last night, though, he didn't sleep at all."

Two days later he added, "Mark and Cindy are doing an exceptional job in confronting this crisis with thoroughness and wisdom. We are impressed at their level of professionalism and diligence. It is difficult to imagine what more could be done on their part. Patience will perhaps be the greatest challenge for all parties concerned."

Monday, July 22 -- *"ASHURA"*

Today is an important festival for Shia Muslims. *Ashura* is the tenth day of the Muslim month of Muharram, when Ali and Hussain's death on the battlefield of Karbala is remembered with much emotion. Typically all the Hazara people assemble in their respective *minbars*, mosques. Here they pray, celebrate, and eat together.

Minbars have a black flag raised outside on a tall flagpole. People who walk by usually kiss this flagpole. I don't remember ever seeing a tall, ornate minaret, or hearing a call to prayer on a loudspeaker during my time

32

Kidnapped!

in the Hazarajat. Each *minbar* has a caretaker who lives there with his family. When people here pray, they use a *mohr*, a flat piece of pressed clay about two inches square on which some verses from the Quran are impressed. The clay comes from Karbala or Meshed, two holy cities in Iran. This *mohr* is kept in a small, embroidered cloth case in each man's pocket. When it is time for prayer, he takes it out and places it where his forehead will touch as he bows in the direction of Mecca. After the prayer is finished, he touches the *mohr* several times and passes his fingers over his face.

So Khalifa and his family all left for the *minbar*. He had given us some of the medicines that had fallen his lot when our trunk of medicines and supplies had been stolen on July 6. With Doc's help, I labeled each in Persian--the kind of medicine, its use, etc.

When the family returned in the afternoon, I was able to wash my clothes. It had been 13 days since I had last put on clean clothes!

Doc and I sat outside as Rajab Ali came over and I helped him with English. We went to bed soon after a *nan tar* supper. I had discovered that the fleas seemed to bother me less when I took a little kerosene from the lamp and rubbed it on my wrists, ankles, and neck.

Tuesday, July 23

After breakfast Doc and I drafted a letter to Engineer Kabir. Khalifa assured us that he could deliver this letter. This is what we wrote:

> Dear Engineer,
> Greetings. Thank you for your work for our freedom. Please continue your work. We hope you can get together with the old men and solve our problem soon. We offered one of these men 150 *lak* Afghanis if we arrive safely in Quetta with you. (One *lak* equals 100,000.) We offered to pay the remaining Global Partners budget that you have here if we are released. We must be in Quetta before we can get the money. We trust you to make the best

33

THE UPPER HAND

plan for our safe travel. We can give you the money in
Quetta to take to these men. When we make an agreement,
we will promise before God, you, the old men, and these
men to pay the money. Please write an answer to us now
in English. Please write your children's names.

Sincerely,

Doctor Lewis and Joel

Late in the morning, Khalifa took me out for another bath--this time in
a stream. How beautiful it was outside! Kindly, Khalifa led me on a longer
way home so we could pick some mulberries. Doc bathed in the courtyard
again.

As "Mrs." Khalifa brought us our **nan tar** lunch, she asked with a
smile if we liked it. We gave an enthusiastic "Yes!" It was good to see that
her fear and reserve was disappearing.

In the afternoon rest God gave me a deep assurance of his power and led
me to pray for spiritual victory.

As we walked around the room together, Doc told the story of buying
his different properties back in Texas, and how he worked to develop the
land and buildings into profitable concerns.

We went into the courtyard in the late afternoon. Rajab came again and
I studied English with him. After a rice supper we talked with Khalifa
about his sick wife. He told us that she was pregnant and he was so
concerned that a child be born safely. Doc gave him some guidance and
recommended medicine.

After we retired, we heard some more firing. The "thieves" must be
active again tonight.

At 11:30 p.m. we were quickly awakened as Khalifa rushed into our
room. "We've been discovered!" he said. "Get your things and come out
quickly."

As we stumbled outside, we saw a mob of men with guns at the gate.
We didn't know what was going on--but I felt like whatever it was, it

34

Kidnapped!

couldn't be worse than what we had now. The men told us and Khalifa to get moving. As I listened to their conversations, I understood what was happening. The men from the villages around had somehow found out that Khalifa was keeping the two American hostages in his home. (News of our kidnapping had caused quite a stir in the area. Everyone was wondering where we were and what would happen. Later I heard that one of the village men had glanced into the courtyard and seen Doc walking.) The men kept repeating how terrible it was that two foreigners had come from a far country to help poor people and the locals had responded by kidnapping them for money.

At one point they knocked Khalifa down, confiscated his gun, and beat him. Khalifa, in turn, was trying to justify himself and lying profusely. He told the men that we had only been there one day. Then he told me that I must also say the same thing. When the men asked me how long we had been there, I said, "I must tell the truth. We've been here six days."

The men turned on Khalifa with more profanities.

But our "deliverers" were a confused rabble. They couldn't agree on what to do with us. We would walk a few minutes. Then we were told to stop as a heated discussion continued. Then it was "go". In this manner we walked about two miles. I tried to explain to Doc what was going on. It was difficult since I wasn't quite sure myself! Anyway, I felt that these events would work out in our favor.

Finally we stopped at a small bazaar on the hill. We were there a long time as the men excitedly discussed what to do. The night air was cold. Several of the men gave us their shawls to wear. We started towards a village above the road and it was decided that we would spend the night in the *minbar* there. The next step would be decided from there.

As we walked, a village head man asked me if I would prefer being handed over to Akhund Salim, Wasim, or Sheikh Fazal. I said that the first two had not been good to us, so Sheikh Fazal sounded best.

As our group neared the village in single file, the village sentry called out, *Daresh!*, Halt!. The men explained who we were and we proceeded on to the *minbar*. Inside, heated discussion continued until morning. Tea and bread were brought several times. Doc soon went to sleep. But I was

35

THE UPPER HAND

interested in the discussion. There was a lot of rhetoric about how bad Akhund Salim was, etc. I made some remarks about how un-Islamic it was to kidnap people and demand a ransom. I said that I feared the Akhund would come there by force and take us back into captivity.

The men responded, "Don't worry in the least now. We have freed you and you cannot be taken again." Those were comforting words for me.

We had a phone conversation this evening with an Englishman who had been held hostage in the same area in 1990. He told of some physical abuse after which, "I became quite nervous; I was intimidated." After that, he negotiated a sum of money for his own release. He stated that the commander who held him (and who also is one of Dr. Bill's and Joel's captors) was immune to outside pressure, but responded well to money.

We were disturbed by this conversation, and decided to analyze some of the differences in the two situations. Thankfully, Mark had signed agreements with all the parties involved, except HIA. Reports indicate that Dr. Bill and Joel were being treated well--even being allowed to go on a one-day fishing trip to the river! The Englishman had been facing an imminent winter, whereas the high mountain plateaus of the Hazarajat are actually one of the most pleasant places to be in the hot summer months of July and August.

On the other side of the equation, Afghanistan was probably more politically stable in 1990 than it is now.

We closed the night around 1:30 a.m. with fervent prayer for the hostages and their captors and for all those involved in securing their release.

B. The Commander's House   (Chilbaghtu)

July 24-Oct.13

Wednesday, July 24

My first whole night in a village mosque hadn't included much sleep! Special tea was brought for us with bread and a hunk of fat from a sheep's tail. I went outside to the bathroom--but the men didn't want Doc going outside. They brought a can for him to use as a toilet.

We could hear and see men assembling with their weapons. Several young men came in to talk to us. "The men who took you captive are very foolish." They went on and on badmouthing the Akhund. Most of the time we were left alone as we waited for the announcement of our fate. God gave us a peace.

At noon we were ushered outside and, without a word of explanation, given to Akhund Salim and his army. I found out later that a messenger had informed the Akhund earlier that morning of what had happened. He quickly assembled all his available troops and weapons--along with soldiers from Wasim's Nahzat-i Islami in the area. In all there were over 30 men--heavily armed with rocket launchers and automatic weapons. There had been some discussion with the villagers--but they couldn't match the Akhund's fire power and had to give in.

Both of us were bitterly disappointed. Our dreams of freedom and returning home had seemed so real. But instead, we seemed to be in a worse position. I was very glum, indeed. This was no doubt the darkest day of my captivity. None of the soldiers in this group seemed kind-hearted. Khalifa appeared and told me, "See what happened when you didn't tell the men what I told you to say? Now you will have to suffer."

THE UPPER HAND

After walking about an hour we arrived at a group of houses where the soldiers decided they would have lunch. They asked, or better, pressured the people to fix something in each house for eight to ten men. After this *qurti* lunch, we walked another hour to the Chilbaghtu road where two jeeps were waiting. As many as could fit, and more, piled in.

The jeeps stopped near a grassy area in Chilbaghtu and the leaders went to a home below the road for a long discussion. When they returned, they motioned for Doc and me to get into different jeeps. My heart sank further. They were separating us. We had at least been able to pray and draw strength from each other. I could help Doc understand what was going on around us. He was a constant encouragement to me to keep from being bitter and resentful. Where would they take me? Where would they take Doc? I gave our little bundle of toothpaste, toothbrushes, and soap to Doc. Some of the soldiers seemed to enjoy our discomfort. Most of them seemed apathetic.

The jeep I was in drove for only ten minutes. We arrived at a big, two-story house that I vaguely recognized. I realized later that we had come into this very home and the surrounding settlement with our vaccination team. We had made a special day trip here from Sang-i Masha. Some distance up the valley I could see "Mastak", the home of the old Khan where we had parked our jeeps on our vaccination tour just a month ago.

I joined the men for tea as they discussed the day's exploits in detail. They finally left and I had a short nap. This house was certainly a step up from the homes we had occupied in Baba and Siah Zamin. But then it was a commander's home. I discovered that this *aghil*, settlement, was called Boldraghna.

One man led me up the stairs to a long (70 feet), unfinished room. I paced back and forth--trying to let out the anger and frustration that I felt inside. I could think of nothing I could do to change my circumstances. Little did I know then (and it's probably good that I didn't know!) that this room would be my home for the next two months and 20 days.

I was called down for a *qurti* supper and then sat quietly as the men talked and talked. The discussions were suddenly interrupted by the sound of gunfire. Most of the men rushed outside with their weapons. "Thieves", I was told--and probably supporters of Chinese Communists. I slept in the guest room with other soldiers. There were no fleas!

Thursday, July 25

I was able to do my exercises upstairs at dawn while the men were saying their prayers. There was lots of conversation around breakfast. Foolishly I tried to defend my position and convince the Akhund to release me. (It was two days later that I realized that he, and not some older and more distinguished person, was THE Akhund Salim!) This was an exercise in futility as no one else in the group would oppose their leader and the Akhund was too clever to be without some kind of justification for any of his actions.

I went upstairs to walk and then have a time of meditation and prayer. Today I made some friends whom I feel were sent by God to encourage and occupy me. They became some of the best friends I made in my six and a half month stay in Afghanistan. Who were they? The village kids! There were at least 25 that I came to know well.

I wrote the following lines from the soldier's base three months later as I looked back on my time with these friends:

Kids--Kids. Thank God for them.
    Didn't take long for me to get to know them.
    Sometimes pesty,
    But we developed an understanding.
    At first, many would come upstairs
    To borrow my pen and draw.
    Then I would lift them up to hold on to the rafters.
    We'd see how many times I could walk around the room
    Before they'd get tired and I'd let them down!
    Breaks in their monotony, I suppose.

English--All of them learned some English.
    Even two-year-old Arif,

39

THE UPPER HAND

> Whom I carried around.
> He would greet me in the morning with "Hello!"
> And would leave me anytime with "Good-a-bye."
> My name to everyone was **Muallim**, teacher.
> Arif called me "Mali", affectionately.
> It was his own shortened version!

Lunch was bread and milk. After resting and playing some more, tea was brought just for me.

As the Akhund was sitting there and talking, I asked if I could go outside for a walk. He sent Zia with me and told me that I could go anywhere in sight. I enjoyed this freedom so much that I sort of jogged along a field fairly far from the house. When I returned, the Akhund said I had gone too far. So much for the freedom I thought I had! I was always careful to recognize and stay in the boundaries that my captors seemed to set up. I wanted to build trust hoping this would lead to greater freedom.

Supper was **qurti**. I had my own separate dish. I would have preferred to eat with the group (four or five per big bowl) but I realized that sometimes people would object on religious grounds. Not being a Muslim, I was, to some, unclean. I let my sentiments be known. And, after this, I always ate with the others.

As we were eating, shots rang out from somewhere nearby. There was much excitement. Most of the men ran outside with their weapons. The Akhund picked up the rocket launcher. There were more shots and a lot of yelling. The men returned one by one after half an hour. Thieves. But apparently they had escaped. Later we learned that these disturbances may have had something to do with our being kept hostage there.

Tonight I slept upstairs alone. Though the room was unfinished, I found I could rest here much better. I appreciated the time alone--and the good place to do exercises in the mornings.

The Commander's House

Friday, July 26

This morning after breakfast the Akhund and I discussed the proposal for getting money to him in Pakistan. He said he would take a letter to Engineer Kabir today. He finally left in the afternoon--promising that I could have a bath whenever I wanted.

Lunch was bread and yogurt. I wrote another letter for Engineer Kabir. I walked fast around the long upstairs room. Then I was allowed outside for some time to walk and visit. A sick man came bringing my toothbrush and soap from Dr. Bill! He also asked that I write a note describing his problem so Doc could prescribe medicine. Doc hadn't understood him. It was a great encouragement to hear that Doc was this near! He wrote:

> All is well. I have received good care in a friendly atmosphere with much freedom to walk. Plenty of milk and a bath promised today. The flies are alive and healthy.
>
> I trust God all is well with you. May God be praised for His constant care and divine providence. The pain, anguish and lonliness is less today. His everlasting love is all sustaining. May the Lord Jesus come quickly. I am praying for good care for you and no maltreatment in any way. Perhaps you, too, can have a bath.
>
> May God bless our loved ones.
>
> Dr. Bill

I later visited with Anwar from two houses to the West. He was a handsome man with some education and appeared to be the Akhund's second-in-command.

I was called in at dusk. To my delight, Zawar, the Akhund's brother, told me to go into the part of the house where his family lived. There were ladies in there! I wanted to be sure that I was right in entering the room. Zawar and I and some of the boys ate together while the women sat in a circle near us and ate their meal. Just being in a family environment helped me feel more comfortable and accepted. This was a sign to me that Zawar liked me and didn't want to exclude me. As the days passed, I became closer and closer to each member of this dear family.

Saturday, July 27

This morning I asked again about a bath. After a while the kids called me saying the water was hot. Since I only had one suit of clothes, Zawar lent me one of his suits. The "bath"room was in a corner of the barn next to the kitchen hearth. It was a four by four foot cemented area sloping down to a drain which went through the wall. Sometimes the cows and goats looked on as I took my bath!

I had soap and I borrowed a pair of the ladies' plastic slippers. There was a bucket of warm water and an aluminum pot with which I could pour the water over my body. I was glad to have soap!

After the bath, Zawar called me to the upper room on the family side. We sat on the carpet and talked. He ordered bread, butter, and buttermilk for a special snack.

I had rest and prayer in my own room. Then tea appeared. Bread and tea was later served for lunch. I was allowed to watch Zawar as he filled in a doorway with stone and mud bricks. In this land everyone is a mason--or "mud mason", *gilkar*, as they say. I helped him stack the heavy mud bricks.

I had tea and visited with two guests. Then I watched as Zawar plastered the outside of the doorway with mud. After a walk with Reza, we had supper together of rice and tea.

ZAWAR

In my two and a half months in this home I became good friends with Zawar. We respected each other. He was a hard worker and also a great talker. Now he was about 50 years old. He had begun his career in the army. Every Afghan man had to serve two years. He told me stories about how rough army life was. Then he moved to Mazar-i Sharif to work in the

---

coal mines where his two brothers also worked. As the result of an accident there, both bones were broken in his left lower leg. They healed, but would always be somewhat crooked.

Zawar then moved to greener pastures. He worked in Iran for several years. And then got into the business of smuggling. He would get jobs for Hazara people in Iran and help them to get in and out illegally. Also he would bring goods back and forth. He served at least one prison sentence for this; but the job paid well. He visited the tomb of Hazrat Ali at Meshad many times--hence his title of *Zawar*, which means "the visitor" or "the pilgrim".

After the Soviet invasion in 1979, Jan Muhammad Zawar became a leader in the resistance. The locals rose up and united in a plan to terminate government control in the district capital, Sang-i Masha. All the officers were killed, and the soldiers were sent home. Zawar had a fiery temper which helped him motivate people. Although illiterate, he became the local leader for the Hizb-i Islami party.

As time went by, Zawar decided to step down and let his younger brother take the leadership in this new party. Officially, a man named Abbasi was the leader of the party. But he spent a lot of time in Pakistan and the local leadership began to take on more complete authority. Akhund Salim, Zawar's brother, was literate and, more importantly, he had charisma and a clever mind--both for military strategizing and for manipulating people. It wasn't long before the Akhund had established himself so firmly that Abbasi became afraid to return into the area!

Zawar and the Akhund together built the new house where I was now a resident. They got along better than the other two brothers who lived nearby. For three or four years they had been busy fighting to defend their party and base against other parties who were united against them. They seldom were able to be at home. The women were left to run everything on the home front and do some of the actual building of the house! But the previous year the Akhund had made peace with Wasim, the strong man of Nahzat-i Islami. Now Zawar was managing the home estate since his brother was away traveling most of the time.

Zawar was always kind to me. I didn't understand why he didn't intervene on my behalf and seek my release. Maybe he had decided to leave

THE UPPER HAND

all politics in his brother's hands. Soon he considered me part of the family and allowed me to be around his wives and the other household members. Knowing I liked to be outside, he would try to take me to different places or, at least, let me outside when he was working.

Zawar had no children by his first wife, a strong and beautiful lady who was originally from a village near Sang-i Masha but had grown up in Kabul. The family called her "*Bole*", meaning a cousin by a mother of two sisters who married two brothers. Zawar married the daughter of a nearby friend in order to father children. His new wife's name was *Dilkha*, "Heart's Desire". She also was beautiful, but slightly more frail. She had borne Zawar one daughter and three sons. A fourth son was born while I was there.

I wrote the following lines about Zawar several months later from the soldier's base:

Zawar--Zawar reminded me of my Uncle Myron.
  Simple, down to earth, and hard-working.
  He had definite ideas about the way things should be.
  We had many long talks.
  "I like you."
  "God knows I hope and pray for your soon release."
  "This is a land of much toil, and little reward."
  "All of us are liars. Don't trust us."
  "This is a land of thieves."
  "You'll remember later
  What this crazy man in Afghanistan told you," he would say.

Sunday, July 28

I spent a lot of time singing this morning. Juma was around. I could keep him and the other kids happy by giving them bits of paper and lending them my pen to make drawings. I began to make a list of the Christian songs I could remember.

The Commander's House

Psalm 121 became even more of a favorite song. Every place I was kept, there were mountains around. Sometimes dark against the pink sunsets. Sometimes snow covered. Always beautiful. Singing this psalm encouraged me to lift my eyes above the mountains to their Maker who was my Keeper. I was reminded not to rely on human means, but to look to God alone.

"I will lift up mine eyes unto the hills,
from whence cometh my help.
My help cometh from the Lord,
which made heaven and earth.
He will not suffer thy foot to be moved:
he that keepeth thee will not slumber..."

I thought of Psalm 23 often. And I was surprised to realize how many different songs I knew which were taken from this favorite psalm. It was a great assurance to think of the Lord as my Shepherd.

Commander Salihi was resting downstairs. He came regularly to spend the night as one of my guards and today he was sick. We ate together a lunch of delicious fresh thick bread with milk and tea. He advised me a little of the "mistakes" our organization had made--that is, in essence, working with Engineer Kabir instead of Hizb-i Islami.

After my rest Juma appeared again. He greeted me by kissing my hand! I was impressed with this custom.

I went outside to see some more masonry. Then Zawar's father-in-law appeared. I had a long talk with him and we established a friendship that strengthened over time. He sympathized with me, but advised that I quickly pay the money and go free. "Don't let this upset you," he said. "Quickly pay the money so you don't have to waste any more of your precious time here."

I was allowed out in the late afternoon to walk around the hills behind the house. I recognized the homes nearby from vaccinating animals there before my captivity. In fact, I had taken pictures in front of two of the homes. Today I met my special friend, Ali Shah, for the first time. Of all

45

THE UPPER HAND

the kids, he seemed the most sympathetic, understanding, and bright. Today I taught them six English words: tea, house, nose, donkey, eye, and apple. In the upstairs room I watched as the kids played some of their own games: hop tag, blind fold tag, carrying each other, etc. They had so few toys, yet they could play and entertain themselves so well! I was led downstairs and, as we waited for the men to come, I had a good chance to talk with the three girls in the house--Nafisa, Naseema, and Razia. Their initial fear of me was disappearing and they had lots of questions. "Where are your mother and father?" "Aren't you afraid at night by yourself?", and so on.

Monday, July 29

After the routine of exercises, outhouse, breakfast, meditation, walk, and songs, some visitors appeared. They were Hussain and Shorty (called *Munshi*, or "scribe"). These men were related to Zawar's family by marriage. It was so interesting as Shorty told of his first trip to Iran when he was 15 years old. Coming from the "backwoods" of Chilbaghtu, the change had been really something!

SHORTY IN IRAN

Shorty said that when he saw the electric lights of Zahidan, on Iran's border with Pakistan, he thought they were like stars. On the bus ride to Tehran he went the three days without food because he didn't know about eating Iranian food--and he was afraid to take the money out of the hiding place where he had sewn it in his clothes. In the big city he was terrified of the traffic crossings. He would dash madly across the road, sometimes knocking people down! He felt he would surely die in this strange, new world.

He had a telephone number of a relative, but had never used a phone. An Iranian lady helped him. But the number had been changed. He had nowhere else to go! He was so overcome with hunger that he felt he had to

---

46

eat. But what? And how? He followed people to what seemed like a restaurant. The first thing he did was walk into a clear, glass door! Finally he figured out how to open it. He didn't know what to order, but said the same thing as the person in front of him. There were none of the local Hazara dishes offered--like **qurti** or **nan buta**. He had never used silverware before--nor had he had this kind of food! But he tried to copy the people around him.

He had taken a bottle of pop, but didn't know how to open it. After he finally succeeded, he took a sip and immediately gagged at the carbon dioxide. He thought it must be an alcoholic drink! This strange food hurt his stomach.

He couldn't finish the whole meal. It was now time to pay. The cashier told him it was something like five rials and two **zari**. He thought the **zari** meant 'thousands', so took out two thousand and five **rials**. Fortunately the cashier explained that a **zari** is the coin smaller than a **rial**, and gave the extra money back.

Not long after this, Shorty witnessed a demonstration in the streets. As he watched the people go by, he recognized a relative from Chilbaghtu. What a relief! The relative helped him find a place to live, get proper attire, and begin working. (Most Afghans work in Iran as laborers on building projects.)

Gradually Shorty adjusted to the new culture. He recounted another shocking experience. One day while riding on a bus a beautiful, young Iranian lady sat next to him. He was so embarrassed. He looked the other way. When it was time for him to get off, he climbed over the seat in front of him rather than speak to the lady!

Shorty joined me for lunch and then we rested together. I found out that he had married a sister of Dilkha.

I walked some more in the room then "studied" with Reza and his cousin, Shah. Then I went down to the guest room to join a guest for tea. It turned out that he knew Mark. Mark and Engineer Kabir had stayed in their home on their hike from Chilbaghtu to Malistan in the spring. He is a **Sayyid**, or a descendant of the prophet. These people are not necessarily wealthy, but they command great respect from the people. Most people when greeting them kiss their hands. (Two times people kissed my hands, thinking somehow that I was a *Sayyid*!) They are called by the title, *Agha*. They even have their own language, although in their homes they speak *Hazaragi*. Because they are considered close to God, they are often asked to pray for others. They generally wear black turbans.

After talking for sometime, this man, Inayat, explained that he wasn't powerful enough to help me. Local politics and pressures forced him to be with some party--and he had joined Hizb-i Islami. But he would take a note for me to Engineer Kabir, if I wanted to write one. I immediately went upstairs and wrote a note in Persian for the engineer. I said that Inayat could read it if he wanted to, but it turned out that he couldn't read.

The full moon was decreasing tonight. After supper and some conversation there was nothing to do but go to bed. I would often look at the stars and mountains outside, and think and pray before rolling out my mattress, pillow, and quilt on the floor.

Tuesday, July 30

Today I made an attempt to spend time studying Persian. I read all the way through Reza's second grade Persian reader (published in Iran) and wrote down the words I didn't know. One of the regular nightly guards, Zabit, had been friendly and brought me a fat *Persian* to *Persian* dictionary. I amused myself then by looking up all these new words. These days Reza was going to school everyday. Sometime later he stopped as a result of fighting in the area.

Juma and Yaqub came to entertain me for a while. Lunch was yogurt and bread. I rested, then Reza appeared with tea.

The commander's home had a large, walled courtyard that I could look down on from my windows. There were only a few newly planted apricot and apple trees--plus some patches of vegetables that didn't do very well because of a lack of water. Whenever the ladies were drawing water from the well, they would be careful to cover themselves because they knew I could look down. Today I had been watching and noticed that the rubber cord, which connected the two rubber buckets for drawing water, had broken. One of the buckets was left down in the well. Dilkha didn't know what to do.

From above I offered to go down into the well and get the bucket. They unlocked my door and I easily made the descent into the well. Foot holds were carved in the shaley rock on both sides of the narrow hole. The water was about ten meters below. My initial attempts to get the bucket only resulted in it sinking down under the water! Dilkha then sent down a stick with a crotch at the end. I managed to snag the bucket with this and pull it up. Dilkha mended the rubber cord with a couple of nails.

Late in the afternoon I was allowed outside on the hills behind the house. There were a lot of kids around and we had more English lessons.

I had rice, bread, and tea downstairs by myself because most of the household had left for a **Muharram** feast. During this holy month, everyone of means in the village must host a dinner for the rest of his neighbors. If he can kill a sheep or goat, it's better; but if he can't, he can serve **nan buta**, a special kind of bread soaked in buttermilk, or **sheer brinj**, rice pudding with a hole for butter in the middle. Also, if a person couldn't fit in his invitation in the month, he could give a rain check!

There were many shots tonight from over the mountains in Chilbaghtu-i Pashi. I went to bed alone in the dark.

Wednesday, July 31

Two guards instead of four stayed for breakfast. A patient came wanting me to write a note for him to take to Doc. A change of clothes arrived today from Engineer Kabir, so I was able to send back Doc's outfit with this man.

The Akhund's sister came to talk for a while. She lives in another village. She seemed very sympathetic.

After I had lunch with two guards, the patient returned. I explained what Doc had written. He thought the man had malaria. The man was grateful. Later I found out that someone had taken one of Doc's written prescriptions to the medical shops in the bazaar at Sang-i Masha and no one could make out what he wrote!

THE UPPER HAND

I sang through the first column of songs that I had listed (30 in all). I have found this a good exercise to pass time and direct my thoughts to things above.

After some exercise and playing with Juma, some men appeared telling me to go and meet Doc in front of Mastak, the nearby Khan's house. What a wonderful surprise! We were thrilled to be together again after seven days of separation. The old Khan had milk and toffees sent out. Hafiz Naimi had brought Doc down. It was my first chance to meet this man, a powerful local commander of the Nahzat party. Zawar was with me. Hafiz and Zawar went to talk alone. Then they returned with their proposition. We should write a letter to Engineer Kabir, telling him to come quickly so that "our problem" could be solved in an "easy" and quick way. These two assured us that if the engineer would come--and surely he would--there were no big obstacles at all to our being freed. So I wrote a letter for them to take to Engineer Kabir. Doc and I prayed and parted very encouraged.

Later I found out that Hafiz Naimi and Zawar's family were arch rivals in the area. There was still bad blood between them. Yes, there was a truce, but each side was still being careful. Hence several other soldiers were with Hafiz Naimi now as his body guards.

I joined Zawar for a supper of *sheer brinj* before bed.

Thursday, August 1 -- my birthday!

Not a very busy birthday. I had an English lesson with Reza. He doesn't go to school on Thursdays or Fridays. Then I joined Isa Khan, a neighbor, for lunch. Isa made a contract with Zawar to bring down all the loads of dried mountain leaves from the family's allotted land on the mountainside. Men had earlier cut the leaves and left them to dry. Isa Khan would tie this fodder in huge bundles and bring it down on his back. He could manage three or four loads a day since the area was about two miles away from the house on a steep mountain track.

We had an interesting talk. I grew to like this cheery man. He had worked several months for a German family in Kabul and still remembered many English words!

50

The Commander's House

This morning Zabit and another guard arranged to take me up the valley to visit Doc. It was a beautiful walk and I was so happy to get out.

Although we had already had breakfast, we stopped at Zabit's house on the way for yogurt and fresh bread. Zabit's brother, who had a staph infection causing skin irritation, accompanied us in hopes of getting some help from Doc. When we got near Naimi's house, we stopped in some trees and waited for quite a while. Finally Doc appeared with two of Naimi's brothers. Tea followed.

Doc and I visited and prayed. In a discussion that followed, Naimi's brothers were so adamant and close-minded that I left discouraged. They detailed the injustices of Engineer Kabir and others of the "royal" family: they had not fairly distributed aid and they had kept the lion's share for themselves. There was no way Doc or I would be released until all their rights from the last six or seven years (which Engineer Kabir had "eaten") were given to them.

I tried to reason that whatever anyone else may have done, Doc and I were innocent. But I could have saved my breath.

On the way home we had *sheer rogho*--like *qurti* except that the bread crumbs are soaked in hot milk, and hot butter is poured into a hole in the middle of the bowl.

Zabit's brother, Ali Daryab, walked me home. He had been to Iran and spoke of the civilization there being far superior. He was anxious to leave this backward area as soon as he could.

After a rest in my spacious room at "home", God sent Lala to me. Lala's real name was Ali Juma. He was an elderly man who had served five years in the British army during World War II. He had learned Urdu in the Indian army. He had been on the Burma front--and told me all about his exploits. Later his son came. He tried to console me, but I was feeling down and it didn't help to hear any more of others feeling sorry for me. I often couldn't tell whether this sympathy was contrived or real. I felt someone should do something--take a stand for what's right--rather than just saying, "Tsk, tsk, it's terrible that the Akhund is keeping you here." Later I

THE UPPER HAND

discovered that Lala himself was a man of true sympathy, but didn't have any political clout.

> There are reports of heavy fighting between the resistance and Kabul government troops in Ghazni province. Another report spoke of one of the kidnapping commanders being killed in the Sang-i Masha bazaar. The assumption of the UN is that a solution to the hostage crisis is very close. I am trying to prepare myself for a sinking feeling in my stomach that comes with bad news. At the same time I am hopeful that good news is forthcoming.

Saturday, August 3

After breakfast Zawar let me join him for a morning walk around the farm. I told him of my discouragement from the day before. He told me, however, that the issue raised there was not important. If Engineer Kabir would come, the solution to our problem was very easy.

Sometime later the Khan's grandson, Salahuddin, came over to study English and have tea. He had received permission from Zawar some days earlier. We had some time alone, and I was quick to ask if he knew anything more about our release. He only knew that the leaders were demanding money. Engineer Kabir was working hard, he said.

Charsi, one of the Akhund's most experienced lieutenants, happened to appear as we were studying and talking. He called for Salahuddin, and, in no uncertain terms, told him to leave and not to come back.

I then wrote some English words--with drawings and corresponding Persian words--for a little friend from next door. After yogurt and bread for lunch, Mubariz came to visit. He was a friendly young man. His father had moved to Pashtun country in nearby Uruzgun about 40 years ago to work as a laborer on land owned by Pashtuns. This same land had been seized from the Hazaras in the time of Abdur Rahman Khan, the king before Zahir Shah. About one and a half years ago, however, war broke out between the Pashtuns and Hazaras. Mubariz and his family were forced to leave everything behind and retreat into the safety of Hazara territory.

The Commander's House

After a rest I worked on my diary. I heard shots. But there was no cause for alarm. It was just the traditional way to celebrate a wedding. I walked and jogged around the room. Then Zawar's brother-in-law appeared and I was allowed outside. Supper featured *nan buta.*

Sunday, August 4

My prayers this morning were that I and others would know the power of the risen Christ on this Lord's Day.

Today turned out to be a breakthrough. I was allowed out in the morning to watch the time-consuming job of plastering the threshing floor with a mud and straw mixture. From today on I was allowed more freedom to be outside when the men were working nearby. I found that this kind of distraction helped time to pass much more pleasantly. I played with the kids. I even talked with the ladies as they asked me questions! They had been curious about me and now they had a chance to joke with me a little. The ladies imagined in their minds how different today's task was from anything that would be done in America.

We had tea and *nan*, bread, together at noon in the shade of a small tree. I was so glad to see the more informal family atmosphere--with men and women sitting together. I also realized that on days of hard work, the men would eat bread and tea before they began, then again at 11 or 12, then have a bigger meal (usually *qurti*) around two, have tea and bread again at five, and then have supper just after dark. This could be counted as five meals!

The plastering work just finished at dark. I had been outside the whole day! I spent some time walking, teaching the kids English words, and playing. I started something today that was to become a daily routine for the next two months. Holding on to their hands, I swung some of the kids around in circles. From now on the kids would come to me throughout the day saying, "*Muallim* (my name here meaning "teacher"), please give me a *charkhak*, swing around." I would reply, "Wait till the evening." Then I would give each kid a turn.

Gradually the swinging around in circles developed into a more lengthy repertoire. They would hold onto my thumbs as I lifted them up. They

53

THE UPPER HAND

would jump off high rocks into my hands. I would hold a hand and a foot and swing them around for a *tiara*, airplane. Then, to close the session, I would go through different animal noises in turn.

Today I noted that Ali Shah said to me, "If you were my captive, I'd let you go."

The apricots on the few trees around the house were beginning to ripen. There were many apricot trees at a slightly higher altitude and the kids often brought some down to eat. Because this area was considerably higher and cooler than Sang-i Masha, every kind of fruit ripened later. Mulberries, grapes, and peaches wouldn't grow here.

We ate apricots together before a supper of *nan buta* was served. Two new soldiers appeared as guards.

Monday, August 5

There were nine of us men for breakfast this morning. We ate a little later and enjoyed fresh bread. As I spent time singing, many new songs came to mind. I prayed for my family, co-workers, and friends that every home would be a place of worship and prayer.

A man from Inayat's village behind the mountain, Shatoo, came for a visit. The kids were playing a lot. I shooed them off so I could have a rest. Ali Daryab, Zabit's brother, returned for a talk.

As we were talking, we heard the noise of the Akhund's jeep. It was full of soldiers, as usual. Whenever the Akhund returned from his excursions, I became depressed. I would hope against hope that he would have some good news for me. His coming seemed to always make the wounds from his threats and my captivity fresh again.

The soldiers were all in great spirits. I was glad to take the invitation to go out to the hills with them and walk while they played the popular game of *sangeeruk*--that is, setting up two target stones about 50 meters apart and then throwing stones to try to hit them.

There was a big group for supper. We had *sheer brinj*. The local mullah was also a guest. I felt depressed and really separate from this jolly group. At one point the mullah asked me some questions.

"What organization are you working for?"

The Commander's House

I tried to explain.

"Are you sure it's not CIA?" he countered.

It was interesting that tonight was the first night I had to use the bathroom in the middle of the night because of stomach problems. Necessity quickly helped me overcome my embarrassment and I went downstairs in the dark, and shook one of the shrouded forms on the guest room floor.

"It's me, Muallim. I have to go outside."

The body was Arif's. He got his flashlight and kindly showed me outside.

A messenger arrived in Quetta who had seen Dr. Bill and Joel. He reported that they were fine, although being held separately. They were in the same village, he said, but held by different parties. The messenger said, "Ninety-nine percent of all the people including the Hizb-i Islami are against what the two thieves have done. If you pay money, you will never be able to work here again."

Tuesday, August 6

There were 12 of us for breakfast. Fresh, thick bread, milk, tea,--and sugar! The Akhund had brought a new shipment.

I spent time walking upstairs and singing. The soldiers left. Later on a peddler, *pingi farosh*--or "hairpin seller", arrived and created quite a bit of interest. They carry things around in a wire basket and a sack. Main items are thread, needles, soap, batteries, candy, and other luxuries. Payment can be made in eggs instead of money!

From my second-story vantage point I watched a man and his wife making their threshing floor. Almost every family has their own. Zawar told me that Engineer Kabir will come tomorrow with Akhund to settle things. I'm encouraged.

Bright, young Muhammad Ullah, the 12-year-old brother of Dilkha, came for a visit. He and a brother attend a school at Sang Sulakh, an hour's walk away.

THE UPPER HAND

I took time out for exercise--feeling cramped in the room. Totalled 78 times walking fast around my room, and 91 pushups.

Zawar appeared so I was allowed outside for talking and playing with kids. I could hardly believe it when Zawar told me to go into his room for supper. Dilkha had baby Unis last night. There she was--sitting and nursing. We had a nice, relaxed visit. I was even able to share some of God's Word.

After supper there was the customary *shab shini* or all night party. I stayed for part of it. I was surprised at the games and songs, the relaxed, festive atmosphere. And I kept thinking that if I were a new mother, I certainly would want a peaceful sleep--rather than people partying around me! I learned some puzzles from Mubariz' older brother, and taught them some I knew. Finally, I went off to bed. It was a late night for rural Afghanistan. No soldiers! I really enjoyed going to bed alone--though the kids would say, "Aren't you afraid to go upstairs alone with no light?"

The day ended well. Thank you, Lord.

Tomorrow Dr. Bill and Joel will have been held captive for a complete month. It is certainly not insignificant to these friends and their families. It might appear that nothing is being done. However, efforts are underway on many fronts. With the frustratingly slow and sketchy communication limitations, it is difficult to see any results.

Cindy and I were reminded of His providence in all of this yesterday as we were delayed in getting to a government office by a guest. When we arrived at the office we realized that only moments before a mob had ransacked the building and many of the cars around it. We recognized that He is certainly intervening to protect and guide us in our daily lives. Most certainly He is in control and actively at work in the lives of our two friends in captivity.

Wednesday, August 7

Only three of us for breakfast this morning. The local *akhund*, priest, dropped by. Zawar was trying to sell his donkey--so I accompanied him

56

The Commander's House

outside to show it to a customer. It was a good time to borrow Zawar's first wife's nail clippers--made in USA .

I went back to my room for a quiet time. I was encouraged in seeking God's face. He's in control! I wrote these words to the tune of *"Thank you, Lord, for saving my soul"*.

> *Thank you, Lord, for walking with me.*
> *Thank you, Lord, for being my friend.*
> *Thank you, Lord, for promising me*
> *That you will walk with me to the end.*

Some time later my singing and studying was interrupted by a welcome and familiar figure below. It was M. Atiq Salimi. Doc and I called him Mark's brother because he helped Mark on his trip this spring--and he is light-skinned and red-haired. Mark thought he spoke English with a Texan accent! Atiq had come to "offer congratulations on the birth of Zawar's son."

I knew that Atiq had left for Pakistan shortly after our kidnapping and I was glad to see him back. He was able to tell me a little about Pakistan and the progress in our situation. He said he had a letter to give me later. We couldn't talk freely, but it was a great assurance to know that I had a "supporter" so close by. From my upstairs window I could see Mastak, the ancient fortress with a lone tower which was Atiq's home.

Another pleasant surprise today. Zawar's father-in-law came to invite me to lunch! Zawar wasn't there, but I was allowed to go! It took us 20 minutes to walk to the lush village of Qabar Qul, nestled higher up the valley beside a small stream.

We had an enjoyable walk and fellowship. I told Atee Aziz that I didn't want to go without Zawar's permission--but he assured me that everything was safe and okay.

The home was beautiful--constructed only several years earlier. Afghan carpenters do wonders with only basic tools. Large glass windows. A large cupboard in the wall with glass doors. And the walls, although only mud plaster, looked as smooth and finished as any cement wall in Islamabad! A

57

THE UPPER HAND

large Persian carpet from northern Afghanistan was in the center of the guest room. All around it were beautiful sitting mats and cushions to lean on. Potted plants were on the window sill. Posters of places in Iran and Pakistan were on the walls. I felt privileged to be here.

After some conversation, one of the boys appeared with a basin and pitcher for washing hands. This was always a sign that the meal would be served soon! And what a meal! *Shorwa*--bowls of broth came first into which we broke up bread until the mixture became semi-solid. When we had eaten this, along with onion sprouts, the mutton was divided and eaten with bread and salt. There were some delicious chunks of fat, too! After this was, of course, tea. It had been weeks since I last had meat.

When I returned home at 2 p.m., I went back to my room to be locked up. I noticed men plowing outside. Guests had arrived--an elderly man and his grandson, Naimat (12). I was to get to know them well in the next few days, and see them later in Patu, their home.

After playing with the kids at sunset, guess what we had for supper! More meat! Guests had come for another night of singing and celebrating the birth of little Unis.

Thursday, August 8

I suppose because of the guests we had a special breakfast this morning. It was *chob josh*, or Hazara *parathas*--a kind of fried bread.

The ladies cleaned the guest room today. After singing and playing with the kids, my lunch (or so I thought!) appeared. Bread and yogurt, which I quite enjoyed. It wasn't very many hours later when a big bowl of hot, fried rice appeared. I couldn't finish it all--so Reza helped me!

Today God encouraged me in a small but meaningful way. The soldiers had taken Doc's pen but had left mine. I knew that there wasn't much ink left--but still I would let the kids draw pictures on bits of paper whenever they wanted, unless I was writing in my pocket notebook. Well, today my pen ran out of ink. And today one of Naimi's soldiers came with supplies that Engineer Kabir had sent. Toilet paper, a flashlight, soap, and...two pens! Someone was watching over me.

58

The Commander's House

After watching the men plow, and then harvest *adas*, a small, soybean-like bean used mainly for animal fodder, I had a chance to talk some more with Atiq. Zawar had invited him for supper. Clearly the issue of our freedom was becoming more complicated. In spite of God's assurance of his love today, I went to bed discouraged.

Friday, August 9

Bath day again! The second since my arrival on July 24. I surely appreciated the bucket of hot water--and the privacy of the whole barn/kitchen. Now I changed from Zawar's suit, which I had been wearing since the last bath, back into my own clothes--kindly washed by the ladies of the house.

I spent some time writing a letter to Doc. I tried to include some verses I remembered as well as a hymn or two--since Doc had told me that he didn't remember hymns too well. Certainly we could encourage each other at every opportunity--and we did!

Today Zawar, Zabit, and I were invited to Atiq's tower for lunch. What a wonderful break from the routine at Boldraghna (the Akhund's house)! We drank tea, listened to music, and looked at books. I was fascinated by an atlas of Afghanistan printed in Iran.

I asked to go out to use the bathroom. Shamsuddin showed me the way and this was the opportunity I was looking for to give him the letters I had written. He had no fresh news to tell me. I had written the following lines to Mark:

"We are well and grateful for all you are doing on our behalf.
We want to be set free in the way and at the time that gives our
Savior the most glory and advances His kingdom the most.
May God guide and sustain you."

Lunch featured really delicious *lobia*--a kind of kidney beans, and meat.

An interesting thing about this room was the presence of a chair! I don't know how it got there. But it was one of the few chairs I saw in my time in Afghanistan. Atiq jokingly said that it was for special people--like the mullah, when he visited.

59

THE UPPER HAND

Back home I joined Baba and Naimat for tea. Baba had eye problems. I told him about Dr. Friesen in Peshawar and, at his request, even wrote a letter for him to Dr. Friesen. I doubt he'll ever make it to Peshawar. I also told him that Doc might be able to help him--so we planned to ask Zawar if we could make a trip to see Doc together--with accompanying guards, of course!

After supper I sat for a long time in the upstairs window watching the continual flashes over the eastern mountains. Sometimes when I had seen this earlier I had wondered what kind of storm could have so much lightning. But it wasn't lightning. It was fighting around Ghazni. I went to bed with a heart full of thanks to God for safety, and a deep feeling of well-being.

Saturday, August 10

Zawar agreed today for Zabit to take me to see Doc. I managed to have some quiet time before we left with Baba and Naimat. On the way there, we met one of Naimi's relatives going the opposite way on a donkey. Obviously, he was a man of means! He beckoned Zabit and they had a private talk. The result was that Baba and Naimat were not allowed to go with us. Naimi didn't want people from other areas taking advantage of Doc's medical services.

Doc and I were allowed some time together alone. He took me to a favorite haunt--the pea patch! The fresh peas were really good. Doc was thankful that his stomach could handle quite a lot of these--and he knew he was getting vitamins. We shared and prayed. God had been ministering to Doc and encouraging him. He mentioned that once the first month of our captivity had passed, things seemed to be easier somehow. I felt the same way. But the time was all too brief. Back for tea with one of Naimi's brothers. This time there was no confrontation. I knew there would be no benefit in bringing up our problem.

On the way home we stopped at the house of one of Zabit's friends. They had recently joined the Hizb-i Islami group to try to get some support for a land disagreement they had with some of Naimi's relations.

The Commander's House

Soon a *qurti* lunch appeared. I was getting bored by all the talk--so covered myself with a sheet at the end of the room for a nap and prayer time. The men had begun playing cards.

Later I was allowed out in the meadow to walk around. I felt really down. But singing helped. Later my spirits lifted as I watched the family butcher a sheep for an evening feast. I realized later that this is all a part of the local system of justice. If you have a problem, you call the elders and powerful men who will be in your favor, give them the best meal you can, then, hopefully, they will help you!

Many guests had come to discuss the land problem. I knew we wouldn't make it home tonight--so I slept fitfully in a room full of other men.

An envoy from Jaghori arrived in the Hizb-i Wahdat office in Quetta saying that the hostage problem is solved. The American people will be here in two or three days. Now there is no problem.

I am very hopeful. I am making reservations for Dr. Bill and myself to London. Ed Rasmussen, a senior TEAM missionary, and possibly Joel's father will travel with us to Quetta. We are not informing anyone in Pakistan until we have the men on Pakistani soil.

Sunday, August 11

I didn't sleep too well, but I was grateful for the morning. It's a little cooler here--I guess because of the slightly higher altitude. There was frost on the ground this morning. I ran back and forth on the path for exercise--careful to stay in view of the house.

Breakfast was leisurely with a lot more talk about the land dispute. One man was assigned to take me home--and I was glad to go! Amazing that even in captivity I had become used to one place and felt more comfortable there than in a constantly changing situation.

On the way home we had tea in my escort's house. He had returned from work in Iran just days earlier. It was interesting to talk to him about the situation for Afghans there. It seems like most people I had talked to who had worked there had at some time or other been put in prison.

61

THE UPPER HAND

Sometimes, if they didn't have the proper permission, they were forcibly sent back to Afghanistan.

When I arrived "home", I saw Zawar breaking down the temporary mud wall that blocked a door on the eastern side of my upstairs room. He had made a contract with a relative, Jan Ali, to plaster the walls and floors of the big upper room.

I immediately liked Jan Ali and his son and helper, Aziz. They were no-nonsense people. They were kind and direct. Jan Ali had worked many years in the southern part of Pakistan as a *mistery*--a mason using mud or cement. It was amazing how fast he worked and how good his work turned out! We often talked in Urdu together.

Jan Ali took three days to finish the rough plaster of the walls and floor. Zawar had to provide the mud when Jan Ali needed it. Zawar kept busy mixing straw and dirt--then bringing it to the mason in a wheelbarrow. The girls, Razia and Nafisa, were busy hauling water, and I helped them in this. I claimed that drawing water from the well and then carrying it around the house and up the steps was good exercise for me. And it was! I appreciated Zawar's attitude towards my help, too. He liked it when I helped--but never forced me to do manual labor. We had a mutual understanding. He knew that I didn't complain to others about him or his treatment, but rather was thankful for his kindness.

The Akhund appeared at dusk in the jeep full of soldiers. My heart sank and I pleaded with the Lord for courage and endurance. The talk around supper was interesting. God had helped me to face my captor once again.

A message from a Hizb-i Wahdat leader arrived saying that the party was raising the full US $15,000 to pay for the release of the hostages. The Wahdat office in Quetta said over the phone that there is a 99% chance that the hostages will be free in the next 36 hours.

Another traveler arrived from Jaghori today and told friends in Quetta that the Americans are free.

The   Commander's   House

Monday, August 12

It was humorous this morning when Zawar got the soldiers to help him harvest wheat after breakfast. Most of them are young guys under 20. They're used to traveling around with their guns, sitting hours on end, talking, and drinking tea. Some of them, granted, work hard on their land when they're not on soldier duty--but most of these guys were on permanent assignment. They didn't relish the idea of hard work! When they came home mid afternoon, they were tired and hungry. And some of the light-hearted joking had stopped!

I could have gone with the soldiers, but I opted to stay with Jan Ali and Aziz--and watch their work. I enjoyed their fellowship.

We had a delicious lunch of rice and cooked greens. Sometimes they cook fresh potato leaves, tender parts of alfalfa, and even poppy leaves! My stomach began to feel upset and gassy.

God gave special grace at supper with the Akhund and his soldiers. Jan Ali also stayed the night. The soldiers wanted to learn some English. I helped them some--writing some things down for them to learn. Little did I realize that soon I would be spending three months with just soldiers! Jan Ali kept the conversation going after supper with stories from Pakistan and from his days of working with Americans in Kandahar. He couldn't say enough good things about their character and the work they did.

Tuesday, August 13

Stomach problems bothered me last night. After an emergency rest stop in the middle of the night, I felt better. I was thankful that I was alone upstairs--and that the floor had not yet been plastered! There was about six inches of loose dirt all over.

The breakfast conversation drifted to religious topics. Of course everyone was curious to know what I believed about certain things. It was a good chance to share things important to me. But, as usual, I sensed more curiosity than deep yearning to know the truth.

Today Aziz didn't come. So I gladly became his father's helper. He wanted to plaster the whole floor today. First, by ingenious use of his

63

THE UPPER HAND

string and level, he determined that the dirt floor was far from level. I hadn't even noticed this. Remember that my room was about 70 feet by 20 feet! We spent quite a lot of time wheel barrowing dirt around and spreading it out until Ali Jan was satisfied at the even level.

The next step was to put handfuls of mud at regular points in a line, pat them down flat, and using the string and a straight stick, make sure they were at the same level. This was enough for a professional mason. Zawar had been madly mixing the dirt, water, and straw in the next room. Now we started wheeling in wheelbarrow after wheelbarrow of mud. Jan Ali spread it out and, using his long "two by four" stick, made it smooth and level.

Of course we had a tea and bread break around 11 a.m. Then we had a rice lunch when we finished around 2 p.m.

Jan Ali was concerned about my plight. "The Akhund is my relative. I will put a word in his ear that he should release you. The money he gets for you will not be worth it."

I appreciated his concern. But I had come to know the Akhund now and realized that Jan Ali's suggestion wouldn't bear much weight.

After a time for rest, prayer, and writing in my diary, I went out to watch Zawar and others harvesting wheat in nearby fields. I took notebooks with me that Abdul Hussain and other neighbors had given me. They wanted me to fill them with English so they could study it in the winter when there was nothing to do.

TEACHING ENGLISH

I discovered that, after writing many pages of English for different ones, that I was developing a certain format--an English teaching technique! For the little kids who couldn't read, or could read only simple things, I taught words in groups and drew a picture for each word. I started with "eye, ear, nose, mouth, hand, and foot." Then it was, "How are you? Fine, thank you." I would write every word in English, then write the English in Persian script, and then write the Persian word.   Later, for soldiers or others who gave me a notebook or a lot of paper, I would write a page on each of the following topics:

ALPHABET	CONVERSATION	FRUIT	NUMBERS
GREETINGS	VEGETABLES	FAMILY	REQUESTS
DISHES	BODY PARTS	ANIMALS	FOOD
CLOTHES	NATURE	TOOLS	SCHOOL
TRAVEL	PERSONAL ITEMS	SHOP	COLORS
OCCUPATIONS	PEOPLE	TIME	HOUSE
QUESTION WORDS			
CONVERSATION IN A RESTAURANT			

By popular demand I also had a section on WAR words!

It was amazing to me what kind of people took an interest in learning English. Mullah Ali Reza said he wanted to master the alphabet so he could read the labels on medicine bottles. While living at the Commander's house, my star pupils were little Ali Shah, Reza, and Juma. I think they were challenged to use their fertile minds and thrilled at how much they could learn. And there was the element of competition. Zawar learned many of the basic words because he heard them from his kids and he loved to have the kids repeat English words to any guest who happened by. He was proud of their accomplishments.

The girls were keen to learn, too. Especially things like "tea, bread, cup, teapot," etc. They liked to visit with me and often asked me the name of item after item in English. I knew there was no way they would remember them all!

The kids also realized early on that I was trying to learn their language. They saw that I wrote down every new word that I learned. And every time I came across a word in their conversation that I didn't know, I would ask them what it meant. They became trained and excellent language helpers! And they loved to come up with words that I didn't know and needed to write down.

The part of my English notebooks that attracted real interest was the page on "tools". The village people were tickled to see my drawings of the

THE UPPER HAND

tools that were so common to them, to read their names in the local dialect, and to realize that they had equivalent English words!

Later on, when I received two strong, small notebooks sent from Pakistan, I dedicated one to be a *Hazaragi* dictionary. I took all the words that I had written so far on scraps of paper and put them both in alphabetical order and in categories according to their meaning. I usually kept this notebook with me to be ready for new additions. And this became an amusement for the people around me. Many times soldiers would be sitting around and one would say, "Muallim, let me see your notebook." They would read some of the entries and laugh and laugh. It was funny for them to see many of their colloquialisms written down!

As I had discovered before in my work in refugee camps in Pakistan, I found that some of my closest and most enduring friendships came through teaching English. Though a captive, I was able to help people. People realized that I wanted to go home. They appreciated me spending my time for them. And, of course, being involved in a worthwhile project helped me to pass my time!

Another benefit of teaching: everyone called me *Muallim*, Teacher. They knew that I was an English teacher in Pakistan. Someone had begun a rumor that Doc and I had been the former US ambassador and a US spy in Iran. My English teaching helped folk to realize that what I said I was, was true. I was for real. It helped to prove my integrity as well as to show that I was a follower of Christ who went about doing good and forgiving his enemies.

I talked with a group of men from the surrounding houses. They were very sympathetic. They often said to me that they prayed and hoped for the day of my release.

I went for a walk carrying little Arif. Yaqub was with me. Supper with Zawar and his family was bread, milk, and tea. Even if his kids didn't have milk, Zawar insisted that I have at least one cup before we started drinking tea. Zawar encouraged me tonight to trust in God and keep hoping. He knew that I prayed often and wanted to give God glory in my life. He said God would hear my prayers. He would often say, "There's only one thing that cannot be solved. That's death." Interestingly, his words did encourage me to cheer up and trust in God.

I sat in the window and meditated a long time before going to bed. The stars are so bright when there's no moon. And every time the full moon comes around, I think of how many months I've been in captivity. Will I be free by the next full moon?

Only Zawar and Mubariz were my guards tonight.

Wednesday, August 14

I dreamed last night of teaching English back in Islamabad!

I slept well. And today my stomach is much better. After breakfast I spent time writing in the upstairs window--my diary and a letter to Doc. I spent some time thinking about Revelation and Isaiah 6.

Ali Juma came for a visit and lunch. He's the one who had been in the British army in World War II and knew Urdu well. While chatting I took the opportunity to briefly share the good news about Jesus. He mentioned that he would invite me to his home for dinner soon. I heard nothing about this from Zawar in the next couple of days--so assumed plans had changed or I wasn't allowed to go.

Zia, the Akhund's nephew, took me out in the afternoon for a walk. We ate some apricots from trees around the house. Then I returned to be locked up in my room. After a while I felt cooped up. Thankfully Zawar returned from the water mill before dark and I could go out and play with the kids.

Thursday, August 15

Last night I dreamed of going home. Since my captivity, my dream life seems to have become more active! Even in afternoon naps my thoughts often go back to some aspect of my past life.

Since the floor of my huge upstairs room had been newly plastered, I had been sleeping in the upstairs stair well--just enough room for my *toshak*, or mattress. Today the floor plaster had dried sufficiently to walk on it. In fact, Zawar thought that walking on it would make it stronger--so I assured him that I would pack it down well! I spent time singing and

THE UPPER HAND

walking around. The new and special song that came to my mind today was, *Take Time to be Holy*. The words were a great encouragement and helped me in praying for others. I spent time praying for Afghanistan. I went outside to watch the wheat harvesting in a nearby field. The neighbor two houses down, Anwar Raziyee, invited me over for a visit and some big, juicy apricots from his carefully protected garden. He seemed to be a nice guy. I remembered that he had been in the jeep with the Akhund when Doc and I were whisked away at night from Patu to Baba.

After a snack of bread and tea, I watched as Zawar and others made supports from fresh poplar trunks for branches of Zawar's apple trees. It really looked like there would be a bumper crop in a few weeks.

Dear Ali Shah asked me today, "Why don't you escape?" Then he added, "If I were bigger, I'd help you." He's about 7.

After a late lunch and a rest, I went to watch Zawar and Atee Muhammad Ali cutting wheat in a different field. Zawar reprimanded me for talking to Raziyee. I hadn't realized it before, but since my captivity, they had become enemies. Zawar was angry and somehow expected that I had known I shouldn't be talking with Raziyee. This displeasure upset me, but I committed the matter to God.

After a delicious supper of greens and bread, I sat for a long time in the window upstairs thinking of new songs. The new moon soon disappeared behind the mountains across the valley.

Friday, August 16

This morning I had breakfast very late in the fields with the men. Being Friday, Reza didn't go to school. Sometimes he could be a real pest. I returned to my stair well since the floor in my room wasn't dry enough yet to sleep on. I wanted to have some time of quiet prayer, but Reza insisted on coming along and pestering me. I tried to pray but couldn't concentrate as Reza kept singing and bugging me. Finally I asked forgiveness from him and the Lord. I helped him with his English first--then spent time in prayer. I asked that my friends might walk with God today.

Out with the workers for a tea and bread snack. Lunch later was one of my favorites--*sheer brinj*, milk rice. This afternoon Arif's pants fell

68

down into the well. I volunteered to retrieve them. I was really surprised to see four frogs in the well. Up to this point I had considered the well a source of purest drinking water--and I used it to brush my teeth, etc. I reported to Zawar that I had seen frogs in the well and now wanted to use water from the nearby *karez* for my teeth. Everyone thought this was hilarious. They all knew that frogs are clean animals. This story was repeated many times later for other people!

There were stories about Doc, too. I wrote the following lines from the soldier's base months later:

> Stories--Our hosts delighted in telling certain incidents about Doc and me.
> The audiences would roar and howl with pleasure.
> Doc didn't know how to ask for an egg,
> So he flapped his wings, crowed,
> And brought forth an "egg" in his hand!
> His hosts understood.

I was permitted to borrow Dilkha's sewing machine for some much-needed repairs on my two suits. It was fun to do something different! And how grateful I was for Mom, who taught me to use a sewing machine when I was in 6th grade.

Repairs done, I was feeling frustrated that I couldn't go outside. After some time I was let out to play. Commander Salihi joined us for supper in "Reza's house". Zawar had great affection for Salihi.

Today a man handed me two small notebooks through the briars that blocked the door on the far east side of my upstairs room. These were from Muallim Wahid in answer to a request I had made.

Saturday, August 17

I woke before dawn as I heard some men talking below. I heard my name mentioned and my heart sank. "Maybe they'll take me away again," I thought. But nothing happened. Reza came to wake me some time later. As was my routine, I got up just after the men rose to say their prayers.

THE UPPER HAND

After 20 minutes or so of exercises--stretching, push ups, sit ups, back exercises, running in place, kicks, etc.--I would go outside, get a full jug of water from the well, and make my way to the outhouse. There was no door on this small room that faced the side of the mountain--so I tried to remember to cough as I approached to escape the embarrassment of finding it occupied! By the same token, when I was inside, I would cough if it seemed anyone was approaching!

The pile of refuse kept getting nearer the hole in the raised outhouse floor. I wondered what would happen. I was pleasantly surprised that not too many flies kept buzzing around the refuse. Bees were more of a problem. One day Zawar mixed the refuse with dirt and carried it off to the field on a donkey.

While on this interesting topic, the outhouse was mainly for guests. The family used rocks behind the house as cover and the smaller kids went to the bathroom almost anywhere they felt like it. I never saw a lady go into the outhouse.

After the outhouse, I would use my soap sparingly to wash my hands and face. Then I'd go up to my room until I saw some of the kids carrying the tray of breakfast things from the house to the guest room.

Because the men were working today, they didn't have breakfast before they left. I prayed part of the Lord's prayer for my family, fellowship members, and co-workers in Islamabad. "Lead me not into temptation but deliver me from evil." Just as I finished praying, tea, milk, and hot *nan* arrived. How thankful I was for God's abundant, good and timely provision of food!

I noted in my diary that I was up to 465 songs today in the list I was making of songs I remembered and would sing through. Some of my favorites were:

"When morning guilds the skies"
"Peace, perfect peace, in this dark world of sin"
"Great is Thy faithfulness"
"What a friend we have in Jesus"
"Lord, have mercy on us"
"God moves in a mysterious way"
"How good is the God we adore"

The Commander's House

"Jesus, you're the sweetest name of all"
"Wherever I am, I'll praise him"

I watched plowing practice outside. The big project today was threshing a soybean-like bean on the threshing floor. After the treading of the oxen, the beans were separated from the chaff by winnowing in the wind. Everyone went inside for *qurti* at 10 a.m. It hadn't been long since my breakfast!

After this it was interesting to watch the sale of one of Zawar's oxen outside. Half the payment, or so, was made with literally bundles of money. Afghanistan's paper money has so little value.

Host Ali Juma arrived at noon to take us to his home for lunch. I enjoyed the walk with him and Zawar to his small settlement up a side valley called "Sokhtanak". Three of his sons were there. We had a nice visit with WONDERFUL food--meat, broth, cooked greens, yogurt and onions.

Bath day again! The sun felt good afterwards, and I sat near the threshing floor playing games on paper with Ali Shah. Later I walked and played with the rest of the kids.

Sunday, August 18

Had breakfast in "Reza's house" with the workers this morning. For big tasks, Zawar often gets one or two workers to help him for a day. There is a daily wage--usually 800 to 1000 afghanis. (The exchange rate at this time was approximately 1000 afghanis to one dollar!) Meals and tea are also the responsibility of the one who hires. Sometimes wages are paid in wheat, or some other exchange is made.

We all walked together to the fields above Mastak, Muhammad Atiq's home . This was land that Zawar was renting from the local "feudal lord's" family. Interestingly, the boys from this family had been our English students in Islamabad. I remember one day when they had invited us for lunch in Islamabad. They had shown us pictures of Jaghori. At that time I had no idea that I would ever see the places they were showing me.

THE UPPER HAND

Zawar pointed to a ruined house up the valley. "That was Jalil and Khalil's home." He knew that I had known these boys in Islamabad.

I was glad for the chance to be outside and felt guilty that the three men were working so hard and I was just sitting around. I took an extra sickle and attempted to cut wheat with them. Zawar gave me a few tips--but I wasn't doing so well! I realized there was a real art to harvesting wheat. Finally Zawar said, "You'll hurt yourself. Just sit and watch us." I spent some time alone writing and praying.

Razia and Nasima soon appeared with tea and bread. On the trip over they had broken "my" cup. I feel they kept this cup for me partly out of respect and partly so no one would be offended that they were drinking from the same cup as a *kafir*, unbeliever. So I didn't mind that much that it was broken!

I spent several hours walking back and forth along the stream and singing. On our way home we walked a different way--passing a big *nahoor*, irrigation pond, where boys were swimming. We stopped at the Khan's pea patch to get a few peas to take home. Then we passed someone else's apricot trees--and ate our fill of delicious apricots.

It was 3 p.m. when we got home. I took a nap, enjoyed some more tea and bread, and then played with the kids outside.

Monday, August 19

Dreamed last night of friends in Peshawar.

Spent a long, uninterrupted time in prayer for a heavenly perspective. Breakfast was brought to me very late. Sometimes I would think that the ladies had forgotten me. But I don't think they ever did!

The harvesters were working in a different area today. I discovered a fairly level path on the slope on the other side of the stream from where they were working. This made a great place for me to walk back and forth and sing and pray. The men could see me, so weren't worried about my running away. The kids walked with me for a while--but soon got bored and went off under the trees to play their own games. They made a seesaw out of some of the poplar logs that had been felled there!

The Commander's House

I had made a list of all the prayer supporters and friends I could remember back in the States and other places. I prayed through this list and felt a real peace and blessing from God through this intercession.

Razia brought *nan tar*, bread crumbs over which buttermilk is poured and then the mixture is eaten with big spoons. Also there was tea and peas that had been cooked in the pods. These were yummy! We all ate together in the shade.

The men were often amazed that I could walk back and forth for hour after hour. I explained that I appreciated the chance for exercise. And really, singing and praying, I didn't notice the time very much. I discovered that the exercise helped to release mental and emotional tension.

The menu today featured *nan buta* for lunch and supper. I quite enjoy this dish--although all the locals talk of it as being very "heavy".

As I was carrying water in buckets from the *karez* for use in the house, one of the neighbor girls told me that she was against my being held for money. Then, as I passed two older ladies, they said that they were always sad when they saw me and always prayed for my quick release and reunion with my family. Everywhere there are people with kind hearts!

> Another day! I have avoided this hostage log over the past three days because of the discouragement of our dispelled hopes of an immediate release of our two friends. I continue, however, to keep notes on various conversations.

Tuesday, August 20 -- My brother, Tim's, birthday!

The harvesting was going on in the same place as yesterday. I walked back and forth along the same path I used yesterday. The discussion over the morning tea break turned out to be quite heated. I expressed my anger at injustice--and that it was all done in the name of religion. The men sometimes implied that really Engineer Kabir was at fault for all that had gone wrong. This made me madder! Engineer Kabir was the person who seemed most concerned about his people's welfare. He was trying to help them. But it was people like the Akhund who, for personal gains in money and power, prevented the poor from getting help. I stated in no uncertain

73

THE UPPER HAND

terms that I felt the real problem of Afghanistan was that people did not fear God. Outwardly they were religious, but they didn't care about the important things like mercy and justice.

At this time Zawar encouraged me to get Engineer Kabir or anyone else involved to quickly pay the full amount demanded so I would not waste anymore of my time in Afghanistan! Later he commented that I was right in my views, but he said I was too intense.

Walking until two helped me to get some of the anger out of my system. I thought through as much of the Bible as I could remember from Genesis to Moses. The kids brought a delicious snack of *pirkee*, known in other parts of Afghanistan as *bolani*--vegetables surrounded by dough and fried. In this case the vegetable was alfalfa greens!

Someone communicated a rumor today that Abbasi or some others of the Hazara Hizb-i Islami leaders in Pakistan had been imprisoned in order to help get me released. At supper Zawar said something encouraging about the possibilities for my freedom. I went to bed encouraged.

Today I noted some of the questions that the women folk asked me "Do you speak *Hazaragi* in your home?" "Is it really night in America when it's day here?"

I explained to many people at different times how the earth rotates around the sun--so half of the earth is light while the other half is dark. I would often use a tea cup and tea pot for a demonstration!

"Is it true that it is night for six months of the year somewhere in America?" "Do they really irrigate by airplane in America?"

I had great joy in growing closer to this village family. When I had first moved into the commander's house, the ladies all stayed carefully covered. They sent the kids with my meals. I never went to the kitchen. But all this changed with time. It wasn't long before one of the ladies said, "You're like a brother now--part of our family."

A rumor went around Quetta that the hostages were released to the Gilani party.

I spoke with the director of the coordinating body for Afghan work in Quetta. We are having a meeting tomorrow of agencies at work in Jaghori.

The Commander's House

We are trying to shut off all projects in the area. This includes projects of five different agencies.

Wednesday, August 21

I was alone in my room all day until 5 p.m. Zawar had gone to a medical store. I prayed for faith like Moses for me and others I upheld regularly. It could have been a frustrating day, but it wasn't. I walked around the room hundreds of times, singing and thinking. I thought of God's goodness to me all through my life. I decided to write to seven people who had especially helped me spiritually. I wrote to Dad and Mom first, then to a man who had helped me as a child to understand faith in Jesus Christ.

When Zawar returned, he knew that I would be tired of being inside. He invited me outside to watch as he made a door. Tea and bread were served there as the kids and I watched him. I picked up the interesting word in *Hazaragi* for hammer--*algha*, which is exactly the same as the word for the palm of a hand.

As I was playing with the kids later, Naseema was being a little terror. I warned her not to hit me again. She did, so I grabbed her and spanked her. She really got mad. And I had the terrible feeling that maybe I had lost a friend. Soon after, one of the ladies told me to walk in a different area. I felt humiliated. But it wasn't long before my relationship with Naseema was restored.

My private room changed to barracks tonight. Four men slept upstairs with me. I resented losing my privacy and didn't sleep too well.

Thursday, August 22

I had breakfast alone when the men left. Zawar left for a fatiha, funeral, in Shatoo. He was away until late--so I was kept inside until 6 p.m.! I spent my time writing English in notebooks and writing *Hazaragi* words that I had learned.

I noticed a man ride up to Mastak on a motorcycle. Somehow my attention was drawn to him--partly because any sight of a motorcycle or car

75

THE UPPER HAND

was a rare occurrence! I watched as he began to walk towards our house. When he got near, I recognized him. It was Aminullah, Engineer Kabir's brother-in-law. I watched him from out of sight. Nadir, the Akhund's brother, was home and Aminullah talked with him. Then they called for me to come into the guest room downstairs.

We had a short talk. Nadir agreed secretly to help Amin and for only a "small" amount of money, have me transported secretly to Sang-i Masha. At the time I was encouraged, but later, as days and days passed, I realized nothing would come of this. I don't believe Nadir was really sincere.

Amin brought Doc's New Testament for him, a letter from Phil, my brother, for me, and a book, **Robinson Crusoe**, for me! Phil's letter was the first news I had from home. It was hand-written on July 23. Tears came to my eyes as I read the words:

> "We've been thinking of you a lot recently. We are concerned for your safety, sanity, and physical well-being. We were very relieved to hear recently from people who have seen you that you are being treated well and your needs and some desires were being met. We have a high level of confidence that this favorable situation is continuing. It's difficult being in the dark--especially in your situation where you don't have a lot to distract you. We know you are good at making the best of any situation and are certainly glad you are not alone.
>
> We are looking forward to your return and will have to start planning a celebration. We anticipate that things will return to normal for you soon.
>
> Hi! from Barb (Phil's wife). Trust that your spirit is holding up. We know that there are so many things to be thankful for. You are in our thoughts constantly and are cared about very much. Zack misses a beard to pull on and the sound of your watch--beep, beep. We're looking forward to having some *chai* with you at a grungy *chai* shop soon.
>
> Message by phone from Dad and Mom: Love and prayers from Dad, Mom, all family, and many, many friends. Psalm 91:1.

76

The   Commander's   House

When Aminullah left, I spent time in prayer before lunch came of buttermilk, bread and onion sprouts. I read some from the New Testament and then copied James 1--knowing that I needed to pass on the NT to Doc as soon as possible. What a treat it was to read the Word of God--especially some parts I had been thinking about but hadn't remembered exactly.

I was allowed out in the courtyard to walk. Hussain Ali, a relative of Zawar's first wife, came on a visit from Sang-i Masha. He and his brother have a goldsmith shop there. I had tea with him and a good talk. He was very sympathetic and offered to take any letters I wanted to write.

At supper time Zawar wasn't around. Dilkha spoke to me saying that she was sorry for my plight and that I had been in all day. She said that all the ladies in the house thought it was wrong for me to be kept as a captive. Amazing how such sympathy would lift my spirits!

Friday, August 23

I slept better last night even though two other soldiers were upstairs. In my prayer time this morning I read over Peter's first epistle from the New Testament. I thought over the topics of God's holiness, Christ's precious blood, and the exhortation to fervent love. I had been reading First Peter during the days of our animal health project.

When I was alone, I wrote notes for Hussain Ali to take to Engineer Kabir and to a boy who had been one of our students.

Of course, everyone was interested in my new book--***Robinson Crusoe***. I enjoyed it tremendously--and didn't want to read too much of it at any one time so it would last longer. Many things in the book encouraged me to wait and trust in God. Also to be thankful and make the best of my situation. As I started reading it today, Reza was nearby making drawings.

77

THE UPPER HAND

A man and his nephew came to visit Zawar. The nephew had originally signed up to work with the animal health project. He told me that one of Engineer Kabir's mistakes was not choosing a boy from the Hizb-i Islami party to be one of the students.

I wrote a letter to another man who had had an impact on my early spiritual life. This was a continuation of my plan to write letters. Then I copied Philippians 1 from Doc's New Testament to study.

I was allowed out to walk around in the courtyard. I was full of pent-up energy. When Zawar returned home, I was allowed outside.

After supper I was frustrated as it seemed like men had decided to permanently spend the nights in "my" room. They kept talking for a long time. I couldn't go to sleep so got up and paced the floor until they decided to bed down.

Saturday, August 24

I dreamed last night of Murree Christian School, the school I had attended in Pakistan from first to twelfth grade!

I talked for quite a while with Zawar this morning about the report of a meeting arranged "to solve our problem".

A man appeared wanting me to write a note to Doc about his sickness. Soon after, Doc himself appeared accompanied by several soldiers. We visited together until 11 a.m. and had time to pray alone. Doc was overjoyed to receive his New Testament.

After Doc had left, Nafisa asked me to take care of Arif. I was happy to do it. She didn't have the key to unlock my door--so she handed him to me through the window! Arif was a good kid and didn't take much entertaining. Besides, he liked being with me.

Two hours later I was allowed outside to walk. After playing with the kids, it was my custom to help Razia and Nafisa and others carry their buckets of water from the *karez*. Today some of the people asked me not to carry water. "Our enemies are reporting that we're forcing you to work," they said.

Tonight I was frustrated again by the soldiers talking on into the night. But I committed the problem to the Lord and was able to sleep well.

The Commander's House

Sunday, August 25

I dreamed of our family being at Aunt Doris' home in New Jersey for a dinner!

I exercised downstairs since there were five men upstairs.

Today was bath day again.

Arif came up to my room and enjoyed a two to three hour nap!

Muallim Wahid, our chosen project supervisor under Engineer Kabir, came to visit with Shamsuddin, Muhammad Atiq's nephew. He hadn't come earlier out of fear of what might happen. He lives about an hour's walk away in Chilbaghtu. They brought no new news, but gave me a pen, which I needed.

I read more of **Robinson Crusoe** and was locked in until dusk. I was mad. But soon I repented of this wrong attitude. Later, as I was walking around, a very distinguished-looking guest arrived on a donkey. He was Agha Sahib--Inayat's older brother from Shatoo. He was a *Sayyid*. I didn't warm up to him very quickly, but later really enjoyed his visit. He was an educated and open-minded man. He had lived much of his life in Kabul before the Russian invasion.

There was almost non-stop talking through the night and the men were up in "my" room. I knew something was going on at Mastak, the Khan's fortress, that was now Muhammad Atiq's home, but it wasn't clear exactly what until morning. A messenger came breathless with news. Many soldiers from Chilbaghtu-i Pashi had surrounded Mastak. They were demanding that Muhammad Atiq's niece be given to a man from their area in marriage, as she had previously agreed to do. Rumor had it that now she was unhappy with the man and wanted to run away to Pakistan. The soldiers wanted to take her by force!

Monday, August 26

We had six soldier guests from Chilbaghtu-i Pashi for breakfast. They had agreed to abandon the use of force and wait for a decision from the elders and commanders about the bride-to-be.

79

THE UPPER HAND

For my morning meditation I thought and prayed about Philippians 1:11 "...*that you may be filled with the fruits of righteousness which are by Jesus Christ to the glory and praise of God.*"

I went out to walk and watch five men wrap up Zawar's wheat harvest.

In the afternoon I spent time at the threshing floor where two oxen were hooked up to pull a *chapaar*--a bunch of thorn branches that had been pressed flat and had some weight so as to break up the wheat straw. As the oxen dragged this over the straw again and again, the wheat straw became finer, and the wheat kernels were slowly pressed out of their husks. Sometimes the kids put little Arif on the *chapaar* to ride. Once he even went to sleep there!

Supper was potato and squash *qorma*, stew. It was delicious and a nice change. I talked at length with Agha Sahib after Zawar went up to sleep. He gave me one of the best perspectives I had heard on our situation:

"Engineer Kabir made a sincere mistake. The groups of soldiers here are hungry. When they see some money, they want it for themselves. They have guns and no fear of God. Enlightened people must work in appropriate ways to help. Therefore, don't harbor bitterness in your heart after this event is over. But continue in an attitude of service."

Tuesday, August 27

A breakfast guest this morning from Sang-i Masha reported privately to me that the local populace is very sorry for the kidnapping.

In my prayer time I thought about Paul's great desire that Christ be magnified in his body. I asked God for joy in spite of problems.

I went outside to watch the threshing. I took a turn driving the oxen around the circle as they stomped on the grain and straw and dragged the *chapaar*, mat of thorns. I read and wrote some with the kids around.

Supper featured bread, butter, milk, and tea.

We visited a high Pakistani government official in Peshawar. He telephoned the leader of the Hizb-i Islami party. The leader stated that he had never been informed about the details of the situation, but said, "If they are with my people, I will take care of it."

An informant for a mine clearing agency who worked in the area of Jaghori brought a letter from Joel and Dr. Bill. The informant emphasized that money should be paid quickly. He even suggested the possibility that the captives could be shifted to Iran if we are not quick in our response.

Joel's brother, Jonathan, recently arrived from the US for a family visit. Jonathan and his wife, Sue, and Don DeHart, Joel's father, recently came to check the letter sent by Joel. They confirmed its validity, its spirit, and the handwriting.

Wednesday, August 28

I had a good sleep, thank God. Zawar and I ate breakfast together. He gave me some background on the history of parties in the area. The Hizb-i Islami certainly had an uphill struggle as they are connected with a Sunni party while the rest of the Hazara parties are supported from Shia Iran.

Today's thought and prayer was focused on James 1--joy in trials.

Then I went outside to spend time at the threshing floor and to walk around.

For lunch, Atee Muhammad Ali and I were asked to go into the Akhund's room. It was my first time in here! The ladies of the house were with us for our *qurti* meal.

The big event today was the arrival of Firoz--the Hizb-i Islami commander of Echa, beyond Baba. They were guests of Anwar Raziyee and his father--the rivals of Akhund and Zawar. In the afternoon they had quite a long discussion with Zawar and friends in the guest room. I happened to be near the door as the soldiers were coming out. Firoz addressed me and said that he hoped my problem would be solved soon. I thanked him and my spirits rose. I had heard from others that he was more sympathetic than some of the other players in the Hizb-i Islami.

THE UPPER HAND

Thursday, August 29

Before going out to the threshing floor this morning I thought about Christ's victory and made this the theme of my prayer time. I spent some time singing.

Today was to be a strange trial. It was my turn to drive the oxen around the threshing floor with a stick. I was amazed to look towards the house and see a group of armed men coming toward us. After a little while I recognized Sheikh Farid. Then I recognized Zia, a former animal health student. I had never seen him with a kalashnikov in his hands and bandoleers across his chest. Doc and I had met Sheikh Farid in Engineer Kabir's house when we were starting our project and deciding which boys to take as students. He seemed a kindly and good man. Later I learned that he was a respected religious leader in the area, having studied in Iran, but that he had virtually no political power. He was from Jodri--half way between Chilbaghtu and Sang-i Masha.

Sheikh Farid saw me, came up, and greeted me warmly. He expressed deep sorrow that I was still a captive. Then I exchanged greetings with Zia. But this was all I had time for. People came running from all directions. Dilkha tugged at me and told me to go to my room. Atee Abdullah appeared panting with his gun. Everyone was excited. I realized later that they thought Sheikh Farid might try to take me by force when he had actually been called to visit the neighbor for a conference.

I followed orders and went up to my room. An older man who was with Sheikh Farid was also a relative of the Akhund's extended family. He was obviously a respected man. He was excited and loudly proclaimed how horrible it was that those who had come to help people were now captives for money. Finally the Sheikh's group left.

I had not been too upset by the goings on. I was just trying to figure out what had happened. Imagine my surprise and dismay when Zawar and Atee Abdullah marched upstairs, guns in their hands, and anger written all over their faces. They began condemningly:

> "Is this what we get for being nice to you and trying to treat you with respect? We wanted to send you home with honor. But you

82

had to betray our kindness by writing a letter to Sheikh Farid and
telling him to come and get you. Did you ever think you'd get
away with that? Now we'll have to be much more strict with you.
No more writing. No more going outside. We'll have to treat you
like a local prisoner. Go over there by the wall!"

I followed orders meekly with a sunken heart. Zawar took my pen and
the papers out of my pocket. Then he went over to the bundle of my stuff
and took all my books and notebooks. He carried them downstairs.

When he came up, he and Atee Abdullah sat down and continued talking
about the incident. They were bothered that Sheikh Farid and his men
seemed to sneak up on them. They talked about what a bad person he was.
They talked about what they would do to me. Finally I could take it no
longer.

"I didn't write a letter to Farid," I blurted out.

"What do you mean you didn't write to him? We know you did!"

It was no use. I kept quiet. All the while I was committing the matter
to the Lord--dreading a worsening position but yet comforted by the
knowledge that I was innocent and that I could do nothing. God would have
to intervene.

Tea arrived. I was invited to join them. I began to feel better already.

Finally the men left and I began my familiar routine of pacing around
the room, singing songs that came to mind, and pouring out my heart to
my God.

Kids showed up to read and play with me. Welcome distraction.

Zawar was walking below and made another comment about how I
should be careful in sending out information. When he was finished, I
pleaded innocence. I think he suspected that I might be telling the truth
from his knowledge of my character.

Later Zawar sent more tea to me and said I could go outside to walk.
Many soldiers came for a consultation in the guest room. There was a
threat of war in Baba. The Akhund was there and some of the elders were
opposing him. I felt much better outside. Another reassuring gesture was
Zawar's invitation to the usual room with his family for dinner. The storm

THE UPPER HAND

of anger had blown over. Things were back to normal. I was allowed to take all my possessions back to my room.

Downstairs a heated discussion continued as I retired. I gave God deep thanks for His help through the day.

Oh, yes! Today I finished **Robinson Crusoe**!

Friday, August 30

The last couple of days I've had some diarrhea.

I watched the threshing this morning--plus the six or eight men who were working together in a clover field below. They wanted to plant wheat there and first had to dig out the clover roots. They dug every square foot with their hand tools--*chap choors*, a tool something between a pick and a hoe. People who didn't have oxen and couldn't borrow them sometimes had to do all their plowing by hand with their *chap choors*. It was hard work--but the men and boys were joking with each other and tea seemed to come pretty often.

Zawar and I were invited up the side valley to Qabar Qul to Dilkha's uncle's place for a *khairaat*, free dinner for some special purpose. It was delicious *sheer brinj*. It was a long visit, but I was growing to like Dilkha's family.

Saturday, August 31

I had a good sleep and I felt very well. I had dreamed of having a potluck at my Aunt Doris'! Now, as I prayed for others, I thought of grace and peace, and the need to abound in love.

Breakfast was out on the threshing floor. I wrote some, then spent most of the morning walking back and forth on the path from the house to the threshing floor and singing.

Lunch was a delicious new treat. **Koocha** was a mixture of wheat, peas, and *adas*--like small beans--cooked together. We ate it with big, dipper-like spoons called *chanchas*. The family had learned some of my peculiar ways so, while everyone else passed the spoon around and took turns, I had my own spoon!

The Commander's House

Had a nice evening with the kids and family. There were no guests. Supper was a delicious pea *qorma*. I noticed that the stars were so clear and bright tonight.

This last day of August is the last page in my little pocket notebook where I have kept my list of songs. When I started writing my diary in it there were so many blank pages--and I thought I'd be in Pakistan long before they were filled up. God has given me daily grace.

Sunday, September 1

In my meditations this morning I prayed for myself and others that we would have a song in our hearts. I decided to work on memorizing Philippians 1. From this day on until my release, going over this chapter--and later the second chapter as well--was part of my daily routine. Repeating these verses almost every day often encouraged me. I thought of Paul's own trials when he wrote this letter. His obvious joy challenged me to rejoice in the Lord in my situation. Paul's prayers for the Philippian church encouraged me to pray daily for believers back in Islamabad.

I wanted to be filled with the fruits of righteousness, and prayed this many times for others I knew (ch. 1, v. 11). I thought of God's upper hand controlling things when Paul said that the things that had happened to him resulted in the furtherance of the gospel.

I thought of others praying for me when I read v. 19 of chapter 1. Paul was confident of his salvation through the Philippians' prayers and the supply of the Spirit of Jesus Christ. Paul wanted Christ magnified in his body above all. This challenged me to pray for God's glory more than my own release. Like Paul, I felt like my staying alive was needful for others (ch. 1, v. 24). I had a confidence I would stay alive.

Christ's humiliation and exaltation in chapter two was a challenge to humility. Timothy and Epaphroditus were good examples of faithful servants of Christ. I thought on to the lesson Paul learned about contentment in every situation. Could I even be content in captivity?! God made this possible many times.

Out to the threshing floor! Zawar's apples were just getting ripe. I had my first one today. Although Zawar chased away kids and others, he kept

THE UPPER HAND

encouraging me to eat apples whenever I felt like it. Later, the kids, realizing my special privilege and longer-reaching arms, would urge me to get apples for them.

After lunch there was some activity over at Mastak. Doc appeared! The local representative for the UN Mine Awareness program, Yaqub Ali Alemi, had driven up to Naimi's home to meet Doc and check on his physical condition. He had been asked to do this by his boss back in Pakistan. Yaqub was from Daud--over in Commander Wasim's territory. I was called over to a grassy spot between Zawar's house and Mastak. Here Yaqub asked some questions and "briefed" us. He wanted to know if we were having any particular difficulties. He assured us that he had spoken with Wasim and ransom was not the issue. It was just unfair distribution of our project's aid. Wasim just wanted to get some assurance that our organization would help in the "truly" needy areas. Yaqub asked if we had ever been asked to give money. I had to say, "Yes."

Doc and I had no time together to talk or pray. But we were nevertheless encouraged by the visit. Yaqub drove back toward Sang-i Masha and Doc and his escorts headed back up the valley.

Zawar and I walked over to Kharba, above Mastak, to cut some willow branches for the sheep. Eating willow leaves before winter prevents sheep from getting certain diseases, Zawar informed me.

Outings to get branches became quite common. I quite enjoyed it because I like climbing trees and Zawar didn't. He would let me climb up and hack down the branches. Then, together, we would gather them and tie them in such a way that we could lift it onto the donkey's back so they could be dragged home.

The Akhund came home at dusk. It was always hard for me to be around him, but God helped me with my attitude.

Zawar and I were the only ones sleeping in "my" room.

Monday, September 2

The commander and his soldiers' home coming was cause for a special breakfast. We had *bosragh*, a kind of bread rolled up and fried. I had my "quiet time" while the young soldiers were playing cards nearby upstairs.

The Commander's House

Outside there was not enough wind to winnow. No *barakat*, blessing, today, they would say. I walked and sang--then watched as Nadir butchered a sheep. Guests came in a jeep from Rekhi for lunch. I'm not sure what the special occasion is today.

I helped dig potatoes for the big evening dinner. Potatoes here are small but very tasty. When the leaves are fresh, they are sometimes cooked as greens. Interestingly, one *Hazaragi* word for potatoes is *patata*.

There were 35 at dinner tonight. I knew almost all of them now and felt comfortable. I prayed that Christ would be exalted in our midst. We had squash, greens, mutton, broth, and rice. A tasty meal!

Tuesday, September 3

Today I took part in another wedding ceremony--my second in Jaghori.

As I was out walking the Akhund spoke to me congenially and positively, as if he were working hard to see that I could go home soon! After some time Zawar said, "Come on! Let's go to the wedding."

We headed off toward Mastak. As we walked Zawar happily congratulated me because, he said, Doc and I would be freed soon to work for his party. Doc would do veterinary work and I would be the principal of a school. This was interesting, but I just wanted to go home!

At Mastak we met M. Atiq, (I use an M. as an abbreviation for "Muhammad") all dressed up in new clothes. I was introduced to Muhammad Ali of Jodri, who joined us in the upper room in the tower. We looked down on the colorful group of people. Guns were very much in evidence. M. Atiq explained that the guests were from Chilbaghtu-i Pashi--the same group who had come at night intending to take the bride by force. They would take the bride back to their home for another big feast.

We enjoyed a really fantastic dinner. For a while, when Zawar stepped out, M. Ali told me of efforts to release Doc and me. He said that 25,000 dollars was being demanded. He asked what I thought if he would bring some soldiers and plan a rescue for me. I was not keen about a plan like that.

I got back earlier than the men. I enjoyed tea with the kids and ladies. Later for supper we had *kala pacha,* cooked skull and hooves of the sheep

87

that was butchered yesterday. This dish is a favorite of mine. Commander Salihi was with us. The skull was his portion. It was comical to see him sucking and licking it!

A traveler from Jaghori reported to sources in Quetta that Wasim had promised to release the captives on Sept. 1. Another traveler brought the same word the next day.

UN friends reported that one of their representatives had a meeting with the hostage takers. The report was, "The hostage takers do not want money any more." He said that the hostages were very well, almost happy. They see each other every day.

Wednesday, September 4 -- *Char Shanbe-i Suri*

I prayed for the furtherance of the Gospel this morning.

After breakfast with Zawar and his family, Arif and I headed off for the threshing floor. I alternated between watching the winnowing and the ladies making *halwa* in the kitchen. Today is *Char Shanbe-i Suri*, a special day for Hazaras when every house cooks *halwa-i samanak*--a special sweet dish made from wheat sprouts, flour, and butter. Amazingly no sugar is added, but the dark brown mixture tastes sweet. It takes a lot of stirring. It is served on a big platter with a depression in the middle filled with hot, melted butter. *Halwa* is a favorite of mine, and this was no exception!

I was surprised when everyone stopped work about 11 a.m. and all we men went together to Sar Bashi's house. He was another brother of the Akhund. There were 12 or 15 of us. We went through the normal hand-washing ritual, then dug in to the delicious *halwa*. Bread was served along with it. I enjoyed it and ate quite a lot. Little did I realize that the custom was to eat some *halwa* in each of the village homes!!

We went to three other homes where we were also served *halwa* and bread. *Halwa* is heavy food, and it wasn't long before I was stuffed. In one home I didn't notice a bee on the *toshak*, cushion. I stepped on him and got stung on the bottom of my foot. Old Atee Qurban is known as a religious man and one who has studied the Quran. When he saw that I'd been bitten, he chanted a few verses and blew on the bite--so it would get better fast.

Guess what we had for supper? Yes! *halwa!*

I found out that the Akhund's wife gave birth to a baby girl around noon. In the evening ladies and girls from the neighboring houses came to sing and celebrate all night.

Thursday, September 5

Had an apple after my exercises this morning.

I thought and prayed about fixing my eyes on Christ.

The wind was not blowing in the right direction on the threshing floor. After a while Zawar and I walked up to Qabar Qul with Atee Aziz to watch him and his sons cleaning the last of their grain. I realized that every family who can afford it, invites neighbors for a special feast when their grain harvesting activities are completed.

I saw a few lone apricots still on the trees around the *khurmo joi*, threshing floor, so I enjoyed them. Then we went to Atee Aziz's brother's home for a *halwa* lunch.

In the evening we came back to the same settlement as guests for a *nan buta* feast left over from the holy month of *Muharram*.

The men were talking together about a surprise attack tonight planned by Wasim and the Akhund on homes of people of other parties. They planned to take away their weapons.

Friday, September 6

Thought and prayed about boldness this morning. As I went outside I felt depressed.

At one o'clock Reza and I headed off for Qabar Qul. We were invited to a *nazar*, a feast marking the end of the wheat harvest.

I was locked in for part of the afternoon, but had a good time of singing.

Before bed tonight Zawar explained some new thinking about Doc and me. Wasim had a proposal that if we would help in certain ways, we would be released.

THE UPPER HAND

> Another disappointing week!
> We have been waiting for the promised release--which should have meant the captives would have arrived here several days ago.
> An "eye-witness" report arrived saying that Dr. Bill was very busy treating patients and that he had learned some Dari.

Saturday, September 7

I thought of some favorite verses in Psalm 84:
"For a day in your courts is better than a thousand..."
"For the Lord God is a sun and a shield..."
"Blessed is the man who trusts in Him."
I was just finishing a time of prayer and meditation when M. Atiq appeared with a bundle of things from Engineer Kabir. Some clothes and a letter. We didn't have long to talk. The Engineer didn't have much to say, but how much I appreciated his concern for our physical well-being.

After some time by the threshing floor, I went in for a delicious potato *qorma* lunch. Mid afternoon I went up to Qabar Qul with Abdullah, Dilkha's younger brother. I walked and sang there a lot around a freshly plowed field. Later I met some elders inside when we had a *halwa* dinner. I was given a separate dish, for a change, and I found out later that it was because Mulla Fazal was present and he didn't care to eat in the same dish as a non-Muslim. The conversation, however, was pleasant.

A baby boy had been born to Aziz--Dilkha's older brother.

Sunday, September 8

I thought of people worshipping in churches all over the world this morning and prayed for the groups I knew. I prayed that God would help me to love others as He loves me.

The men were pleased today as a good breeze was blowing. Zawar had moved the pile of wheat and chaff in order to take advantage of wind from the west. Originally he had hoped for wind from the east. At some threshing floors I noticed a stick with some dried manure on top. This, they told me, was to invite a *barakat*, or good wind from the right direction. It was interesting to me to note that when people came up to others working on the threshing floor, the common greeting was "*Barakat!*" or "*Barakat-i khormo!*", meaning, "Blessing of the threshing floor!"

Zawar and I talked some as we were alone upstairs before going to bed. He was telling me some things that were very bad in their culture--like passing gas and flicking food back into the common dish. Sometimes I had accidentally put my thumb between the index finger and long finger of my fist. This, I learned, is very bad.

Monday, September 9

A man joined us for breakfast and reported that Commander Wasim had been at Naimi's and had talked with Doc. Doc had promised that our organization would be willing to continue aid if we were released.

My meditation this morning was on thankfulness to God for all He has done. I wrote in my diary, "overflowing with thankfulness."

I watched men and boys loading manure from the pile near the house to spread out in the fields. Two donkeys were going at one time. This is an important step before plowing.

Then I went down to help Zawar as he was making one sloping field slightly bigger by moving some big rocks and building a retaining wall. They were using pry bars, huge hammers, and *chapchoors*, the tool something between a pick and a hoe. My shoes quickly filled up with dirt. I had only one pair--running shoes that my brother, Phil, had given me. From lots of use there were holes in both sides of both shoes!

In the afternoon there was wind for winnowing.

We enjoyed boiled potatoes, bread, and salt for supper. To the amusement of others--especially the kids--I ate my potatoes with the skins on and told them that the skins had lots of vitamins. My thirst for tea seemed almost unquenchable tonight. Zawar told me that this was because I had been working for a change.

THE UPPER HAND

Tuesday, September 10

I spent the morning with Zawar and Atee Muhammad Ali as they
continued to work on extending the field. We moved more rocks and dug
out two fairly big poplar stumps. I admired their way of carrying heavy
stones. By inter-twining their fingers behind their backs they could carry
two or three heavy stones with much less effort than it would take carrying
them in front!

We had tea and bread twice down at the field.

In the afternoon there was no *barakat*, good wind, so plans for
winnowing had to be cancelled. I spent time writing letters on the threshing
floor. About a week ago I decided to start writing letters to all those I could
remember on the list of my prayer supporters. Before this I didn't have the
motivation because:

1. I thought we would be released anytime.
2. I wasn't sure if I could keep things I wrote.
3. I didn't have my own paper.

Now I found letter writing a useful way to fill up my time. It helped me to
think about others. I usually quoted a verse or two from Philippians which
helped me in my task of memorizing. It may be hard to imagine, but
having a task to keep me busy gave me a new sense of self-esteem. My
time and schedule was not completely determined by others now. Some
days I managed ten or more letters.

Atee M. Ali had made a lean-to of tree branches by the threshing floor.
Until the harvest was completed and the grain stored, he would sleep there
every night to protect the wheat from thieves or animals. He was Zawar's
permanent farmer on contract for a year at a time. A certain portion of the
grain went to him.

Tonight we had supper of potato *qorma* in the lean-to. The men were
prepared to winnow at night if there was wind. We talked a long time but
no wind came so off to bed we went.

92

The Commander's House

Wednesday, September 11

My thoughts and prayers this morning were around Philippians 1:25
"...I know that I shall abide and continue with you all for your furtherance and joy of faith."

There was a good wind this morning, so Atee Aziz and Inayat came to help winnow. I wrote letters for part of the morning. After lunch I had a bath! And then I helped drive two bulls and one donkey, all tied together, over the remains of the wheat left from the first threshing.

After the regular play time with the kids our supper menu was boiled potatoes, milk, bread, and tea. Zawar and I were alone for the night.

Thursday, September 12

Had a good sleep. Several times I would get up before Zawar and begin my exercises. He saw the whole repertoire and his response was a mixture of amusement and unbelief! Once he asked me to do some of the exercises for two visiting friends. I was interested to note that when others weren't around, he was not so interested in getting up for the early prayers.

I thought especially of this line of a song for my prayers this morning, *"For His love surrounds me like the sea."* So true, I thought. Even in Chilbaghtu.

Today was the final winnowing. I enjoyed a special snack with everybody else--roasted wheat. It was really good.

After a supper of yogurt and eight-day-old *halwa*, I helped Zawar, Atee M. Ali, and Nadir butcher a big sheep for a special *khairaat*, a feast given for neighbors in order to gain blessing. It was fun helping the men and women in this family setting. Knowing the custom in Pakistan, I asked, "How do you cook the testicles?" They responded that they didn't eat them, but I could if I wanted. I made kabobs with them over the hot coals. They also roasted the fresh liver. Both were tasty.

We topped things off with a small watermelon that Zawar had planted in the front yard. It tasted good even though it was smaller than a soccer ball.

93

THE UPPER HAND

I heard today of Doc being taken to Nawa and speaking over the radio to Pakistan. Later this turned out to be a false report.

Friday, September 13

Today was a festive day indeed. We had a *Quran khwani*, feast, and the cleaning up of the wheat harvest.

A group of students who had reached a certain level in their Quran studies had been invited along with some others who were known to be able Quran readers. A *Quran khwani* is a gathering where the whole Quran is read through in one sitting. It is supposed to bring special blessing. It's also a help for forgiving the sins of departed loved ones. I asked Zawar if this was an essential part of the celebration at the end of a harvest.

"No," he replied, "but it guarantees a blessing on the crop next year."

Also, the generosity of this feast bodes well for prosperity.

I ate breakfast with the students and then sat in on the first part of the recital. I was asked to read, but declined. Atee Muhammad Ali, his father and his three sons all took part. It doesn't matter how many are present. The Quran is divided into 30 separate parts. This is a special kind of Quran--often kept by the local mulla. Each participant gets at least one part. Sometimes they may get two or three--depending on the number present. Faster readers may finish three before another slower reader finishes two. Some like to read loudly and in a beautiful sing-song. Others read quietly. The point is to get through the whole Quran. Everyone is reading at the same time and no attempt is made at explaining or thinking of the meaning of anything read.

At the end of the *Quran khwani*, sweets are passed around--especially for the participants. Also some money is given to the mulla to divide among his charges.

I left early to walk back and forth outside. The whole recitation took about three hours! I joined in an early lunch of bread soaked in mutton broth--followed by chunks of mutton and fat. Each bowl of broth and plate of meat was to be shared by four or five people.

Out on the threshing floor the measuring began. We all took a guess at how many *kharwaars*, donkey loads, the pile of cleaned wheat would

94

amount to. Ever since the first day of winnowing when a small pile of grain had been separated from the chaff, a Quran was placed on the top of the smoothed out pile. For good luck, I was told, as well as to protect the grain. Who would dare to steal someone's grain that was under the Quran? Later, as the pile grew bigger, the five names of the friends of God--Muhammad, Ali, Fatima, Hassan, and Hussain--were also written with a stick in the grain.

The wheat was measured in a special basket. And piles were made all over the threshing floor. It was interesting seeing different ones figuring out the total. There were no calculators! There were some strange ways and some wrong ways of adding numbers together. I think the total for Zawar was a little more than 13 *kharwaars*--a good harvest, especially considering that other areas of Jaghori had poor harvests because of a blight which caused the wheat grains to become red and worthless.

Atee M. Ali was happy with his part--one third of the total. This was his share as the one who farmed the land. Some of the wheat went for the blacksmith's annual fee. Some went to Aghae Mubaligh, the local mullah, and, in many cases, the *chaipo*, shepherd. When the wheat was taken to the mill, the miller got a certain percentage as his wage. Some was also distributed free to poor people. The rule for *zakat*, or alms, is that one-tenth the value of the wheat is to be given as wheat, money, or goods to the poor or to the local *minbar*, mosque. I think that Zawar considered giving a radio away as part or all of his alms.

A special root was burned today. Its smoke was a good omen.

Also at the time of measuring wheat, fresh bread is made from the new grain and passed out to everybody.

We stayed around the threshing floor until it was dark. There were 12 guests in Zawar's room in the evening for *kala pacha*, skull and hooves.

Our local representatives in Jaghori have been dealing directly with the captors. At least three times the negotiations were near completion when people either sent from Pakistanis or Americans or just self-appointed entrepreneurs came and interrupted the negotiations with their own offers. End result: Joel and Bill not free.

THE UPPER HAND

All political parties in Jaghori are preparing for war. Thus many feel it's better for Dr. Bill and Joel to come out soon. Once fighting starts it will be very difficult to negotiate.

This call for prayer was sent out to many friends in the US:

"This is a call for extraordinary prayer for a very serious overseas situation in which lives are in jeopardy. Because of the sensitivity and complexity of the problem, we cannot give more information at this time. However, we urge you to focus your prayer attention and spiritual energy on this crisis."

Saturday, September 14

Zawar was still under his quilt and I was exercising when I heard a voice calling, "Zawar, Zawar!"

"Tell him I'm not here," Zawar mumbled.

But he had already been let in. It was a kindly older man. I found out later that we had vaccinated his animals. We ate breakfast together.

My thought this morning was on trusting Christ in our frailty.

Zawar and I went down to the field where Atee M. Ali was plowing. We moved some stones for the retaining wall. After lunch we returned here. Atiq from Mastak showed up. Zawar and I went back to the house with him for tea. Atiq discussed a right price for Zawar's big, fat ram.

After my time of playing with the kids, the Akhund appeared with his usual entourage. Reza and Nafisa were always delighted at his return.

I went to bed feeling down after another confrontation with my captor and no news about my release.

Sunday, September 15

The Akhund and his band set off this morning for Trugh--a small settlement between Boldrughna and Naimi's place. They were hopefully going to settle the land dispute that had been a concern for weeks now. I was told that I could go along for an outing and visit Doc. I had been asking for such a visit since I hadn't seen Doc for 15 days.

The Commander's House

At Trugh the Akhund and most of his soldiers entered the host's house to begin negotiations. The household there busied itself preparing a mutton feast for lunch and supper. Two soldiers were assigned to take me to Doc's. On the way we got lost. As we approached a small threshing floor, we noticed Naimi himself there. A few pleasantries were exchanged. Naimi told me how he had obtained vaccines and now only needed the syringes before Doc and I could start vaccinating together in the area.

On to the house where the soldiers kindly gave Doc and me a long time together outside. We talked about many things. Doc told me about Wasim's visit there and how everybody had treated him with great respect--almost reverence. Doc was feeling very bored and desperate. He said that he didn't feel he could last through the winter. He had written Mark and his family pleading that they do all they could to free him before winter. I took a letter that he had written to his wife. I would try to send it out by some trusted person.

I wanted Doc to read some conditions I had written for our release. I wanted the captors to admit their wrong-doing before our organization would continue any work in the area. Also I wanted all of our stolen things returned. Doc convinced me that these things were not so important. All that really mattered was our getting out. We could let them save face.

There were tears and prayers before we returned to the house upon a call for a *qurti* lunch.

It was just an hour or two later when I had another lunch back at the house where the land settlement was under heated debate. Doc had given me *On Wings of Eagles* to read. This book is the true story of how some American businessmen managed to escape from Iran at the time of the Iranian revolution in 1979. I went outside to walk, sing, and read. After dusk, I walked home with some soldiers.

Monday, September 16

This morning I sensed my sin and frailty in a strong way. I prayed for forgiveness, cleansing, and strength.

After breakfast with the soldiers I walked with Reza to Kharba to watch Atee Muhammad Ali and his boys plowing. Reza wanted to go home, so

97

THE UPPER HAND

told me that I had to go, too. Did I have to obey a 12-year-old? I tried to reason with Reza that Atee M. Ali could watch and take care of me. I wanted to read and write until lunch. Finally, he let me stay.

We came home fairly early and I carried the plow. When I first picked it up, it seemed awkward and heavy. Then Zawar showed me the right way to carry it on my shoulder.

We had a delicious squash and yogurt dish for lunch.

Zawar had been frustrated by having to police his apple trees. Kids and others would "steal" apples whenever they could get away with it. Some evenings Zawar would send Reza or Jawad or Razia out for an hour or so with instructions to sit quietly under the trees and throw rocks at any sound! So now Zawar had found a man willing to contract for the rest of the apples on the trees. Today the trees were picked clean.

As the sky darkened we busied ourselves with another activity. Wasps had been plaguing us--building nests in many holes in the walls. Many of the kids and some adults had been stung. Zawar wanted to control this problem, so the first method tried was stuffing plastic bags in the holes and burning them. This technique was called *"welding"* in Hazaragi!

But the wasps were too smart and industrious to let this foil them. They worked hard night and day until they had made other tunnels in the mud. So for several evenings we kept busy filling the holes with mud, and using various other techniques. Finally it seemed like the wasp plague was over.

Tonight Arbab invited us for an end-of-the-harvest feast. His home was a stone's throw from our house. I went along with the Akhund, his soldiers and the neighbors. Two huge bowls of *nan buta* were served. About eight men could eat at once. There were two shifts. I really had a good time with the men. And I had come to know Arbab's two sons quite well. The younger, Ismail, about six, was a keen English student.

Tuesday, September 17

On this visit the Akhund had not spoken to me directly. I felt that it would be good to ask him in a straightforward way about my situation. So, as we were all eating breakfast I asked,

The Commander's House

"What is the progress on my situation? You told me some time ago that you were working towards a quick solution."

Surprisingly, the Akhund seemed to answer my question in a very civil way.

"A representative from Hizb-i Islami in Peshawar is coming to discuss your release. We are trying to arrange for you and Dr. Lewis to start vaccinating animals in this area again--so that the vaccine doesn't go out of date. Yasin Ali, who spoke with you and Doc and took a message to Pakistan, hasn't returned yet. Your friends Engineer Kabir and Aminullah have made our work more difficult because they have told everyone that we are holding you for ransom."

I realized that these commanders had no scruples, but they wanted to be perceived by the outside world as respectable people.

A sub-commander present then with the Akhund encouraged me later that he would do all he could to work for my quick release.

The Akhund left with his noisy crowd. They were going to Ghazni now to pick up a load of arms from Hizb-i Islami in Pakistan, I was told.

I helped Zawar outside to saw some logs with his Russian bow saw.

At noon Atiq joined us for a walk up to Sokhtanak to Ali Juma's ("*Lala*")--the kindly old man who knew Urdu--for another harvest feast. After the meal I was given permission to climb up to the top of a rocky outcropping far above the threshing floor. Two younger boys came with me. When was the last time I had been able to climb? It was an exhilarating feeling. I wrote a letter and read some before I heard the cry to return.

The measuring and activity on the threshing floor took a long time. I kept busy writing English and letters. When all was finished, Zawar and I walked home via Qabar Qul, where Zawar made an arrangement with his in-laws to borrow their ox tomorrow for plowing.

99

THE UPPER HAND

Wednesday, September 18

Today was a busy and full day. Zawar owned some trees at Cheshma, a settlement in another little valley. He had hired Atee Ahmad Shah to work for him for the day to fell, saw, and carry this wood over to Kharba to a place where it could be picked up by the new owner in a truck.

After one or two trips with Zawar, Reza, and Atee Ahmad Shah and the donkeys, I became an experienced donkey man! I was responsible for one of the donkeys and its heavy load. The load had to be properly balanced all the way--and then flipped off at the end. Several times I ran back ahead of the empty donkeys for half a mile up and down the little valleys. Several times I rode the donkey back.

Several of the stumps were so big that a donkey couldn't carry them. They had to be split several times. I marveled at Atee Ahmad Shah's dexterity and strength. First they determined the best place to drive a wedge in. Then, when the iron wedges had gone in and the wood hadn't split, they drove in larger wooden wedges that they had just made. One stump took a great effort to finally split.

The tea and bread that we had twice during the day tasted so good! At night Atee Ahmad Shah joined us for a special supper of *sheer brinj*.

Thursday, September 19

I wrote some letters this morning and spent time on the threshing floor. Atiq came by with a letter from Engineer Kabir. Nadir was around and both of us talked with him--then had lunch in his house. I was concerned that Zawar not be angry when he found out where I had been.

The other important event today was Doc's arrival with Naimi's son and some other soldiers. Naimi's son studied in Sang-i Masha. He knew a smattering of English, and was a help to Doc in communication. Doc told me of the visit made by two leaders of the *Shura*, Council, of mujahideen commanders in Peshawar. They were Sunnis and had come to enquire about Doc's health. One was a judge, Doc said. They had asked him some questions on cassette tape. Doc had sent the message that he was being well-treated and that he had not been asked for money. He also added a word

for his family. Doc told me that this visit had been a very emotional time.
He had started crying during the questioning.

After a meal of *sheer rogho*, bread crumbs in milk, we said good-bye
to each other.

Friday, September 20

Atiq appeared early this morning with the message that Engineer Kabir
was at his house. He told Zawar that the Engineer had received the
Akhund's permission to see me and give me some supplies. He invited us
for breakfast.

Zawar was very reluctant, but eventually we went. What a boost it was
to see Engineer Kabir, and to realize that he was still working hard for our
freedom. We discussed his trip to Pakistan in the next day or two, and the
three-point proposal he was taking along. He had talked to the Akhund
recently. The idea was that if our organization would make a school and
clinic in the area, our captors would be happy to release us.

I spent some time there writing my first letter to send out to my
family. Zawar was reluctant and suspicious about this, but finally gave in
and let me write. This is what I wrote:

Dear family,

Grace and peace from our wonderful Lord.

This morning I received your letter, Jonny and Sue, and some things
you sent. Many thanks. I am really sad that I will miss you in Pakistan,
but I believe that God's plan is very good--better than we could ever devise.
I'm so happy about the addition you're expecting! And congrats, Mike and
Sar, on the birth of Philippa! I like the name. How do you feel, Joel and
Nate, about a sister?!

I am quite healthy and have had more freedom to be outside and walk,
etc. So I appreciate that. Negotiations seem to be making some progress.
I'm glad to hear that now the groups are not asking for money.

THE UPPER HAND

I keep busy by singing. I've listed almost 600 songs and choruses. I've been playing with kids and teaching them English. Ten days ago I started a letter-writing project to my friends in the States. I hope to mail them when I'm free. I have more time to pray.

My present host is very kind. I've sort of become a part of the family which, you know, I like a lot. They treat me very well and give me the best food. I'm grateful.

Mom, glad to hear your medical tests seem good. I see Dr. Bill quite often--every two weeks or more often. He has really experienced God's grace. But boredom is a big problem. He gets emotional whenever we speak of his family.

I don't need to write a lot of details because (read the second part of Philippians 1) I have confidence I'll see you again. You are all in my thoughts and prayers every day. I feel there's no danger to life but just a matter of patience.

Love,

Joel

The supplies I had received were two sweaters, two news magazines, toilet paper, soap, pens, and letters from my brother, Jonny and his wife, Sue, and Mark.

I said goodbye to Engineer Kabir with high hopes, but I found out some time later that he never went to Pakistan. And the proposal he carried was not an honest or serious one.

The rest of the morning I spent with Zawar, Jawed, and Arif up at Qabar Qul. Zawar had purchased some straw there and was carrying it down to his barn on donkeys. Amazing what volume one donkey can carry!

I had fun with the kids in addition to doing some reading and writing on my own. Had a nice visit with Atee Aziz.

Supper featured delicious broth with bread and meat.

The Commander's House

Saturday, September 21

Reza is sick today. It started a few days ago.

I helped Zawar making chimneys in the room above the kitchen and barn.

I wrote, then had lunch alone and spent some time walking. The whole neighborhood gathered in Reza's room to show their sympathy. Each person, of course, gave his own idea of what should be done! At the request of the family, I had sent a note with Mubariz for Doc to come down. He showed up, to my surprise. He examined Reza and felt like he should keep a close watch on him because the symptoms were not clear. Doc didn't stay long.

Atiq was also there. He was the local person who knew the most about medicine, having worked at the hospital in Sang-i Masha before it was closed by the Nahzat attack. I admired his real concern and desire to help others.

We all sat there together until about midnight.

Sunday, September 22

After exercises and my morning rituals, I had breakfast in Reza's room. He's no better. Sometime later in the morning Dr. Ghulam Muhammad arrived from Sang-i Masha with some medicines. Word had been sent to the Akhund, who had sent the doctor.

Dr. Ghulam seemed capable. He noticed that Reza's neck was stiff and concluded--as Atiq had supposed--that the problem was *meningit*, spinal meningitis. He left some medicines and injections. Atiq became the chief nurse, and I his assistant!

Many visitors came. Much tea was served. I went out in the afternoon to walk and write. Then inside from dusk to 10 p.m. with Atiq and Reza. Reza was really in bad shape--delirious, and saying all kinds of strange things. Zawar's first wife and the Akhund's present wife served Reza lovingly and tirelessly.

The ladies woke me up at two to give Reza more shots. We used a regular disposable syringe that we "sterilized" each time, along with the

THE UPPER HAND

needle, in a bowl of boiling water from the kettle. Sometimes the water had the faint color of tea! From now on I gave Reza his shots.

Thought today of the fragility of life.

Monday, September 23

Had breakfast in Reza's room with visitors. I gave him his pills and shots. Reza could be pretty uncooperative, cursing and crying--and refusing to take pills. Atiq, in his good-humored way, would say, "Watch out, Reza! A wasp is coming!" Then he would give the injection and say, "Oh, these terrible wasps! You should be more careful not to disturb their nest!" Reza was also on an IV drip. This was very painful for him. Sometimes it was hard to find his veins.

Shams and Sultan came for an English lesson. I was going through the book that Shams had been studying in Sang-i Masha. It was an excellent book--the kind used at the British Consulate course in Kabul. I saw definite progress in Shams' comprehension and memory.

After they left, I had some prayer time thinking of God's faithfulness. I kept thinking over these words of a song:

"Morning by morning new mercies I see,
All I have needed Thy hand hath provided
Great is thy faithfulness, Lord unto me."

I went in for the next injection time at 10 a.m.--and then visited some with Atiq and others there. The next shot time was 3 p.m.

I was in Reza's room at 5 p.m. when the Akhund arrived. As soon as the IV was empty, he took Reza in the jeep to Sang-i Masha. Reza seemed to have improved today and to be resting better. Zawar went with the Akhund to town.

I spent some time talking to Latif's brother. Latif was the soldier who took Doc's watch and my money. Latif's whole family had come because of Reza's illness. Latif's younger sister was engaged to Reza!

Today Nadir brought up the subject of money and asked why I didn't just pay and end the whole matter.

The Commander's House

Tuesday, September 24

Had a long prayer time this morning thinking of Jesus carrying his children in his arms all the day long.

Had another English class with Shams. His brother, Salah, was with him, too.

I knew something was going on in the afternoon, but didn't figure it out exactly. Then I heard. Everyone was getting ready to go to Jasha for a wedding. Nadir came to me and said, "Change your clothes and let's go!"

I was really pleased to be out. It was my first long walk in two months except for the hour's walk up to Naimi's place several times. I enjoyed the long one-and-a-half hour walk with the other men of the *aghil*, village. They took their guns, of course, but they were not too worried. It was Charsi's son who was getting married, and Charsi was a loyal follower of the Akhund.

I was given special treatment at the feast--although I didn't want it. Some folk there knew me and almost all had heard of me, I think. Muallim Wahid was sitting at the end of the tablecloth at the other end of the tent. I acknowledged him with only a look--not wanting to get him in trouble. I sat next to "Dr. Sharif"--not a real doctor, but an educated man who sold medicines. We had a good talk. I was served separately and the men made sure I got some of the best pieces of meat. I was pretty free to express that I felt it was a shameful thing that I was being held for money, but also that God was helping me and I was trusting Him for my freedom.

It was a treat to have several kinds of desserts!

Nadir said we shouldn't stay, so he and I and another soldier took off after the feast and walked home by the full moon.

Wednesday, September 25

I had breakfast outside with Atee M. Ali, since Zawar hadn't returned yet from Sang-i Masha. Then the family granted me permission to spend the day with Atee Ahmad Shah. Jawad went with me across the fields and through the wooded valleys to Cheshma. Atee Ahmad Shah was working with maybe ten other men to irrigate their fields on a dry hillside. It was their turn for using the water from the channel. Some of the men used high rubber boots--"Wellingtons" made in Iran--so their feet wouldn't get wet.

After watching this for a while, Atee Ahmad Shah took me for a visit to Muhammad Qariadar's home for a nice visit and a *halwa* lunch. A *qariadar* is a local elected official in the former government responsible for looking after local matters and reporting to the government.

My stomach had been upset since this morning--and I knew that *halwa* was not the best thing for it. The rest of the afternoon and evening I was in great discomfort.

Atee Ahmad Shah continued working on irrigating different fields. I sat with the men for a while--and then went to the shade of a tree and bushes to read *On Wings of Eagles* and frequently relieve myself!

I was home before dark. I didn't have any supper because I was feeling lousy. Got up twice in the night to visit the bathroom.

Thursday, September 26

I just had tea for breakfast, since my tummy was still upset. I thought through Psalm 1 and the prosperous man who trusts in the Lord.

After a little bread and tea for lunch, I had no more stomach problems.

Shams came for another English lesson. Then I spent some time walking.

There was a cold wind blowing today. After playing with the kids and visiting the spring I felt like I needed to go inside to warm up! It was now that I discovered the benefit of the ingenious architecture of Afghan homes. The kitchen was at a slightly lower level than the "living room". The chimney from the kitchen fire was directed under the floor of this room and up the opposite wall--acting as a smokeless and spaceless room heater! One could adjust the heat by sitting in different places in the room. Right over the chimney, of course, was warmer.

After a supper of bread and tea I visited a little with the ladies. Zawar had not returned yet.

It was cold upstairs. I used two quilts tonight. I had just two guards.

The Commander's House

Friday, September 27

Rain began early this morning. It was the first real rain I had seen in Afghanistan! The roof on my room hadn't been plastered, and leaked at different places. I pulled my bedding to a dry place. It wasn't a hard rain, but it continued steady and cold for some time.

My thought this morning was, *"Let God arise and let His enemies be scattered"*.

Liaqat and Shah brought the sad news that little Hamida, Nadir's four-month-old baby, had died last night. Also Mubariz had cut off his finger while chopping branches off a tree. Later I found that it was a serious cut, but it had not been totally severed. It was a sad sight to watch the funeral procession heading for the graveyard in the cold drizzle.

I joined a group assembled in Nadir's house next door to sympathize with the family for the death. I ended up answering lots of questions about America. There wasn't a lot of sorrow expressed, or efforts by the group to comfort the family. I was surprised about this. Perhaps this was another outworking of a fatalistic world view.

After a *qurti* lunch there, I went to the guest room, under my room, to rest and write. It was cold! We had had rain, but snow had fallen on the surrounding mountains.

The evening meal was at Nadir's again with all the people of the village except, notably, Rizayee, Misteri, and their families. There wasn't much of the serious talk that I expected. It seemed, rather, just more time to wile away with idle talk.

I felt badly because I had offered Nadir several days earlier to have a special prayer for Hamida. He had agreed. But the time I suggested then was not good for him. I felt he might be reluctant so decided to let it go until he would bring it up. Now the chance was gone. I consoled myself that I had prayed for Hamida in my time alone.

Saturday, September 28

A cold day! I thought of Jesus as our best friend and the One who gives us good friends.

THE UPPER HAND

Shams and Salah came for an English lesson. We had it downstairs because of the weather.

Lunch was **nan** and tea. I walked and sang for an hour then wrote letters. I also had a bath!

The Akhund arrived with Reza and his troops. Reza was doing much better--but still had restricted movement in his neck.

Atiq had kindly sent a plastic container over for me to fill with drinking water. I took this to the *karez* to fill. All the kids wanted to look at and carry my new container!

I had a tasty dinner of meat and broth with the soldiers. I slept downstairs because of the cold. It was hard to relinquish my upstairs independence. Would it be winter from now on?

Sunday, September 29

I woke up to find a dusting of snow over everything outside. Snow continued to fall for part of the morning.

In my prayer time upstairs I thought of James 1 and patience. I was discouraged. I guess the weather was part of it. My patience and faith was wearing thin.

What a boost it was to have M. Atiq come for a visit.

The Akhund let me go with him for lunch of *suji halwa*, a sweet dish made of cream of wheat. It was delicious! More important was the lengthy time we had for private, frank discussion. We discussed Atiq's plans to visit Pakistan soon--and how I could send letters along. Atiq expressed hopes that the groups against Wasim and the Akhund might gain control of the region.

Some time later at the Akhund's house there was a big to-do. Mamur Yaqub, a Hizb-i Islami commander from near Anguri, came with his jeep and a group of soldiers. He was somehow junior to the Akhund in authority, but he impressed me from the first time I saw him with his education, reason, and wit.

I had no desire to be in with all the soldiers and visiting dignitaries, so I helped out fixing dinner in the kitchen. I helped peel potatoes and onions as a mutton dinner was being prepared. Both potatoes and onions were tiny. I had only seen small ones in this region.

Supper was delicious. I had a good conversation with two of Mamur Yaqub's soldiers who were sympathetic. The Mamur and Akhund had left for a private talk in another room.

I went upstairs to sleep. It was cold, but so good to be alone.

We received very positive letters from Bill and Joel dated Sept. 20.

One person reports, "Wasim is tired of keeping the Americans." He implied that the captor would accept 20% to 50% of the demand. He said, "Give me the money and I will have the men out in five days." He claimed that the Kabul regime had approached Wasim asking him for the Americans, but we think this was just a scare tactic.

Monday, September 30

After breakfast with the soldiers I was much encouraged by Mamur Yaqub taking time to talk with me privately. He explained the efforts in process for Doc's and my release. He told of his own disagreement with the action of capturing us. He promised continued, dedicated efforts for our freedom, and that he would contact Peshawar and try to get a message to me in a week or two.

The Akhund and Mamur left shortly for points east. I had a feeling of relief and hope.

In my prayer time I thought of being "doers of the Word". I had lunch alone with little Juma.

I started reading from James A. Michener's *Space*, that I had received from Atiq to pass on to Doc. Shortly after, Zawar called me to accompany him to Kharba to cut some more willow branches. We made a detour on our return to Mastak. How grateful I was that Zawar let me stay here for a while. Atiq had water heated and asked if I wanted to take a bath in his bathroom. What a treat! I hadn't used shampoo since our capture three months ago. After my bath I shared melon from Sang-i Masha and tea with the men. Shams and I then had our English lesson.

THE UPPER HAND

Shams escorted me home at dark. How unusual not to have guards with guns along!

I joined the family for a potato supper. Zawar wasn't in, and I slept in the guest room alone.

Tuesday, October 1

Today I gave shots to Reza several times and visited with him.

In my prayer time I thought of *"not terrified by adversaries"*, and prayed this for my family and friends.

After some writing, I drew some water from the well and brought it to Zawar. He was doing some mud masonry in the barn to make new stalls for the animals. Then I drew about 20 buckets of water out of the well trying to empty and clean it. But I didn't seem to make a dent in the water supply!

Shams came for his English lesson, which we had over bread and tea.

After an hour or so of walking on my usual route around the threshing floor, Zawar invited me to go over to Kharba to get some more willow branches for the goats.

We had a lot of lady guests tonight for some reason. We men benefited by being able to enjoy a *sheer brinj* supper!

The men stayed talking for a long time. A lot of things were going on in local politics. Yesterday when the Akhund was on his way to Nawa, he was unsuccessfully ambushed. There was much talk of who did it and how to get revenge.

> Message from our representative in Jaghori: "We fear that another military commander may take the Americans hostage to another place, beginning an entire new round of negotiations.

Wednesday, October 2

I had early breakfast with the soldiers and then gave Reza his shot.

I thought this morning about following Christ, who *"knows the way in the wilderness."*

The Commander's House

I was totally surprised when Nasrullah and Walid came for a visit. In the conversation that followed, I found out that Nasrullah had been chosen as Mark's "special envoy". Mark wanted him to be a messenger, and take care of any needs we might have. This was the first time I remember seeing Nasrullah--although he spoke of having seen me in Islamabad, where his family was living. Walid was our hard-working animal health student from Sabz Chob.

Nasrullah showed me a picture of Mark with my brother, Jonathan, in Quetta. Then he told how Mark had sent him to work on our problem because he knew Akhund Salim. Another job Nasrullah had was to try to get pictures of Doc and me. He had been given a camera for this purpose, and he went about using it in a very sensitive way. His pictures of us turned out to be a great help.

I insisted to Nasrullah that I didn't need anything at present except batteries for my flashlight. He gave me the ones from his own flashlight.

Nasrullah gave news of the outside world and efforts for our release. Zawar was sitting with us, so I know Nasrullah felt that he couldn't say everything he wanted. I also sensed a distance because Nasrullah was from the *khan khel*, the traditional local aristocracy. Walid was also from this family. Later Zawar told me that youngsters like Nasrullah couldn't do much to solve a problem like mine.

Nevertheless, this visit was a great encouragement.

Nasrullah was going to try to see Doc that afternoon or the next day.

Zawar, Atiq, and I were invited for lunch today to Atee Aziz's at Qabar Qul. Afterwards we went to the small *ziarat*, the grave of a *Sayyid*, where the family wanted to offer some special prayers. They had brought along some rice to eat here and share it with others after the prayers.

Lala's house was nearby. I ran over to say "Hi", but insisted that I couldn't stay for tea.

In the evening we were guests again! This time at Mastak, M. Atiq's house. It was good to share a special meal with his family and Nasrullah and Walid. We had chicken *qorma* and rice *boota*.

After giving Reza another shot, I went upstairs to sleep alone.

THE UPPER HAND

> WAR HAS BEGUN in Jaghori. This changes everything.
> A messenger said that the two Americans were together now in Naimi's house. They are vaccinating animals in Chilbaghtu along with five body guards. They are very far from the fighting.

Thursday, October 3

Today I thought especially of the song, "*We rest on Thee, our shield and our defender.*" I felt my weakness, but I wanted to go in His strength.

I watched Zawar and Ishaq as they built new stalls and walls in the barn area next to the kitchen.

Shams came for his English lesson after lunch. Nasrullah was with him. He took some pictures, promising to send prints in a few weeks to the kids who were in the picture with me.

After playing outside with the kids, I went in for a supper of milk, bread, and tea. Later I helped some more on the construction work, and wrote some more in my *Hazaragi* Dictionary.

Friday, October 4

This morning Zawar scolded the ladies of the house for not working harder at the job he had given them in the kitchen and barn area, clearing out old rubble and manure for the manure heap. Then Zawar left for work elsewhere. I felt sorry for the ladies as I saw them working with the shovel, *chapchoor* and wheelbarrow--so I volunteered my services.

One of the ladies told me, "You see how hard women have to work in Afghanistan!"

It was hard work scraping, shoveling, and carrying loads outside. It wasn't long before I had big blisters on both hands. If I had known then how long they would take to heal, I would have been more careful! But the ladies appreciated my help. I felt close to them as sisters and they had said that they considered me like a brother.

In the afternoon I watched some more of the construction. I gave Reza his last shot in the series he was taking. He was glad to be finished!

The Commander's House

I went out with Zawar again to cut some more willow branches. On the way back Reza and I went to Mastak so I could have my English lesson with Shams. We also had a snack there, of course!

It was dark as Reza and I made our way home. We arrived to a flurry of activity. The Akhund had sent word that he was bringing his second bride home the next day. I discovered later that he had married this lady from Patu a year ago, but had not brought her to his home. This was a common custom. I discovered it when several days later Zawar told me that the Akhund's new wife had just had a baby boy the night before. I thought he must be joking. I was under the impression that they had just been married! After a tea and bread supper, I helped the men butcher a calf. There was lots of work to do. We got to bed late.

> Received news that both Dr. Bill and Joel are being held in Akhund Salim's house. The people in Bamian are talking about Joel who is digging, cleaning, and working manually to assist with general farming chores, etc. without being forced. He just wants to help.

Saturday, October 5

I enjoyed breakfast with the ladies! I had a quick prayer time, then joined in the intense but fun-filled preparations for the coming guests. I helped cut up the meat, then peeled and cut up a pile of miniature onions.

Another trip for willow branches.

After a meat snack I changed clothes in the new stables downstairs. I was getting ready to leave when the Akhund's first wife came in crying. She probably expected to be alone. When she saw me she shared some of the burden that was on her heart:

"A family unit with two wives never works out happily."

I could feel her heartache as everyone else was celebrating.

We heard some shots in the distance. The wedding party was coming! Someone even fired a rocket launcher. When two jeeps appeared over the far ridge, there was great excitement. Many shots were fired. Everyone was in their best clothes.

THE UPPER HAND

The male guests were ushered into the guest room. I watched as some ladies helped the shrouded bride from the back of a jeep into the house. I only realized later that she had made that rough trip just days before her baby was due! I joined the guests for tea and *bosragh*, a special fried bread.

It was quite a while before supper. I was able to get some time to rest and write. Then I walked back and forth outside, and went over to watch the boys playing *sangirak*, rock throwing.

I went back to the kitchen. I preferred to be there helping than in with the guests. Several times folk insisted that I have choice morsels of meat! I enjoyed the activity there. The people preparing and serving had become my friends. Most of the people of the village were there to help--and of course, to eat!

At a moment when the Akhund saw me he volunteered that Doc's and my position was looking up. Why did simple words from a man I didn't trust make my spirits soar so high?

It was a great night. I ate too much. Eight others shared my bedroom tonight. Thankfully the weather had warmed up some.

> No statement on VOA or BBC should occur until the war is over.
> Now the situation is extremely unclear. We do not need to send in a letter to someone who may not be holding our people by the time the letter gets there.

Sunday, October 6

I chose not to do my exercises in front of all the guests this morning! After a *chob josh* breakfast, I had a chance for some time alone. I thought of Christ's humility and of being shining lights.

I wrote some letters, read my book, and then walked back and forth for a long time. I would sing several songs together with a common theme. One favorite thought was God's almighty power. I would sing:

"He's able, He's able, I know He's able
I know my Lord is able to carry me through."

The Commander's House

"Ah, Lord God, Thou hast made the heavens
and the earth by Thy great power
Nothing is too difficult for Thee..,"

"Faith, mighty faith, the promise sees
And looks to God alone;
Laughs at impossibilities,
And cries it shall be done."

"Got any rivers you think are uncrossable
Got any mountains you can't tunnel through
God specializes in things thought impossible
He does the things others cannot do."

I enjoyed a lunch of **shorwa** and bread with Zawar in the kitchen, then had an English lesson with Shams. I was surprised by a call across the fields from the Akhund. When I arrived, Atiq was there, too. Akhund told me that Doc had come for a visit and was at Mastak. We had a good but brief time together. Doc told of a visit by a doctor connected with MCI (Mercy Corps International) and another representative. We prayed together.

Doc wasn't allowed to join us for supper, and he wanted to get home before dark since his weak eyes made walking at night difficult. But Jawad and I stayed for a delicious supper of calf feet!

When we got home we joined a group for tea. Serious and tragic news had arrived. My one-eyed guard, Salihi, had been gunned down in the middle of Sang-i Masha bazaar by three men who made a quick get away. Salihi had been considered one of the Akhund's best men. Last year he had fought the Pashtuns with great cunning and bravery. Everyone knew how many men he was reputed to have killed.

It had been Hafiz Naimi, his brother's murderer, who had brought the body back to the family home in Chilbaghtu. It was a gesture of good will which some were suspicious about.

There was much serious talk about what should be done. Inayat and his brother, Agha Sahib, from Shatoo were guests. I was touched that Agha

THE UPPER HAND

Sahib had brought me a magnetic chess and checkers game to help me pass my time. He hadn't forgotten me since our first meeting weeks ago.

Someone visiting Hazara in Quetta said that the Americans will be back here in Pakistan in two weeks.

Monday, October 7

After a special breakfast with the guests, I took time alone to think about being lights in a crooked world. Then I went out to walk.

I spent some time talking to more *Sayyids* who had gathered to try to resolve some problem they had among themselves. My stomach was feeling upset, but still I went with Zawar to Kharba for more branches. Later it felt good to just lie down and read *Space* until it got dark.

Tuesday, October 8

Today I'm starting a new volume of my diary--a small notebook sent by friends in Pakistan.

I had a lousy night with a stomach full of gas. I shortened my exercises and then joined the Akhund, Zawar, and the two *Sayyids* for breakfast. I spent time alone, and wrote letters and filled in some of the notebooks my English students had given me.

As I walked outside, I spent quite a bit of time talking with Abdul Hussain, who had finished all his farm work, and was just waiting for the winter snows! I liked him a lot, but didn't want to let on this to others, fearing that he might suffer somehow.

We had a late lunch. I was sort of surprised that Zawar took me right into the room filled with ladies! Customarily, on the third day after the birth of a child, all the ladies from the community are invited for a special meal. We enjoyed rice and bread.

Births are only half the story. Afghanistan has one of the highest infant mortality rates in the world. There are 163 deaths out of every 1000 births. This baby would also die a few months later.

The   Commander's   House

I went outside to prepare an English test for Shams. After our lesson, three ladies came upstairs to see me and to "sympathize" or encourage me.

I walked until dark, then played with the kids and went to the *karez* for my routine of filling my water bottle. As the weather had been getting colder, my hands had become quite chapped. The ladies of the house, especially little Razia, were concerned and gave me some perfumed vaseline to use on my hands.

> Good time of intercession with the DeHart family prior to Jonathan's trip back to the US tomorrow. Joel's brother, Jonathan, has been of tremendous assistance to us. His appeals to the US officials as a family member have been EXTREMELY helpful. He may be able to continue in this role from the States.

Wednesday, October 9

I was tired and had a great sleep, thank God.

I did my exercises and then went over Philippians 1 and 2 before breakfast time.

I prayed thinking of "bright hope for tomorrow" based on Christ.

I wrote some, then organized my letters thinking that maybe Atiq or someone else might be able to take a bundle of them to Pakistan.

After time walking outside, Nafisa brought me a lunch of yogurt and bread. Atiq and Agha Mulla came to see the Akhund, but he wasn't in. We had tea together, and I retired for my lesson with Shams.

Then it was Kharba again for more willow branches. When we got back, we had supper of yogurt and bread together in the room with all the ladies. Folks continued talking for a long time, and I worked on my *Hazaragi* dictionary. I went to bed happy.

Thursday, October 10

We had our morning tea early. Zawar had said he would let me go with a group to the top of the range that marked the northern side of the Chilbaghtu valley. The purpose was to stock up on firewood for the winter.

THE UPPER HAND

This side of the range had very little growing on it in terms of burnable bushes. This was due to the division of the mountain surface area among the people of the more densely populated Chilbaghtu valley. But the other side of the range had an amazingly thick growth of bushes. This area belonged to the *Sayyids* of Shatoo. But Zawar and others reasoned that the *Sayyids* were rich enough, and what they didn't know wouldn't hurt them!

It was a good, steep walk for more than an hour to the top. I was greeted by a stunning view of a huge, snow-covered peak directly north. The men with me pointed out areas of Dai Zangi, Malistan, and Bamiyan.

We descended furtively on the northern side and I watched with interest as the men began chopping up bushes with their *chapchoors*, pick hoes, and stacking them. It was a fine art to get a huge bundle packed nicely so it would stay in place with just one circle of rope and be comfortable on one's back!

It wasn't long before Zawar had my load ready. It wasn't as big as his own load, or any of the other men's. We had a snack of dry bread before heading down.

"Lucky we haven't been spotted," the men said among themselves. "The *Sayyids* sometimes patrol this area with guns looking for poachers. If they catch someone, they really give him a hard time."

I was the first one home! I had a lighter load and enjoyed going at a fast pace, being alone and feeling almost free! Besides, it was the most exercise I had had in ages. My legs were sore.

When the others returned, we ate. Then they went back for another load! I rested upstairs and thought about God's deliverance of Israel at the Red Sea. God has triumphed gloriously.

I saw a jeep coming toward our settlement from the main road. Who could it be? It was Muhammad Ali of Jodri bringing things for me:

cooked meat	apples	sweater
long underwear	2 pairs of warm socks	pocket knife
toothpaste	toothbrush	3 bags of candy
4 batteries	toilet paper	3 pens

The Commander's House

It was fun to distribute the apples among the kids! There were just enough to go around.

After my English lesson with Shams, I went with Jawad, Reza, and the donkey to Kharba to get more willow branches. The blisters on the palms of my hands were bothering me as I climbed the trees and chopped the branches with the adze. I wasn't able to treat the open wounds with antiseptic, as I would have done at home! We were glad that Bole, Zawar's first wife, happened along as we were trying to balance the load and heft it onto the donkey! She was returning from Salihi's funeral.

Bole was a strong and lovely lady with a beautiful character. She seemed to always be unselfishly serving others. She didn't seem to be sorry for herself that she had lost the "favored wife" status because she had not been able to have kids. She had many times gone out of her way to be kind to me.

We were home by dark, just in time for games with the kids.

I joked with everyone that they were now my guests for supper, since I was sharing the meat that had come for me!

Friday, October 11

I arose early to join the mountain climbing expedition again, but Zawar said I shouldn't go. After breakfast I watched the ladies making bread. To their delight I had many questions about names of things and about their techniques.

In time alone, I went over the Philippians chapters and prayed for health for all.

In my walking, my left heel was bothering me because of my tight, new *kalaushes*--Russian, felt-lined rubber shoes that folks here wear in the winter. My old jogging shoes were certainly more comfortable to walk in, even though they had big holes in the front.

After a *qurti* lunch with the workers, I got to join them on their second escapade of the day. I made it clear to Zawar that, since I understood the issue now (that they were actually stealing wood from the *Sayyids*) I would not set foot on the other side of the range nor bring a load of contraband back. I would only go along for the walk.

119

THE UPPER HAND

My full water jug was finished off by the 15 men before we got to the top! I rested and read *Space* while the men and boys cut and made their bundles of fuel. They were really scared that the *Sayyids* might spot them and take some action.

To my chagrin, I realized that Zawar had tricked me. He had prepared a bundle for me bigger than the one yesterday! He said, "If any one of us locals had legs as fat as yours, we could carry very big loads."

I decided to oblige and carry the load. Again I was the first home, but this time much more tired. I enjoyed tea and dried mulberries. Supper was a really delicious potato *qorma*. As we sat around afterwards, Madad, one of the day workers, was a great help on my *Hazaragi* dictionary.

Saturday, October 12

In my prayer time this morning I thought of the verse, *"Work out your own salvation with fear and trembling."* After all that Christ has worked in us, our part is to humbly work out the practical implications of our salvation.

Downstairs with the ladies for breakfast, we got into a discussion of marriage customs.

Sometime later I went outside to walk. There was a lot of activity at A. Hussain's house. Guests were coming that evening for a wedding, to take his sister. The whole community was helping him with preparations. It was nice to see! I helped to peel and slice onions for an hour or so and talked to the men.

A boy handed me a sealed envelope. It was a letter from Doc, the last I would get. Zawar opened it, I guess to check it, then handed it to me. It was dated October 10, then a note was added from Oct. 13. Most of the four-page letter was verses copied from Hebrews. I was touched as I read the added note:

> I think the date is correct but have been partially incoherent for three days so may have missed a day. Flu, I think with instability but much better today other than phlebitis and erysipelas in left calf.

The Commander's House

> I am too weak and lame to visit you so please come to see me if at all possible...
>
> I must be a mess. My hosts have suggested I take a bath but the severe chills have prevented that. I have been too ill to worry about appearance but I trust God to see me thru this too!
>
> Come, if at all possible.
>
> Love,
>
> Bill

This letter put me in a serious frame of mind. "What if Dr. Bill died?," I asked myself. I told Zawar that Doc was sick and I wanted to visit him. Zawar gave no definite answer.

I had been asking Atee M. Ali to give me a haircut for quite some time. There were no barber shops in the valley. Atee M. Ali often cut people's hair and didn't seem to take any money in return. Now he mentioned to me that he had time. We received permission from Zawar and headed across the fields to his house. I felt much better after the job was done. I didn't mind at all sitting on the ground outside while he operated.

What barber will serve you yogurt, bread, and fresh carrots after a haircut?!

My student, Shams, came by looking for me. We went back to the house for what would be our last lesson together.

Aziz, Dilkha's brother, was giving Jawad and Juma haircuts in the sun. He stayed for the evening, so we had a good time talking together. I had supper of *shorwa* and meat with him, brought down from the feast at A. Hussain's. I was invited to the feast, but didn't know about it until the last minute. I guess festivities were still going on when I went up to bed alone.

Reflections on the current situation by Mark's boss:

After several weeks of daily contact with Afghans and Pakistanis, several impressions have been formed. Inevitably when the subject of kidnapping comes up, the following solutions are proposed:

1. Immediately pay a cash ransom.

2. Send armed police, Mujahideen, or independent soldiers for a rescue.

3. Capture family members of the captor and arrange a trade.

4. Hire someone to eliminate the captor.

This summer, as the Hizb-i Wahdat leadership was involved in other battles, Wasim struck an alliance with other independent commanders to become the most aggressive and powerful leader in the valley.

Unfortunately this occured during Joel and Bill's visit to Jaghori. The last few months, on at least ten occasions, individuals representing different groups have each met with Wasim to deal with the hostage situation. We have heard of different money offers.

Multiple organizations, parties, and institutions are applying pressure on the captors through a variety of methods including:

1. Witholding basic human necessities such as humanitarian assistance programs.

2. Witholding funds by employers.

3. Stimulation of pressure from within the masses of Afghanistan as a result of a compilation of methods.

4. Military intimidation by 1000 hostile troops within the Hazarajat.

5. Military intimidation by multiple political parties with many more thousands of ethnically antagonistic troops outside of the Hazarajat who are anxious for an excuse to kidnap or murder Hazaras, invade Hazara villages, and loot Hazara lines of transportation.

We now have a package of personal items from Joel's parents for Joel and know of a local man who may be going in in a few days. Should we purchase anything for Bill? Last time we sent him the camera, books, film, etc.

C. The Soldiers' Base   (Patu)

Oct. 13--Dec. 26

Sunday, October 13

Today began normally, but was to be a day of one of the greatest changes in my captivity. A new chapter would begin!

Nafisa brought me tea and bread in the middle of my prayer time. When I finished breakfast and prayers, I began work on my dictionary and diary. Men were downstairs discussing something. I wasn't paying particular attention to them. But Zawar came up to my room and sat down next to me in the window.

"We want to send you to the *paigah*, military base, for a few days in order to ensure your safety," he said. "There's a war going on now with the *Shola* Communist groups. Many soldiers have left Chilbaghtu. There are not enough left to properly guard you. What do you think? Do you agree to go?"

"I've come to like it here," I replied. "I like the family atmosphere and I've come to know the people here. You know that I don't like being around soldiers. So, no. I don't want to go. But I am your captive and will do what you say."

"It will only be for two days. Three at the most. I promise. Then you can come back here until the time when you can go and rejoin your family."

Zawar was firm. Obviously a decision had already been reached.

It was about 10 a.m. I packed things to leave and the things I would need for two or three days. It was cold and I wore my long johns for the first time. Also all the layers of sweaters, etc. that I had. I wrapped a few things in a large, embroidered cloth that Engineer Kabir had sent once with

123

THE UPPER HAND

supplies. The book, *Space*, my wool shawl, flashlight, soap, toothpaste, toothbrush, socks, and some toilet paper.

It was about noon when I set off with five soldiers. The ladies of the house gave me some dried meat and bread, since I hadn't had lunch. I said good bye to a few kids I saw as I was leaving. I wished I could have said good bye to everyone. I wonder if I'll ever see them again. But these things were beyond my control. I had to go and trust God.

I was glad that I knew all these soldiers. But I was still angry and frustrated inside. I didn't like being forced. I longed for freedom.

After an hour's walk we stopped at Charsi's for tea. This was the same village where I had come for the wedding several weeks ago. After tea, the men just sat around talking and talking. I didn't understand why they wanted such a long break. I wanted to get on with the trip!

I asked for permission to go outside. Then I sat on a grassy strip next to a stream and read *Space*. I nibbled at my bread and meat, and gave a little to some nearby kids.

It was time to hit the trail again. We went at a good pace, but not too fast. I was thankful for the training I had had the last two days going up and down the mountain! It was a lovely walk over mountain ridges along a well-marked trail.

As we descended into the Baba valley, I recognized some of the terrain from our six-day stay in Safed Sang.

I saw an old man in the distance working outside a newly built house. I recognized him as Baba, the father of the four brothers who had kept us in Safed Sang! I greeted him warmly.

It was almost dusk as we arrived at a huge fortified house. I recognized it as the house we came to first in Baba months ago. The host had insisted that we couldn't stay there. This was the home of brothers Qurban and Mulla. One had a shop in the bazaar.

We had tea immediately, then a *nan buta* supper later. God helped me to feel a sense of well-being as the men continued talking on into the night. All the people around were kind to me. Six of us slept in that guest room.

The Soldier's Base

Monday, October 14

At the pre-dawn prayer time I got up with the rest of the men and went outside to the *karez*. I walked back and forth in the almond grove, and did my exercises. I had just enough time to go over Philippians 1 and 2, and pray for my family and friends before the call to come in for breakfast.

After breakfast, the men sat around for more than an hour. I was impatient and wished we would get moving. Finally we set off for Patu. It was a really beautiful walk--across fields and streams, following a stream up over a range of hills, then a steep descent to the Arghundab River. I was ahead some of the time, as I preferred walking faster. I liked Rizayee, and enjoyed his company on the way down.

When we got to the river, we stopped at a large house for tea. The tea and bread was followed by delicious grapes--freshly picked! They were my only grapes of the season.

As we walked up the river, I saw many familiar places from Doc's and my trip three months ago with the lame doctor. When we crossed the river we added another man to our party. Then the real climb began! Atee M. Ali and Rizayee went pretty slowly, since they weren't feeling well. The new man and I climbed steadily, arriving at the base about half an hour before the rest.

We had tea and bread in the "office". I was surprised how many soldiers there I knew from before. After some time I went outside to visit with my friend, Atee Bostan, the cook. I read some in the sun and worked some on my dictionary. I spent time walking back and forth (now one of my favorite ways for spending time--as I could sing and pray and think.)

At dusk I joined the soldiers for a familiar meal of rice cooked in vegetable oil. The talk in the office seemed almost endless. I was frustrated and spent some time trying to read *Space* by the light of the lantern. Then I got up to go and brush my teeth. I was hoping the precedent I had set in Chilbaghtu would be unquestioned here. "I always brush my teeth at night before going to bed."

I went down to the constantly flowing *karez*--about 100 yards from the office, down the hill. I enjoyed the few moments of dark solitude. On the days I had not been wearing my long underwear, I put them on here in preparation for the cold nights. When I returned, some of the soldiers told me not to go there after dark.

Eight or nine of us slept in the small office that night. There were no quilts or mattresses. And there weren't really enough blankets to go around. Rizayee kindly claimed one of the better blankets for me. I was still feeling down about having left the familiar family setting of Chilbaghtu and now being with soldiers.

Rizayee coughed quite a lot during the night. Fleas kept me awake for a while. And the hourly changing of the guard was hard to get used to. As each soldier would come in from the cold after his turn, he would wake the man who had been designated as having the next shift. He would get up and prepare to leave as the other snuggled back into his blanket. Then it would be fairly quiet for an hour!

Somehow I got some good rest that night.

Tuesday, October 15

There was a rush at the **karez** early in the morning as the men all performed their ablutions before prayers. The rocky area just beyond the **karez** was the most popular bathroom spot around. I joined them this morning, and then spent some time walking before breakfast in the office.

After getting an earful of the morning conversation, I asked if I could go out and climb the nearby mountain on my own. After all, they had told me when I came here that I would be free to walk all over by myself. "That's okay," they said as I pointed to the top of the mountain that was behind the base.

After about a 15-minute climb I found a nice level spot among some rocks near an old bunker. I soaked up the sun and was enjoying the time to be alone and pray. As I was finishing, I noticed Atee M. Ali looking around. He was looking for me. He said he wanted to take me to a safer place. "Our soldiers don't all know you. One may see you and shoot. You should stay near to the base."

Thankfully he let me be alone to read and write at a rocky crag overlooking the base. This was to be my morning prayer spot for the first

month. I could watch what was going on below and hear the calls for
meals! I think they felt reassured that I was near enough to check on.

I wrote a letter to Doc here before being called down for tea and bread
around 11. I spent some time visiting with the soldiers. After a rice lunch,
I found a spot where I could stretch out in the sun nearby. After a nap I
finished working on my dictionary, that is I finished sorting the words I had
already compiled.

Before supper I got some exercise by walking up and down the hill four
times at a fast pace. When supper in the office was finished, the soldiers
from Chilbaghtu began telling the base commander about my **Hazaragi**
dictionary. He asked to see it and was quite amused by some of the words I
had collected. He and others especially enjoyed the names for farm
equipment that I had picked up! I had made simple drawings beside the
things that were new to me.

There were eight of us again tonight.

Wednesday, October 16

This morning I went to a nearby field for exercises. This scheduling
seemed to work well since, by the time I had finished, the rush at the **karez**
was over.

Breakfast was late. The commander assigned jobs to different men.
Almost daily a group of three walked for about 45 minutes over to "Number
2", another base overlooking Sang-i Masha. They would return at dusk.
Other men were sent here and there with messages. Sometimes men were
assigned to collect firewood or bring a load of food up on the camp donkey.

I climbed up to the **jaba**, rocky outcropping, to find a sunny spot to
pray. The chorus I had learned from my brother, Tim, and his family kept
going through my mind,

"For Thy daily mercies, be Thy name adored.
More than all we praise Thee for Thyself, O Lord."

127

THE UPPER HAND

After a while Jalal appeared and called out for me. I managed to put him off for a while until I had read some and written some letters. Then I went down with him for lunch.

Two distinguished guests had arrived. Dr. Hakim spoke English very well. He had worked for the Austrian Relief Committee. With him was Muallim Amanullah, who knew a little English. I remembered meeting him in an area near Engineer Kabir's house when we vaccinated his animals.

The Akhund had also arrived with a lot of new people. As usual, when I saw him I began to feel mad and helpless.

Later on, Dr. Hakim approached me as I was sitting alone in the sun. He told me that Mark had sent a radio into the area so that he could communicate with us. But, Dr. Hakim said, they couldn't get the radio to work. He went on to say that the Akhund wanted him to talk to me. The Akhund wanted cash for our release, he said, or else the continued work of our project. We talked over local politics and the chances for our release. Dr. Hakim seemed to be a nice guy. He said he had tried to explain to the Akhund that we couldn't pay money for our release because it would make the situation more dangerous for other foreign aid workers.

I talked some with Muallim Amanullah. He said that the kidnapping was only for cash.

Tonight I had supper with the soldiers in the kitchen. I had a strong desire to avoid the Akhund's presence. After brushing my teeth, though, I went into the office. The Akhund had a stomach ache.

We sent a letter today to Commander Wasim thanking him for keeping Bill and Joel safe and stating, "We know that now is the best time for these men to return to their families." We told him that we agreed with his suggestion that a new survey be done and work be continued in the area, but this could only begin when our men returned to Pakistan.

We told him that we had instructed VOA and BBC to broadcast that Bill and Joel were not being held for ransom.

My own feeling is that flowery radio messages will help greatly to get our friends out.

The Soldier's Base

Thursday, October 17

After exercise this morning I walked up and down the hill twice. Then I warmed myself at the kitchen fire and went in for tea in the office. The men were listening to the radio.

In my prayer spot this morning I went over Philippians 2 and thought of this verse: *"It is God who worketh in you both to will and to do of His good pleasure."* I prayed:

"Lord, you change our desires. Thank you. You make us want your pleasure, then you enable us to do it! Make this a day where I do your good pleasure."

I wrote, read, and then collected some firewood for the kitchen. When I went down for lunch, I sat with Dr. Hakim, Muallim Amanullah, and Yusaf (a relative). Later I had some time to talk with Yusaf alone. He had worked as a mechanic in Sang-i Masha. He said that he and his friends would like to try to sneak me out of the base. But things were pretty difficult right now.

Dr. Hakim talked with the Akhund quite a while in the office. He came out and made his way toward me. "The Akhund says he'll release you and Doc if you do projects in neglected areas like Chilbaghtu, Baba, Patu, and Aicha (these were the areas that Hizb-i Islami controlled!)." Dr. Hakim told me I could write letters which he would take. "Write one for Mark," he said, "and I'll try to send it by radio." I also sent letters with him to my family and Doc.

I took a nap and wrote some more letters to friends back in Pakistan and the States. Seven letters in all today.

A new shift of soldiers arrived today. Later I realized the system. There were basically three shifts. Each would come for a week at a time for "base duty". If one man couldn't come, he had to find a substitute. Each group had it's own sub-commander. In my 3-month "tenure" at the base I got to know most of the soldiers pretty well. As the men came and went every week, I almost felt like a fixture. Men often expressed to me that they were sorry I was being kept so long.

129

THE UPPER HAND

I was chatting with a 15-year-old "*mujahid*" and learning some new *Hazaragi* words. Two new soldiers approached me. The older one I later discovered was a Mullah, and the younger was a teacher, Muallim Hamid. Both became good friends. I was surprised to find out that Muallim Hamid had studied in a Pakistani school in Quetta and had later worked in Karachi. His Urdu was very good, and he also knew some English. He was the cook's nephew. We spoke of the fighting now being based on *uqda,* personal grievances, rather than *aqeeda,* moral or religious conviction.

It was colder tonight. There were about ten of us sleeping in the office.

We had a meeting with the new US Ambassador to Pakistan, Nicholas Platt, and his staff. The ambassador was cordial and professional. We discussed what was being done for the release of our friends and ways of communicating better.

The big rumor today is that Wasim has been killed.

Friday, October 18

I had breakfast this morning with my new friend, Muallim Hamid, on the roof of the barracks which adjoined the kitchen. Then I was off to my "office" on the rocky knoll. As I prayed, I thought of God as my sun and shield. "LORD, energize, encourage, and bring hope, warmth, and light to your people. Protect them from the evil one. Cause rejoicing in you."

As usual, my prayers for others encouraged me. I wrote, read, and climbed around on the rocks. I made it down to the kitchen a little late for lunch. I enjoyed the lunch of delicious *lobia,* kidney beans, with rice, and tea. *Lobia* definitely became my favorite of all the dishes served.

After my nap I watched Atee Bostan make bread. I helped him a little. It really took a lot of energy and skill. And when there were a lot of soldiers, he had to make bread twice a day!

I sang songs until sunset. The sunsets from the base were beautiful. I wish I could draw the breath-taking vista of mountains and valleys topped with ever-changing cloud formations.

130

The Soldier's Base

I had supper in the soldiers' room for the first time. It seemed crowded and less clean. But I came to enjoy it later and consider it my place rather than the office. I much preferred the atmosphere around the soldiers as compared to the "bigwigs". I didn't miss the constant political and military discussions!

The remaining evening hours turned out to be unforgettable. The events that followed turned out to be the main topic of discussion for weeks to come!

Ali Pana was the sub-commander for the group from Sabz Chob, Uloom, and Cheshma. He was a short, friendly fellow. His bravery and skill in fighting under fire were almost a legend. But he had one problem. Occasionally, for unknown reasons, he would go into violent and uncontrollable fits. I still don't know if these fits were demonic or natural.

At any rate, about four of us were sitting in the soldiers room after dinner. Suddenly Ali Pana entered glaring devilishly and breathing heavily. He looked at each of us carefully. We all knew something was different. Then he suddenly started hitting Amin, who was sitting next to the door. Amin did the worst thing he could have done. He started laughing. This seemed to make Ali Pana all the more furious. He beat him some more, then left. Others began to laugh. Ali roamed around outside for a while. Then he was back in the room. He went straight for a kalashnikov leaning up against the wall. The soldier let him take it and Ali pointed it at him. The man lifted his hands and said, "I surrender!" Then Ali went out and fired a couple shots. You can imagine how this charged the atmosphere at the base!

Things seemed to have calmed down. Another sub-commander managed to take the gun away from Ali Pana. I went down to the spring to brush my teeth. When I returned, Ali was chasing people and hurling big stones at them. I climbed on top of a rock to be out of range, then on top of the office roof. There was half an hour of excitement, and then hours of talk about it. Ali went over to the sentry's barracks about 100 yards away. He scared the men there so much that one, Amin, jumped barefoot onto the rocks and took the whole skin off half the sole of his foot! In spite of his wound, Amin ran back to the office for safety and medical treatment. One soldier had some capsules of tetracycline. He opened these and sprinkled the

THE UPPER HAND

powder over the wounds, and then bound them up. There was no first aid kit at the base.

Ali Pana calmed down some and several men grabbed him and brought him into the office where I was sitting with many of the others. They laid him down and tried to soothe him, I was praying for him. I told him to sit next to me and tried to treat him very normally. But some of the men started laughing, and this set Ali off again. Another mad rampage outside. Then he disappeared. Several hours later he appeared--in his right mind, but exhausted.

There were ten of us in the office tonight. Close fellowship! I had peace in my heart from God because I realized that even in strange and violent situations, I was in God's care. Some of the soldiers later remarked how they noticed Ali Pana hadn't acted aggressively towards me.

Saturday, October 19

This morning I walked up to the saddle near my rocky retreat for exercises. I joined the Chilbaghtu gang for breakfast. For my prayer time later I went over the verses from Hebrews that Doc had written out for me from his New Testament. This had been my last letter from him.

I thought of Jesus Christ as our high priest. He was made like us in every way. We are called to be a kingdom of priests. I interceded for soldiers, folk I've come to know here, and for the country. I prayed for others to be intercessors and to be bold.

After writing four letters, I climbed around on the rocks. Lunch was a special treat--*lobia* with its broth poured over broken up bread. I washed my socks and feet at the spring. Then I watched the stone throwing competition. My pen had run out of ink, so I borrowed a sack from Atee Bostan and went out to collect firewood.

I ate supper with the soldiers that night and was surprised how much rice I put away! I did enjoy it. Discussion on America and religion followed.

After brushing my teeth I bedded down with ten others in the office again. There wasn't much room to turn over! I was so thankful to God that he had helped me to adjust and get used to different sleeping situations.

The Soldier's Base

A little later there was a scare as a sentry thought he heard someone. Just about all the soldiers took off with their guns--only to return some time later convinced that it had been a false alarm.

Sunday, October 20

The Chilbaghtu (or "Timbuktoo", as Doc called it) gang had breakfast early. I borrowed Zabit's pen and took off for my prayer spot. I prayed for the current situation thinking of the verse, *"The effectual, fervent prayer of a righteous man availeth much."* I prayed for my family and friends that the character of Christ might be evident in them *"so in the day of Christ I may rejoice that I have not run in vain, neither labored in vain."*

Just as I finished my diary, Atee Qasim appeared--seemingly wanting someone to talk to. He had been away from his family for two weeks now, and was tired of it. Having nothing to do at the base was tiring in itself. We talked until lunch. He encouraged me to trust God. He spoke of the evils existing in the name of Islam.

We descended to the base together. A lot of new people had come. After a rice lunch I went to my second office (the one nearer the kitchen in front of a huge rock). What a delightful surprise to see Nasrullah, Mark's messenger, coming towards me! He had brought me another pair of long underwear and socks. I wrote letters for him to take to Mark, Engineer Kabir, and my family. Nasrullah then took a picture of me in my office, and one of me sitting next to the Akhund in the office.

After a long talk with the Akhund in private, Nasrullah came back to talk to me. The Akhund had written a letter to Mark saying that I would be released if Mark's organization would promise to build a school in Chilbaghtu and send the money to buy the land for it. I would be released when the land was bought, he promised. Even though I knew the Akhund and his wily ways, I could not help but feel encouraged. At least something was happening!

Nasrullah left assuring me that he would be back within two weeks--or quicker, if he could manage.

My spirits had lifted. There were nine of us in the office tonight. I had a good sleep but woke up with a stomach full of gas.

133

THE UPPER HAND

Excerpts from a friend assisting Mark:

"The exhaustion level is taking its toll on the whole family (Morris'). Mark's parents have been here visiting from Africa. They have been a great help in the office and home. I believe that I am the most optimistic person in the house concerning a near term solution to our situation. Part of that may be because the Morrises have been through several false hopes already."

10:45 p.m. A call from the US saying that Bill had been released in Peshawar.

11:50 p.m. Phil DeHart, Joel's brother, calls from Philadelphia. Bill's wife had called him and said, "Bill has lost 40 lbs., but was in good spirits. Someone is going in for Joel." Phil was obviously concerned and I tried to assure him and let him know that we will not stop our efforts here for Joel's release.

Monday, October 21

My tummy was really upset this morning. The men went out after breakfast to gather firewood and bring water. I went up to my office and re-read the verses from Hebrews that Doc had written for me. This one stuck out:

"How much more shall the blood of Christ, who through the eternal spirit offered himself without spot to God, purge your conscience from dead works to serve the living Lord." 9:14

I prayed with thanks for the purging and power of this blood, and for the ability to serve God.

Something was in the air today. Why all the extra soldiers? Why were the leaders holding long meetings? The soldiers told me. There was to be an operation on a village that was full of **Sholas**, Chinese Communists. The accusation was that these people were against Islam. And they were trying to build a following using money that was coming from Communists via Pakistan. Also, some of these men had guns belonging to Hizb-i Islami--yet they refused to give them back and also refused to show up for their turn at guard duty. Later I heard the other side of the story.

The Soldier's Base

The soldiers left around ten at night. Thankfully for them the moon was almost full. They seemed used to such planned attacks under cover of darkness. I remember Munshi, my short friend, debating out loud whether he would obey orders and go, or not. He didn't want to be firing at his own people. He ended up going. About 20 men went--divided into about three groups.

We talked some; then enjoyed a good night's sleep. There were only six of us in the office!

Tuesday, October 22

I exercised on the saddle overlooking the base. There weren't too many of us for breakfast. Afterwards I was told not to go up to my office because of the operation in the Patu valley below. When the bread was baked I carried a kettle along with two other men up to a rocky knoll where the Akhund and others were setting up the Chinese *zeek-o-yuk* antiaircraft gun to fire down on the area under attack. They had heard sounds of a volley of firing below. They were in touch by radio with the commanders of the three different groups who had gone for the attack in the valley.

They thought it strange when I didn't want to sit with them and enjoy the firing of the huge gun. I went off to meditate and the Akhund sent Atee Qasim to keep an eye on me. I sort of resented him being along, but he sat at some distance and let me have some privacy in a sunny place. I was able to refresh myself there in the Lord. I thought of the words, *"For all seek their own, not the things which are Jesus Christ's"*. I prayed for the current battle, and Afghanistan in general.

I began writing a poetic account of my experience in Afghanistan. This is how I began:

A LAMENT FOR AFGHANISTAN

Beauties--Afghanistan, the heart of Asia;
Land of barren mountains and lush oases,
Proverbial cool breezes and clear waters,
Plentiful fruit, precious gems

135

THE UPPER HAND

Colorful people and ancient traditions,

Primitiveness--Modern technology seems to have passed you by.
>   Your wheat is harvested just like it was in the time of
>   Abraham.
>   Your people proclaim whole-hearted allegiance to the
>   Arabian prophet,
>   Your men and boys are all armed and trained in the arts of
>   war.

Lawlessness--Afghanistan, my heart aches for you.
>   Twelve bloody years with no end in sight.
>   A battlefield again after several years of relative control.
>   "The law of the jungle," they said.
>   Might makes right.
>   "You won't believe what we've seen," they said,
>   "Men killed like flies and no one asks why."

Fighting--Now the Russians are gone,
>   But fighting with government troops continues in other areas.
>   Here it's "brother killing brother"
>   In a quest for local power and control.
>   Last year it was the Shia Hazaras against the Sunni Pashtuns.
>   They tell of bold victories and plentiful booty--
>   The wheat that we use for bread at the base is a part.

Infighting--The heavy guns sounded repeatedly this morning.
>   Russians? No. But they say they're Communists.
>   They were with our group before, but now they've joined
>   another.
>   Therefore, "Communists". "And we hate all Communists."
>   A restless peace was broken ten days ago,
>   After a brief break from four years of internal war.

Remnants--To the casual observer, the effect of war is obvious.

The Soldier's Base

Remains of tanks. Gunpowder for blasting rocks.
Bomb cases used for flower pots.
A bullet shell used as a lid handle.
Kids play with rocket holders.

Misfortune-- **Badbakhti**
> Our land has no borders with other countries.
> All my savings from work in Iran were stolen.
> Sixteen of my relatives disappeared when Taraki took over.
> What is our small misery in comparison?
> These words of comfort are often offered:
> "Every man should see every kind of day--good and bad."

Attraction--Afghanistan, my heart aches for you.
> Your land has fascinated me.
> Your people have warmed and drawn me with ruggedness and
> hospitality.
> I wanted to draw close, to help, to see first hand.
> So I came, and was welcomed warmly, it seemed,
> Honored and appreciated wherever I went.
> Until the day before our departure was due...

Then Atee Qasim and I walked on up the hill and down to the kitchen for tea and bread.

After some time, three soldiers returned. Fifteen prisoners were coming, they reported. One boy had been shot, but there had been no deaths. The rest of the soldiers and prisoners came later. Some elders had also come up from the valley--presumably to try to sort out the contention.

Two of the elders came up to me in my office. "We have some good news for you," they said. "Doc has been released. He has reached Peshawar and is well."

"How do you know?" I questioned.

"We heard it on the radio," they replied.

I thanked them. I felt great joy. I took it as a definite answer to my prayer, and an evidence of God's mercy. It was only later that I thought that these men could well be tricking me for some reason of their own. After hearing several confirming reports in the days to follow, however, I began to believe it!

I spent a lot of time walking and singing above the base. The accommodations at the base were really stretched now. I was asked to join a group going down to a nearby house to spend the night. I was glad to go. I enjoyed the exercise and change of pace. We had delicious *nan-i waitu*, a kind of bread with butter mixed into the dough, and tea. This made a good supper for me. The soldiers were dead tired, so there was not much talk. I stayed up praying and thinking for a while. It was great to sleep without being interrupted by the hourly shifting of the guard.

Wednesday, October 23

I enjoyed the change this morning. I exercised in an almond grove. It was now my tenth day away from Chilbaghtu--and Zawar had told me I would be at the base for two, or at the most, three days. I was beginning to think that I might not get back to Chilbaghtu.

Breakfast was supplemented with delicious dried mulberries. I felt good as we climbed the steep mountainside back to the base.

In my prayer time this morning I prayed for people in their groups that they would "stand fast in one spirit, with one mind striving for the faith of the gospel." I was thankful for the partial victory (Dr. Bill's freedom), and prayed for complete victory and glory to God.

The men were playing volleyball. If anyone hit the ball hard, it was off in the rocks down the side of the mountain! They enjoyed the game and some were really good at it. The net? A rope (taken from the base donkey) between two poles. The boundary line? Non-existent!

After lunch I went over some English with Muallim Hamid and two other men. Slowly, teaching English was becoming a main occupation here.

As I sat in my office #2 and read *Space*, some guys came to talk. One was Charsi's brother. "What do you think of Afghanistan now?" they asked. Sometimes my answers were bitter as I used my own case as an example. "Afghanistan will not make progress as long as the leaders only think of their personal prosperity and well-being. They must act selflessly for the good of the common people."

The Akhund and a large group of soldiers left after lunch. I went up to the saddle and *jaba* to walk and sing until sunset. Some thought that I had run off! But they were new soldiers who weren't familiar with my habits and routine.

I had supper with Atee Bostan in the kitchen. He welcomed my company and I felt comfortable there with him. Plus, I was given special attention when it came to food! When the other soldiers were denied bread along with rice because the bread just wouldn't last, I got a little to go along with tea for "dessert"! Atee Bostan had a square rock to sit on near the fireplace. I would sit nearby on an upside down bucket.

I waited a long time for things to quieten down for sleep. But interrogations were going on in the office. Finally I went into the office to sleep. They didn't mind my presence. I thought they would object since they were trying to prove from individual taped sessions the criminal actions of each of the new prisoners. It was hard to get to sleep.

Dr. Bill is Free!

The last 36 hours have been exhausting, exhilarating, rewarding, and frustrating as one former involuntary guest arrived in this country, passed through some additional trials and as of this moment is on a flight accompanied by Cindy Morris to London. The Father gets all the credit although His servants have expended astronomical amounts of energy.

Dr. Bill Lewis completed 103 days with his hosts with high spirits, deeper commitments, a very reduced physical stature, tremendous appetite, sense of humor, appreciation for all who have sustained him and eagerness to get back to home and family. He has had the flu and has contracted an ear disease which he has treated himself.

Bill's companion, however, remains in Afghanistan. His condition has not changed.

Dr. Bill frequently mentioned high spiritual experiences, prayer time, new resolves, insights from time with the Lord, and good times that he and

THE UPPER HAND

Joel spent together in prayer. He had new insights into holiness. Joel had no Bible, so Bill wrote verses from his New Testament for him. Joel sent Bill the words to many songs and Old Testament verses. Dr. Bill is a strong individual who has been through a difficult experience, has a deeper faith, and is willing to share his insights.

Numerous press releases have appeared in the last few days. They have varied in their degree of accuracy.

Interestingly, Dr. Bill started his journey to us the same day that a major prayer effort was organized in the US. That same day, the Peshawar Fellowship also had special prayer for the captives.

Don't have any idea how Joel may come home, but am not seriously concerned for him. A thought has occured to me more than once today since the radio contact. Joel may not be in any big hurry to come home. From what all of his friends say about him, the opportunity to spend a winter in the middle of Afghanistan is the kind of thing he always wanted to do. From his perspective, he and the Lord have the people of Hazarajat surrounded. I consistently hear such things as Joel loves to camp out and takes his vacations hiking through high mountains alone. Joel loves to spend weeks with the village people. Joel has excellent fluency in more than one local language and projects the aura of a religious man. He has no problem living on bread and tea. He sleeps on the floor on an Afghan rug in his Islamabad house. He has few possessions and doesn't mind sharing any that he does have. Dr. Bill indicated that Joel had enough scripture memorized to encourage both of them. When I do get through to him by radio, we may have to politely ask him to come home.

Thursday, October 24

A pre-dawn alert woke everyone up. Someone had heard firing. But it turned out to be a false alarm. It was things like this that made me appreciate the security I had lived with all my life. And God gave me peace in situations like this where others were afraid.

The water container near the kitchen was empty. I thought it amazing that with lots of soldiers around and no particular daily responsibilities, they

140

The Soldier's Base

couldn't keep the container full of water. I carried two buckets of water from the spring to the water container. Usually when the men saw me doing this, they would say, "Don't do that. You shouldn't work." But it was important for me to feel useful, and I saw that the work was not being done by anyone else. I would tell them, "I like doing this for the exercise"--and it was good exercise! The buckets were made of old shortening cans and held about seven gallons of water each.

I had breakfast in the office. Afterwards I got into a discussion with Muawin Saib that turned out to be a confrontation. It made me upset. Muawin was from Baba and was an older man that the others looked up to. He had some responsibilities in administration. He had had some education. He began speaking about areas that had received no help, and how people like me came and helped the already-wealthy. Then he went on to say that bad people like Engineer Kabir would use us for furthering their own nefarious aims (spreading Communism and distancing people from faith in God). It was not really our fault, they would sometimes say, but we were suffering for the evil of people like Engineer Kabir. Things like kidnapping were necessary to draw attention to local needs and injustices.

To my later regret, I was drawn into the war of words. I tried to justify my position. I tried to defend Engineer Kabir. I tried to explain that any true religion had at its base mercy and respect for human life and freedom--not force and cruelty.

But my words fell on deaf ears. I should have saved my breath. I realized more than before the clear differences in our ethical and moral base. They were not bothered by wrong action if it seemed to help them. They could always find some justification. The end justified the means. No one seemed to stand for principles.

I left the office in an angry mood. Graciously God ministered to me and lifted my thoughts to Himself. I thought of Jesus as the eternal king. I reminded myself of one of the verses Doc had written to me. Christ is always alive to make intercession for us. He can save to the "uttermost"!

I was able to vary my activities today to make my time pass well. Interrogations had been going on all day. I was repulsed by the thought of listening to more of this as I tried to go to sleep, so I decided to sleep with

141

the soldiers. It was hard to do at first, but I came to like this situation much better later.

Unlike the office, the soldier's room had a *lar,* a chimney or smoke tunnel that went under the floor then up through the wall. This was a very effective way of heating the room. In fact, tonight I was too hot! I realized later that different parts of the room were hotter or colder--depending on the path of the *lar*. Later on I was able to claim a space that was just on the edge of the hot part. This place was not so desirable to others, so folk came to understand that this was "Muallim's spot". This assurance of personal space at night gave me some sense of security.

I had to get up two times in the night because of diarrhea. My thoughts went to my room in Islamabad with the attached bathroom--an electric light I could switch on, a flush toilet, hot running water, and toilet paper. Now I had to fill the dipper with cold water (my toilet paper had finished a long time ago), alert the guard so he wouldn't think I was trying to escape, find a rock in the moonlight, and crouch behind it in the cold and in my weak body state. Difficult, yes. But it made me think of being thankful for the good health I had generally enjoyed.

Later I adopted a small plastic case (a cover for some kind of ammunition), and kept it as a kind of personal cup for use in place of toilet paper. The water container near the kitchen would be covered with ice in the mornings. I would treat myself to a special luxury of hot water from the bucket in the *tanoor*, oven, which Atee Bostan (and later his son, Bostan) kept for kneading the dough in the morning.

Friday, October 25

I did some exercise, but my upset stomach was bothering me. After tea in the office Muallim Hamid told me that he was going home for a day or two, and asked if I'd like to go along. The idea was thrilling. But I was sure they wouldn't let me. The Akhund wasn't there, anyway. But they did!

We had a wonderful walk. For the first part we were re-tracing the steps that Doc and I had taken when the lame doctor led us to his home after the first few days of our captivity. Then we took a new trail. I enjoyed Muallim Hamid's company so much. He talked about some disputes with family land and how he was forced to join Hizb-i Islami, although he didn't want to. For a year he had taught in a school set up by Hizb-i Islami with funds from outside. But then the budget had been cut.

Although my stomach was not back to normal yet, I was glad I still had the energy to walk. The whole hike lasted about three hours. We had a break at Sufi's house when we got to the Patu--Sang-i Masha road.

When we arrived at Muallim Hamid's home in upper Qunagh, we had a delicious snack of bread made from chick peas with tea. A little later an omelette appeared. On my request I had some time alone in the guest room to look at Muallim's books and nap. I woke up when a guest came. It was the lame doctor! It was good to see him, but I saw immediately that he was in a bad state. He was a man in danger. He was wondering how he could escape to Pakistan. Over more tea he related the details of how he had been arrested and beaten when the Akhund and leaders found out that he had been in touch with some people who were planning to get Doc and me out of the area. Other soldiers had told me that the doctor's beating was the result of stealing some of the party's food, which he was responsible to keep and transport.

I promised that I would tell no one of our meeting, and I gave the doctor my address in Pakistan so he could contact me when I was free.

Muallim and I went out for a walk. He showed me his land and a shop nearby. We dug carrots out of the ground, washed them, peeled them, and ate them. We visited his uncle working on the threshing floor. Then it was back home for dried mulberries and almonds.

After dusk Arif appeared. He was another soldier friend from the base who was on Muallim's shift. We walked together to a large home up the valley. This was the Subedar's home. He had served in the Pakistan army and spoke Urdu. Muallim took part in the *Quran khwani,* reading the whole Quran, with about 24 others. It was finished in about half an hour, and a delicious meal appeared. Cooked apricots and fresh onions were served along with the *shorwa* and meat.

A relaxed discussion on world geography, religion, and politics followed the meal. The Mullah and another educated man were especially interested in learning. The Mullah mentioned having a New Testament that he had read at least parts of.

143

THE UPPER HAND

My stomach was still full of gas. We had a wonderful night's sleep in Muallim's sister's house. What a pleasant change not to be roused regularly during the night by the changing of the guards.

Saturday, October 26

Up later than usual. I did my exercises on the grass near the spring. After breakfast we went to Muallim's house. He had recently finished building it--at least the first story--and was proud of it. All the ceilings were the dome variety. The room I really appreciated now was the bathroom. His mother had heated a can of water. Taking a bath here was the most refreshing thing I could imagine. Even if I had to put my dirty clothes back on. It had been over two weeks since my last bath.

After some fresh bread and tea, we were off on our way back to the base. I had been concerned that Muallim's superiors might be angry that he had kept me overnight. But he said there was no problem.

On our way back we stopped at another of Muallim's sister's houses to fill our pockets with dried apricots and nuts! Another break at Sufi's house for some roasted liver and tea. We walked on to Juma's house. Muallim had spotted a suspicious jeep heading for Patu and was worried. We needed to make it back to the base as soon as possible, he said. Instead of going on the easy and familiar path around the mountain, we went straight up the side until, finally, we reached the trail at the top that led to Base #2.

We saw several flocks of *kauks*, a game bird, on our way. But the one shot that Muallim took at one missed its mark. We passed Atee Bostan on his way home for a short vacation.

I was tired when we arrived at the base mid-afternoon. But a time of rest in my office refreshed me. I came down to watch some volleyball before it got dark.

I slept with the soldiers again tonight, and it wasn't too hot.

144

The Soldier's Base

Sunday, October 27

My stomach is still upset. In my prayer time I thought of the line, *"Hast thou not seen, how thy desires e'er have been, granted in what He ordaineth."* I prayed for the Lord's people meeting in different places. I was called for lunch early. After resting, reading, and writing I went up to the saddle to walk and sing. A messenger came up to tell me to come down. I felt like a prisoner and the realization of my lack of freedom hit me hard. I walked back and forth near the base buildings. Supper featured a change--*lobia*, kidney beans, and their juice poured over bread that we had broken up into the four-five man basins.

I talked a long time with Bostan Ali, the old cook's son and now his substitute. We grew close and spent much time together. He became my best friend of all the soldiers. As I bedded down with the soldiers, I thanked God from the bottom of my heart for a deep sense of health and well-being.

We got a phone call from a trusted friend in Quetta. There was an important secret message that had freshly arrived. The messenger would only give it to us in person.

We got the first flight we could for Quetta, wondering what this important message could be. An hour after we arrived in our hotel there, our trusted friend appeared with the messenger. They both were very serious. Our friend emphasized again, "This is a very secret message. You must read it secretively."

I opened the envelope quickly, and then showed my companion. The messaage was in English. It read:

"Don't believe anything this messenger tells you." That was all!

Monday, October 28

As I sat in the kitchen after breakfast, the Akhund came by. He knew of the promise that I would return to Chilbaghtu. I had asked him when I could return several times. There was no point to asking any more. He asked me if I needed anything. I told him that if I was going to be staying here longer, I wanted all my stuff from Chilbaghtu. At least I could use a clean set of clothes and some toilet paper. He promised that these things would arrive soon. And then he told me not to go up to the *jaba* any more. I was disappointed by these restrictions. It made me feel down. But like so many times in the past, a closed door in one place meant something better to open up elsewhere. I walked down past the sentry barracks and found a nice sunny prayer place among the rocks. It was just as private, and I think the Akhund felt more secure about my being there.

I thought especially of the hymn lines:

> *Here I raise my Ebenezer,*
> *Hither by Thy help I've come*
> *And I hope by Thy good pleasure*
> *Safely to arrive at home.*

I asked God for this day to be one in His courts.

I returned to the base area before lunch to read and write some. I washed my feet and socks again at the spring.

Supper featured *lobia* and *nan tar* again. I helped serve in the kitchen. I had tea later with Bostan and Sufi. I went to sleep with the soldiers and slept well since my stomach seems to be back to normal.

Tuesday, October 29

I missed not going up to the saddle for my morning exercise. After breakfast with the soldiers I stayed in the room and went over Philippians 1 and 2 to myself. I repeated these chapters almost every day. I walked and sang for about an hour, then went back to yesterday's place of prayer. I thought of these words, "Not somehow, but triumphantly." I asked God to increase my faith.

I had lunch on the roof of the soldier's room/store room with Khadim and friends. I thank God that my anger at him for being one of my original captors has gone away. He's just a kid--maybe 18 at the most. And he's proud of being one of the Akhund's bodyguards.

This afternoon I joined in the volleyball game for about two hours. It was fun! I realized that my energy level is down. The other guys turned to the more popular stone throwing. I went away to walk and pray. Later I

talked with Atee Juma, Charsi, and boys. There were some questions about
my faith.

Tonight there was a long discussion in the room about America and
geography. Ali Pana remarked: "It's incredible that you came from such an
advanced country and people here captured you for a little money." Feelings
and words like this kept me from losing faith in the good part of the people
I was with.

Wednesday, October 30

One of my favorite morning songs was:

"Let the morning bring me word of your unfailing love
For I have put my trust in You,
Show me the way I should go, O Lord,
For to You do I lift up my soul.
Rescue me from my enemies,
For I put my trust in You
Teach me to do Your will, O Lord,
For You are my God."   Psalm 143:8-10

After breakfast with the soldiers I had a chance to listen to the BBC
English news and English program!

Down to my new office. I thought through Philippians--Paul writing
to Lydia, whose heart God had opened. Then there was the girl who was
delivered from an evil spirit. And the jailor, saved from suicide, and his
family. Paul's affection for them was so obvious. I prayed for the joy of
family and friends by my release, and the praise to God that would result.

I shook out my clothes and sunned them. I continued writing the
poetic account of events here.

I finished *Space* this afternoon. Also played some more volleyball.

I talked for a while with one of the prisoners. They had it much worse
off than I. It made me thankful. All of them were kept in an underground
room below the office. At first Bostan cooked for them, but they had to pay
a daily fee for this in addition to the huge amount that the Akhund was

THE UPPER HAND

demanding for their release. Soon they had a system going where someone from their village would come every couple of days with a donkey and a supply of home-cooked food. They also began to use their own stove and pots.

At first the 15 prisoners were pretty much confined to their room 24 hours a day. Later they were taken out almost every day to gather firewood for the kitchen. They were also made to carry water for the kitchen. One boy was assigned to be the cook's helper.

Several times elders from Patu came to intercede on behalf of the prisoners. After some days, some of the younger boys were allowed to go. Some time later, some of the men left. But three or four were kept for a long time. They were considered the more responsible "criminals". I found out later that two of the men had been severely beaten to make them confess things (claimed to be untrue by the person I was talking to). Out of fear of retribution they told the elders that they had not been beaten.

It was nice to see in certain soldiers a real compassion for the prisoners. They wanted to make life as easy for them as possible.

Two of the prisoners were brothers of the late Mamur Ahmad. It was his village that had been surrounded and attacked before dawn. Houses had been searched and things taken. A lot of ill feeling had been generated.

I was tired tonight and went to sleep early.

Thursday, October 31

Following breakfast I had a discussion about Pakistan and the US with two prisoners from Baba who had been captured and brought to the base several days earlier. One had worked for Oxfam, a voluntary agency out of Pakistan. Their crime was that they were also supposed to be supporting the *Sholas.* As we got to know each other in the following days, we developed a good friendship.

In my prayer time I thought of the verse:

"I beseech you therefore, by the mercies of God, that you present your bodies a living sacrifice, holy and acceptable to God, which is your reasonable service of worship. And be not conformed to the

148

The Soldier's Base

world, but be transformed by the renewing of your minds that you may know what is the good and perfect will of God."   *Romans 12:1-2*

I wrote my memoirs until lunch and finished my notebook paper. Now I had nothing more to read and no more paper to use to write--except my diary and dictionary.

Supper was an interesting dish. They called it *tafa*. It was a kind of broth made from potatoes, or onions, or many other things. But this was just plain *tafa*. The commander told a joke about *tafa* of *tafa*--which means something like stone soup! Our *tafa* tonight had only vegetable oil and water. We poured this hot over broken up bread in bowls.

There seems to be a perception that Joel is half Pakistani, "...may have a Pakistani mother." We strongly reiterated that he is equally as important as Dr. Lewis who has already been freed. We are trying to get an American-looking photo of Joel to show to various friends we visit.

We learned today that the Afghan Interim Government has sent five letters to the government of Iran to contact the Shia captors and request that they release the captives.

A traveler left Quetta with many letters, books, clothes, etc. for Joel.

Friday, November 1

In my "office" today I thought over a favorite song: *"Every day I look to you to be the strength of my life."* As day after day passed with increasing complexity or no seeming change in the situation, this song helped me to think in terms of a day at a time. A friend in Islamabad wrote that he was praying these lines for me.

Then I read the verse, *"Be ye steadfast, unmovable, always abounding in the work of the Lord."* I prayed especially for the congregations worshipping in Islamabad and Peshawar. Then I worked on a letter list that would also be a prayer list. I've written 147 letters so far, not counting letters to family. These letters and other writings were the most valuable possessions I had in the little bundle I carried around with me everywhere.

THE UPPER HAND

Other things my bundle contained were an extra pair of long johns. They were too small so I used them for a pillow. Soap, my plastic "mug" for bathroom use, tooth brush and tooth paste, flashlight, and the occasional dried fruit that people brought me.

Before lunch I had time to write some English for Commander Ghulam Hussain of Baba in a notebook he had given me.

After lunch and a nap the Akhund told me that I could go down to Rasooli's house for a bath. This was a very welcome treat. Not only could I leave the base,but I could get clean, too! Rasooli was a man with a kind heart. I understood later that he was one of the Hizb-i Islami commanders who was not in favor of the kidnapping action. He was from one of the houses nearest the base, so had responsibility for the actual day-to-day running of things.

M. Juma (Babai) went down with me. As we entered the guest room in the house, it seemed familiar. Then I realized that this was the room where Doc and I had spent our first night of captivity!

After tea, bread, and a rest, Rasooli led me down to the *nahoor*, irrigation pond. It was quite a private place. His wife had heated a pot of water for my bath. Boy, that felt good! Furthermore, Rasooli got out a pair of clean clothes for me to put on after the bath!! I managed to save enough hot water to wash my undershirt, as well.

We were back to the base by dusk. It felt good to be with Bostan again around the kitchen hearth. We sat a long time drinking tea and talking.

Tonight God showed me His personal love for me in a new way. Atee M. Ali was a foul-mouthed and rough character in this team of soldiers. He seemed to always be getting in fights with people. Yet he rose earlier than anyone else in the morning to say his prayers. He would criticize others for not properly keeping their religious duties. Anyway, tonight Atee M. Ali asked me if I wanted an extra blanket. I had one, and I knew there weren't extras to go around so I said, "No, thanks." At midnight, Atee M. Ali came over and put the blanket on me.

The Soldier's Base

Saturday, November 2

I feel great this morning. In my prayer time after breakfast I thought over Psalm 23--and how God's love and blessings reach us everywhere. I sang, "*I will give thanks to Thee, O Lord, among the peoples...*"

I hadn't been in my "office" for long when I was called and asked if I would like to go with the Akhund and a group of men on a trip into the Patu valley. I was happy to go. I don't know really why they wanted me to come with them. I, of course, appreciated the chance to be out.

As we walked down the mountain I mentioned to the men that I had been thinking about a verse in the Bible. What does God require of us? To do justly, to love mercy, and to walk humbly with our God. I was trying to point out the hypocrisy that I saw with all the religious talk and prayers, but then so many actions that seemed unjust and unmerciful to me.

Again, I could have saved my breath. When a man's heart wants something he will make reasons to justify it. I should not have wasted my effort trying to argue my case.

It was a very interesting and beautiful walk to Sevak, where we stopped for lunch. This town was clearly visible from the base, but was further than it looked. We stopped in the home of the commander's brother, Atee Habib. Soon tea appeared. A lot later a lunch of chicken *shorwa* came. It had been a long time since I had eaten chicken!

We walked about three quarters of an hour to the next town, Karez. Here, in the *minbar*, mosque, a meeting was scheduled between the locals and the Akhund to try to solve the issue of the prisoners at the base. The dynamics were very interesting to me, as I was allowed to sit in the meeting. It was here that I first heard the famous Persian proverb spoken in *Hazaragi*:

"Koh-i buland, rah da bale she."
There is a way to the top of even the highest mountain.

THE UPPER HAND

There were many speeches and formalities. There was an atmosphere of superficial politeness. No decision was reached after a couple of hours, so the meeting would continue tomorrow. In this setting I saw the Akhund as a man of great cunning and wit. There was no question that he had a way with words.

We all walked together to Khalili's house in nearby Char Achagh. What a surprise on the way to meet Mamur Yaqub and some of his troops! They had driven to Patu to try to find the Akhund--thinking he would be at the base.

It was a big group and Khalili was a gracious host. He worked for Hizb-i Wahdat in Bamiyan and was now home on a break. Other men from nearby homes helped to serve the delicious mutton meal. As we ate, there was some discussion about America and Christianity. I spoke out unwisely about the lawlessness in the area. I got a burning answer from the Akhund. He said that he hoped to get *sawab*, religious merit, for kidnapping me because, by doing this, he was dealing a strong blow to the Communist Sholas. I could hardly believe he said it, and that no one else seemed to blink an eye.

We listened to the radio together, then I went off with Babai, Atee Nadir, and two others to the guest room of another house. I had a good night's sleep.

Sunday, November 3

I exercised along the bank of a beautiful stream. The group for breakfast was about 20!

The Akhund and Mamur Yaqub had a long talk together before going to the meeting in the *minbar*. The rest of us waited outside. I began talking to Ali Baba Amini, one of the Mamur's soldiers. He knew some English. His brother was an engineer, and they owned a medical store in Anguri. I told Ali Baba that I was an English teacher in Islamabad. He was interested because he had been to Rawalpindi to visit friends.

"I had two friends from here who were studying in a *madrassa*, mosque school, in Rawalpindi. When I visited them," he continued, "they

152

told me that they went to Islamabad every Thursday afternoon to study English with an American."

I asked a few more questions and then told him that I was that American! We were both amazed. I knew that Baqir and Anwar were Hazaras, but I had no idea where they were from.

After talking for a long time, I lay down by a rock in the sun and had a prayer time. I thought of the wonder of forgiveness, and how we can walk in the light. God had forgiven me for my pride last night.

I really appreciated being able to visit alone with Mamur Yaqub and his soldiers in Atee Yunas' house nearby. It seemed like there was always worthwhile conversation around Mamur Yaqub. He was a knowledgeable man in many areas, and he had a great sense of humor. He was also very frank and unassuming. Mamur kindly gave me a notebook and I wrote a letter to my family for him to send.

The Akhund and his crew joined us there for another chicken *shorwa* lunch. When they returned, I had quite a lengthy discussion with Mamur about religion. He was interested and had good questions.

We went back to Char Achagh again for the night, but this time another home hosted us. Chicken again! We slept in the same house.

Monday, November 4

After breakfast a group of us set off to go back to the base. Mamur Yaqub and his troops were with us. On the way our discussion of religion continued. It was a long walk--maybe four hours--but we were not in a hurry. When we arrived, I went off by myself to pray. I thought of the verse,

"No temptation has overtaken you but such as is common to man but God is faithful who will not suffer you to be tempted above that you are able to bear, but will with the temptation also make a way to escape that you may be able to bear it."

I shared a rice lunch with Mamur in the office. Shortly after, Mamur, his soldiers and I left with Rasooli for Rasooli's house. I enjoyed a walk out in the almond groves. Carrots were also planted there. I dug some up and enjoyed them.

Guess what we had for supper? Chicken soup! We had an interesting discussion of politics. We listened on the radio to reports of the attempted assassination in Italy of Zahir Shah, the King of Afghanistan until 1971. I had the radio to myself for some time in the afternoon. I was deeply encouraged to hear most of the song *"One day at a time, sweet Jesus"* on BBC!

Mamur told the story of his days in university when he worked for a local tourist hotel. His job was to approach foreign tourists and ask them in English if they needed a hotel to stay in. One of his friends had the same job. Once a tourist asked his friend, "Does your hotel have bed bugs?" His friend didn't know what "bedbugs" were, but thinking they must be something good, he replied, "Oh yes, we have the biggest and best bed bugs in town!"

We all retired when the gas lamp gave out.

Tuesday, November 5

I went out by the pond to exercise in the almond grove. We had delicious fresh bread for breakfast. We also listened to the radio and visited. Mamur told me that Hizb-i Islami in Peshawar had offered four million Afghanis in military aid to the Akhund for my release. He felt that the whole thing about building a school (as we had discussed with Nasrullah) was a lie. The real issue was money. He felt that the meeting with commander Feroz and the representatives from Hizb-i Islami might help.

Mamur Yaqub and his soldiers set off for Baba. I was left to watch Rasooli build the roof for a new addition to his house that was to be the barn. I had a prayer time inside and thought of God's sovereignty and love. To God all the nations are like a drop in a bucket, or dust in the balance. *"Behold what manner of love the Father has bestowed on us that we should be called the sons of God."*

I helped Rasooli and his worker drag branches for the roof. Then back to the base by dusk. On the way I made a big mistake. I ate a raw turnip. It didn't taste like turnips in America or Pakistan. Later folks told me that eating these turnips raw causes stomach problems. Well, I got a very upset stomach and had to get up several times during the night.

I was encouraged to hear that three more of the prisoners from Karez had been released. I felt sorry for them, and I had a new interest in anyone who was freed from captivity!

A soldier approached me last night saying that he could help me escape if I wanted. I told him that I was not interested now. I didn't trust him, and I didn't want to plan such an escape without consultation with friends and a peace from the Lord.

A messenger we sent returned yesterday from Jaghori. He saw Joel in the mountain fortress. Mr. Joel is well, he said. He was not sad, he was "very happy". The messenger brought some pictures of Joel teaching the soldiers English. He also brought a letter from Akhund Salim stating that the condition for freeing Joel was making a school in that area. Joel must lay the first stone of the school. Global Partners would maintain complete control of the school and personnel. After that, Joel would be released soon.

At the time of the meeting, neither the messenger or Joel knew if Dr. Bill was free or not. Joel told him that he must find out if Dr. Bill were free. If he weren't, Joel said, "You must do everything you can to free him quickly."

During the meeting Akhund Salim showed the messenger a letter from the HIA office in Quetta which told him to keep Joel longer to get some money and weapons.

Snow has fallen in Jaghori. Travel is possible, but getting more difficult.

The messenger reported that the story in Jaghori is that Dr. Bill was traded for 10 kalashnikovs and one large antiaircraft gun.

Wednesday, November 6

I figured out that today is the four-month anniversary of my captivity!

Shortly after breakfast Rasooli asked if I would like to go back with him to his house. I was happy. On the way down we picked up a worker. I watched as they worked together to cover the rafters with brush, then grass and then mud. I left to have some quiet time alone by the trickling brook by the almond trees. I thanked God especially for physical health and blessing. I thought of the verse, *"I am the Lord who healeth thee."*

Back to the work site to help drag some more branches. A mullah was visiting and he asked some religious questions. The four of us had *qurti* lunch together. I borrowed a needle and thread to try to sew the outer strips that were coming off of my jogging shoes. Then I kept myself busy walking, singing, and writing until the men stopped work.

I enjoyed supper with Rasooli, Ali Bazaar (the hired worker) and Liaqat, Rasooli's oldest son. I had the chance to listen to the radio by myself tonight. I heard a Farsi Christian program from Monaco, Monte Carlo, and the Family Bible Hour from Limasol, Cyprus!

I walked out to the *karez* to brush my teeth. Even the dog didn't bother me. (Very few Hazaras keep watch dogs. There is a strong feeling that dogs are unclean and undesirable from a religious standpoint.) I went to bed full of thanksgiving and enjoying good health.

Thursday, November 7

I exercised in the almond grove. It was pretty cold. Breakfast was the ordinary tea and bread--supplemented with dried mulberries.

When the men went to work, I listened to the radio for a while then went down to a quiet, sunny spot near the *nahoor* for a prayer time. I prayed: "Lord, speak to me of what's on your heart. Give me your perspective." As I listened to the trickle of water going out of the irrigation pond, a song came to mind: *"As the deer longs for the water so my soul longs after you."* I don't know why I hadn't thought of this one before in captivity. Now the song was new and fresh. I also thought of Christ's promise, *"Blessed are those who hunger and thirst after righteousness, for they shall be filled."* I thought of God's abundant supply of living water.

I wrote a letter then visited with Irshad, the shepherd boy. Back to the house to watch the continuing work on the roof. In the afternoon a messenger arrived, telling of war in Sang-i Masha. This news encouraged Rasooli to head back to the base as soon as possible. We arrived at dark in

156

time for a delicious *lobia* supper. For some reason I slept in the office alone tonight. It was cold, but at least there were no interruptions.

> We are preparing a statement for a radio contact with Joel's captor on November 12. We should not miss this opportunity. It will be difficult to promise anything. The captor was asking for a school named after Joel. We must be polite, but tough. Perhaps we can agree to consider certain actions when Joel is free.
>
> When our messenger asked why he hadn't just asked for help in starting a school instead of taking hostages, he said the captor replied, "I made a mistake. Now my honor is finished in all of Jaghori. All of my family is against me. I can't even go home now. I don't want money. Just give me a school to save my honor."
>
> As he spoke, he was pulling down on his ears as a symbol of repentence for something done wrong.

Friday, November 8

I had now established a walking trail that went from the kitchen a little ways around the side of the mountain through the hillside strewn with huge rocks. The end of my trail was about 125 yards from the kitchen, and the last one third of the trail was out of sight of the base. It was in this part, on a level spot above the trail, that I now did my exercises. And I began running back and forth five to ten times on the part where I couldn't be seen. I missed the freedom to run for longer distances.

After tea and bread with Bostan, I walked along my trail and sang. Then I went to my office. I prayed for financial needs and thought of the words, *"My God shall supply all your needs according to his riches in Christ Jesus."* After prayer time, I enjoyed some dried fruit, compliments of Muallim Hamid.

Mamur Yaqub and his soldiers came after lunch. I called them up to my office and shared my dried fruit with them. After supper I visited some with Mamur. He spoke of recently talking to the Akhund about my freedom. I also spoke today with my friend, the prisoner from Baba, about

157

THE UPPER HAND

my case--and his case, too, as a payment was being demanded for his release! It was a down day, but became better at the end.

Tonight there were lots of soldiers in the room. I slept in a narrower space, and couldn't sleep as well.

Saturday, November 9

I wrote letters in the soldier's room this morning to Mark and my family to send with Muallim Hamid. I felt he would be a reliable courier.

In my prayer time this morning I thought about the future. God gives us a future and a hope. Don't worry about the future. Live each day to its full. Don't loose hope.

I examined my clothes since I had been itching. In fact I had thought that I might be developing some kind of rash on my arms and other places. I found one tick and five lice!

Mamur and his gang left after lunch.

I had a long talk with my fellow prisoner from Baba as we ate almonds together. The money demand for his freedom had gone down to five *lak* (One *lak* is one hundred thousand). But he said he was still unwilling to pay anything.

I had an English class with A. Hamid. I got cold just sitting as the sun was going down. So I walked up and down the mountain. The soldiers had killed a *kauk*, quail, on their return from #2 base, so we had it for dinner. It made a delicious broth. I sat in the kitchen a long time after supper. Tonight I had much more room and slept well.

Sunday, November 10

I got up this morning to a surprise. It was snowing outside! I did my routine relief visit and had only a brief exercise time. After breakfast and some writing, I decided to venture out. I was glad I did. I had a great time of prayer, singing, and going over Philippians 1 and 2. I wish I had a dollar for every lap I made on my trail this morning! As I walked it was sometimes snowing, sleeting, or hailing. I was glad for my good *chadur*, shawl.

The Soldier's Base

I joined the others for a rice lunch in the soldier's room. It was nice and cozy. Someone had recently nailed a sheet of plastic on the outside of the one window into the room. I went to the office to nap there alone. After some time the commander came in and joined me for a snooze. I spent time there horizontally praying over a list of friends. I thought of Sunday worship and rest. I thought of victory in Christ.

After tea and another walk, I had another English lesson with A. Hussain. It was foggy and cloudy all day. What a change from the almost perfectly clear weather we had been having for months.

Atee Zia and two men arrived in the afternoon. There were more soldiers in the room tonight, but I slept well.

Monday, November 11

It was foggy this morning. The fog would clear at times to reveal beautiful, white mountains to the West. The Chilbaghtu and Baba ranges were really pretty with a new white blanket. I thought of "You are beautiful beyond description, too marvelous for words..."

At 11 a.m. or so I went to my office and soaked up the sun that was now radiating from an almost clear sky. I meditated and searched my clothes again for bugs.

It was one such day when I was enjoying the sun that I thought up these words to fit the tune of a familiar chorus (*"Living under the shadow of His wings"*):

Basking in the sunshine of your love,
Gives me such energy;
Strength to run my daily race and sing
Worship, worship to my King.

In my prayers I thought of John 3:16. God loved and gave. If He gave us Christ, won't he freely give us all things? I sang, *"You did not wait for me to draw near to you..."*

The Akhund arrived in the morning. There was a lot of activity, for some reason.

THE UPPER HAND

Today the two prisoners from Baba were moved in with five other prisoners.

For supper I helped Bostan serve the soldiers rice. He had made a little *lobia* for the two of us to enjoy alone!

I went to bed around 9 p.m., but I didn't sleep too well. I had eaten too much *lobia*!

Tuesday, November 12

I picked a new spot for exercising this morning. The snow had melted enough dry ground in this small, flat place surrounded by rocks.

After breakfast I spent some time talking to Nadir, one of the prisoners.

Later in my walking, I came face to face with the Akhund at one point. I told him of the things I needed but that I had not yet received. As usual, he assured me that everything would be taken care of.

In my prayer time I thought through a favorite hymn, *"May the mind of Christ my Savior"* and prayed for the mind of Christ toward my captor. I thought of four things from Philippians 2:

1. Christ's disregard for reputation
2. Christ's servanthood
3. Christ's humiliation
4. Christ's obedience

I prayed especially for the fellowship meeting tonight in Islamabad.

I had just finished praying and taking four lice out of my clothes when Rasooli, Musa, and Muheeb appeared on their way down to Rasooli's house. They invited me to go along. We stopped at a house on the way for tea and dried mulberries. I saw a scorpion on the wall here--the first I remember seeing in Afghanistan.

I was glad for the opportunity for another bath, and a chance to wash my socks and undershirt. My bath house again was the open air next to the irrigation pool!

After a lunch I went with Musa to buy a goat for an offering to be eaten by the garrison. The Akhund was pleased about some progress in the

160

The   Soldier's   Base

current power struggle. Musa and I took the black goat up the mountain and I helped in the butchering. I joked with the men that this was for the release of all prisoners!

Rasooli brought a special supply of mulberries for me. I was touched, and realized again I was not far from God's love and care.

Time passed well as we prepared and cooked the goat. It was cold and a few snowflakes fell. I was amazed how one goat could provide so many meals for our group. Tonight the meal was rice with some meat.

I slept next to Muallim Hamid tonight. He turned over in the night on top of me! I didn't sleep too well under my *chadar*, shawl.

Wednesday, November 13

I wrote my diary in the soldier's room after breakfast. It was cold and foggy. The absence of the sunlight made me depressed. I wrote some letters and had a long talk with my prisoner friend from Baba. I appreciated his educated company. We talked a little about his work for Oxfam and his travels.

A little snow was falling. I walked for some time, then went to my office for prayer. I prayed that we (my family, my co-workers and believing friends) might be useful in service to God--whatever our situations. Snow began falling on my *chadar*. It was a strangely moving time. It was so quiet all around. And under my cover I was warm.

Snow made me feel depressed because I was hoping to be out of Afghanistan before the passes became blocked with high snows. It was hard to think of staying all winter here.

I walked back to the kitchen through the snow.

White beards from Patu had come to negotiate for the prisoners.

I alternated time between walking outside and sitting in the *gulkho*, inside kitchen now being used for warming the soldier's room. I killed four lice in my clothes.

Some of the fog began to lift. I was invited for supper with the five remaining prisoners. It was quite a feast compared to the regular base fare. The stew contained dried meat, a recently-killed quail, turnips, potatoes,

161

THE UPPER HAND

chick peas, and beans. We talked a lot about their situation and accusations against them. Somehow I was more prone to believe their side of the story! I rejoiced tonight that my friend from Baba had been set free, and also three of the others. But I also wished from the bottom of my heart that my turn would come soon! Yes, I was getting used to ups and downs. But the thought of freedom just out of reach still pained my deepest sensitivities.

Tonight I was against the wall again in the soldier's room. This was my favorite place. I slept better. There were more blankets to go around now that most of the prisoners had left.

Thursday, November 14

It's beautifully clear this morning! The snow on the Baba and Chilbaghtu ranges is melting fast. I feel really well today.

I spent some time writing in the soldier's room after breakfast. A new shift of soldiers arrived. One soldier spoke some English and asked me a few questions. I didn't feel comfortable around him.

After I had been walking for a while, Zawar and three others from Chilbaghtu arrived! It was very good to see Zawar. I think he understands me like few others--even if I'm not sure I can trust him completely. He brought my *kaloushes*, felt-lined rubbershoes made in Russia. This is normal winter footwear here. When there's lots of snow, men wear these with thick wool socks. Sometimes they tie *pai bands*, strips of cloth, around their calves for added warmth and protection from the snow. Also there is a special kind of locally made wool pants for the snow and cold weather. They are made from thick, hand-loomed wool cloth. They are narrow at the calves and baggy at the thighs and waist. They look to me like riding pants!

I found out some sad news from Zawar later. The Akhund's new son--born days before I had left Chilbaghtu--had died of a cold that had been going around. So had his daughter, born to the wife that I had come to know well. Reza, though, had almost completely recovered.

In my office this morning I prayed for compassion rather than bitterness. Three lice. I got back a little late for lunch. A soldier had brought me two eggs. And now, since the other food was gone, one of the men fried an egg for me. That was a real treat. A. Hassan, my English student, was on this new shift. He brought walnuts and apricots for me.

In office #2 I took a nap, wrote a letter, and wrote English in a notebook. Rasooli joined me for a brief visit. Bazaz arrived from Khar Kush and brought me a letter from Engineer Salim. It was good to read his kind words, but there was nothing definite to pin hopes on.

After *shorwa* and a little goat meat in the kitchen, I went with a group to Rasooli's house. They played cards until late. I gave an English lesson, listened to the radio, and then had a wonderful sleep.

Friday, November 15

The almond grove is beautiful this morning. I feel really well. I listened to BBC news, then Radio Free Afghanistan--broadcast from the US, I think. Then Germany's Pashtu program.

I enjoyed a brisk walk back up the mountain. I spent time in prayer regarding my situation and valley politics. I had been asking God for my release by today in view of activities back in Islamabad. I had felt led to pray this way. I was disappointed, but I knew God had his hand on me and my situation. What was He trying to teach me? I asked for a fresh revelation of the meaning of Christ coming in the flesh, after reading verses from Hebrews (the ones Doc had written down for me).

I walked up to office #2 to rest. God ministered to me as I began writing to my family things I was learning about God's timing. I titled it, *"In His Time"* (This essay is included in **WRITINGS FROM PATU** at the end of this journal). I could understand better that the wise and logical thing to do was trust in God's better judgment. I compiled all the thoughts and Bible passages I could remember on this subject.

I thought of the six hard-boiled eggs Bostan had just brought me on his return from home leave (and he apologized that he didn't have anything more to bring!). I thought back to this morning when I was heading off for prayer time in my office. I heard a voice behind me calling, "Muallim, Muallim!" It made me mad that the soldiers would bother me. I ignored the call for a while, then looked behind. It was big Latif of Cheshma. He was walking toward me. "I brought something for you, Muallim." He handed

THE UPPER HAND

me a bar of East German soap. "I thought you might need some more soap soon."

I said a heart-felt "Thank you". Yes, God was taking care of me.

Today three groups left for Sang-i Masha to help Commander Wasim infighting with Hizb-i Wahdat and other parties. The war in the valley had increased in intensity.

The supper menu in the kitchen featured *lobia*, beans, added to the intestines and stomach of our goat all on rice.

Saturday, November 16

Today was a mixture of sun and clouds. After breakfast and some walking, I joined Bostan in the kitchen to watch Zawar make bread. It was Zawar who had put the *tanoor*, oven, in at the base. He told stories of making bread when there were a hundred or more soldiers there at the time when all the other parties in the valley were against them and trying to drive them out. He would teach Bostan how to make better bread, he said.

But as Zawar slapped piece after piece against the wall of the *tanoor*, the dough just peeled off and slipped to the bottom of the oven. He had kneaded the dough too thin. And the flour was *kam gam*, not much gluten, compared to the flour he was used to. After this there were no more complaints about Bostan's baking!

In my office I prayed, "Lord, help us in whatever situation to be content in your time. And teach us in the waiting period."

One louse today.

I visited with Barat Ali--a big, likable guy. He was the brother of Mamur Ahmad, the commander who had been killed three months ago. He had brought a big bag of dried apricots, candy, and almonds for me!

Lunch was delicious *lobia*, kidney beans, on broken up bread. I spent sometime visiting with the last prisoners, who were released later in the day. It was good to see them clearing their stuff out of the room below the office and heading down the mountain.

I watched Zawar knead the flour for bread. Then Zawar, Bostan, and I had tea together. We listened to a blind man who had just walked up the mountain. He had come to appeal to the Akhund for help in an interesting

164

situation. He couldn't do other work, so had taken to buying and selling eggs. Boys had made a joke of him in one village and had broken 150 of his eggs. Could the Akhund punish the rascals and guarantee him security?

I filled up some time walking and carrying water from the *karez*.

A report came telling the commander to prepare for a possible attack. There was a flurry of activity as soldiers prepared to take a big gun to the top of the hill overlooking the base, and to the hut on the *jaba*, rock outcropping. There were loads of guns, blankets, and other things that were carried away. The evening and night were full of interruptions. I thank God for good sleep anyway.

> We had a visit today with the director and staff of the Afghan Construction Logistics Unit (ACLU). The director is a leading member of the Hizb-i Islami (HIA). He stated that it's not the policy of the HIA to kidnap foreigners and demand the building of a school. They were aware, he said, of the situation, and were dealing with it. They had sent a team recently to work on this matter.
>
> We asked the director about the relationship of the national office of HIA to the local commander, Akhund Salim. He replied, "He is not a member of our party. But we know him and give him weapons and money."

Sunday, November 17

Spotty sunshine again today. In my time for meditation I thought of God's mercy. He spared Epaphroditus' life so Paul might not have sorrow upon sorrow. I prayed for God's new mercies today, and for the churches I know.

No lice today!

I had lunch with an older man who was a blacksmith by profession. Some time later I traded A. Hassan my Pakistani pen-knife for his fine one made by this gentleman. The handle was made of beautiful, hard *khinjak* wood--the hardwood trees that grow on these rocky mountains. And the blade was fashioned from the hard metal at the tip of *zeek-o yak* shells. A *zeek-o yuk* is a Chinese antiaircraft gun.

165

THE UPPER HAND

The elderly man had brought me a bag of almonds and *khaista*, dried fruit. I secretly gave him a letter to send to Pakistan to mail to my family.

Later, in office #2, I wrote a letter to Engineer Salim for Bazaz to take. The Akhund saw me as I was getting ready to give it to Bazaz. He suspected something. "What are you doing?" he asked in an angry way.

I just told him the truth.

"Why didn't you tell me?" he continued.

I told him I would read the letter to him. When I did, he let me give it to Bazaz.

I spent much time this afternoon singing and praying as I walked back and forth on my course. I prayed for the names on my list from the letters "H" to "L". I took a break for a hard-boiled egg, almonds, and apricots.

I had a relaxed supper with Bostan and Khaliq, the new kitchen helper. We sat around the fire until late. Bostan was happy to have a helper to train. But Khaliq was not keen to be at the base. He always talked about running away. He was only about 16 years old. He came because his father was an invalid, and couldn't perform his tour of duty.

An HIA soldier who is not loyal to Akhund Salim secretly sought out Joel on one of his unaccompanied excursions around the mountain. He said that Joel is not being watched by bodyguards on his morning and afternoon walks around the mountain. The soldier offered Joel the opportunity to walk out to Pakistan with him. Joel refused because of his anticipation that another deal was nearly finalized.

Monday, November 18

As I walked this morning, I sang a song after each verse of Philippians 1. I tried to think of a song that each verse suggested. Now I have finished memorizing Philippians 2.

Now that I'm accumulating more and more dried fruit and other things, I made an arrangement with Bostan to keep my things in the arms and ammunition warehouse. This is where Bostan stored food supplies so they wouldn't disappear. He kept a key to the door.

The Soldier's Base

In my office I thought of Paul's use of "joy" and "rejoice" in Philippians 1.

    (1) Joy in prayer for the church
    (2) Joy at his freedom and reunion
    (3) Joy that Christ is preached

I prayed with joy for friends that their love might abound.

I took off my long underwear and sweater in the sun. The sun shone brightly this morning, but clouds rolled in during the afternoon. The little shepherd boy came around and we had a nice visit. I shared my dried fruit with him. I wrote some more on the "*In His Time*" essay.

As I walked back towards the kitchen, I saw two men coming down from the saddle behind the base. I didn't pay much attention to them. We reached the kitchen about the same time. The men had been sent by Engineer Kabir. They brought me eight books, 22 letters, a *chadar*, shawl, and a small sewing kit!!

I quickly read the letters from Mark and Engineer Kabir and wrote brief responses for the messengers to take back. The messengers talked to the Akhund then left in a hurry to go to Nawa. As they left, they told me that they were hurrying so that my problem could be solved soon. My hopes shot up as I thought, "Any day now...!"

I had my regular English lesson with Hassan, then rested and read all the letters. How encouraged I was--though I didn't show it by jumping up and down! Several things from the letters really stuck in my mind.

Auntie Phyllis wrote about my "new assignment".

Pastor Ed wrote, "...I believe there are times when we suffer with Jesus for the same reason that he suffered--that others might be redeemed."

Mark wrote, "You can be sure that someone is probably praying for you every hour of the day."

Seven letters were from my family. Ten were from colleagues in Islamabad. Then there was one from Peshawar, one from the US, and one from Lahore. Engineer Kabir and Engineer Salim also wrote.

The books were: ***The Bible*** {Good News)
                     The Pursuit of God (Tozer) two copies!
                     Hind's Feet on High Places (Hurnard)

THE UPPER HAND

Daily with the King (Evans)
The Lift of Love (Baker)
The Grace Awakening (Swindoll)
A Heart for God (Ferguson)

The day before, I had thought that I would need to borrow a needle and thread to sew on a button that had come off my suit. Also I had lost another button. And several places on my suit needed to be mended. Even this morning I had thought that I would borrow a needle and work on mending in the afternoon. In the sewing kit I received there were two buttons, the right color of thread, and a needle. God had provided these things in an unexpected way. I shared this with Bostan.

As the sun began to go down, I was given permission to walk up and visit the guys at the new post on top of the mountain. After the rice supper, I combined my trip to the spring to brush my teeth with several rounds on my walking route. I had a lot to think about and thank God for.

The soldier's room was full. Now, with my books, I could read by lamp light as the soldiers finished their usual hour-long discussion on how to divide the guard duties for that night. The men never objected to me reading as late as I wanted to. After all, when they went to sleep, they turned the lamp down slightly and hung it on a nail in front of the closed window.

Tuesday, November 19

Today also began sunny, and later turned cloudy. I sang songs this morning in connection with Philippians 2. I talked to Zawar in the kitchen about a day of reckoning and the shortness of life.

In my office my theme was 'no separation'--"*I am His, and He is mine.*" Before I had finished my prayers, Atee M. Ali showed up. I invited him to share in my supply of walnuts and dried fruit. I think he was bored, so he was glad for the diversion. I have always been close to him and his family. They are kind people.

After a while, Zawar showed up! I think he was bored, too.

The number of soldiers at the base is really down now because so many have left. It makes for a more relaxed atmosphere.

The Soldier's Base

After lunch I was sitting in the kitchen and reading **Hind's Feet in High Places.** The Akhund came up and asked:

"What are you reading?"

"It's a book about knowing God," I replied.

"Why don't you read the Quran? That's the real way to know God."

The immediate response that jumped in my mind was a bitter and sarcastic one, such as I had regretfully given before: "If you and your actions represent Islam, I want nothing of it!" But God's spirit didn't let me say this. Instead I said, "I've read the Quran and, yes, there are some good things there."

This exchange was a significant turning point for me. God had actually helped in my attitude, and words, as I had been praying! I still struggled with these things later. But now I had an inner peace and joy. Thank you, Lord, for helping me.

I sewed two buttons on my suit and fixed two sleeves with my new sewing kit. I also extracted a splinter.

There were few disturbances tonight, for a change.

Wednesday, November 20

It was sunny and cold. I read today's reading from **Daily with the King**--then Psalms 139, 140, and 91. A verse from Psalm 140 became a frequent part of my prayers--v. 1 and 8:

"Save me, Lord, from evil men..."

"Lord, don't give the wicked what they want:
don't let their plots succeed."

I rejoiced in the thought that wherever I go, God is there to lead and help me. Sometimes I was overwhelmed as God showed me His care for me--even in Chilbaghtu or Patu. David's words in this psalm are so encouraging:

"Where could I go to escape from you? ...
If I flew away beyond the east
or lived in the farthest place in the west,
you would be there to lead me,
you would be there to help me."

THE UPPER HAND

I spent time in prayer, then finished writing *"In His Time"* in my office.

Only two lice today.

It was cold in office #2 after lunch, so I took a short nap in the soldier's room. I asked Bostan to heat up a shortening tin full of water in the *tanoor*, and then took a bath in a small "bathroom" next to where the base donkey lived.

After the shower, Zawar called me. "What for?" I wondered. I went to the office to find Baqir there! He was one of the two Hazara boys I had taught English to in Islamabad on a weekly basis! I had learned of his presence in the area from Ali Baba, one of Mamur Yaqub's soldiers. But I never expected to see him.

We exchanged a few greetings. The Akhund was obviously suspicious. "Why have you come?" he wanted to know. Baqir explained how I had been his teacher, and this seemed to satisfy the Akhund somewhat. He let us go to talk for a while in the soldier's room. But Baqir wasn't even allowed to stay the night. After an early supper he was led down to Rasooli's house to spend the night.

Baqir told me an interesting account. He had been married five days ago. When he and his family found out from Ali Baba that I was the foreigner in Akhund Salim's hands, they were very sad. He wanted to come and see me. His mother told him that he must. So he set off walking at 4 a.m. He had never been in Patu before. He kept asking people how to get to the base. In one way his trip was at great personal risk. He had no idea how the Akhund would receive him, or where he would stay. It would not have been unusual for him to be taken captive.

Anyway, after one detour that took a lot of time, he finally made it to the base. It was about 4 p.m. He hadn't eaten anything on the way. He is very slight and short. He brought me gifts--nail clippers, a notebook, and a pen. Each was something that I needed! Again, I was touched deeply with God's care for me through people's kindness.

Baqir told me that his companion in Rawalpindi, Anwar, was now studying in Delhi. He also told how the family home in Kabul was hit by a rocket and his sister had been injured. Another amazing story was how

170

The Soldier's Base

Baqir had received a letter from Frederick--a Swiss teacher who had been living with me in Islamabad and had taken the boys' English classes for a time. Frederick had not known their proper address. Nor had he known that mail is not delivered outside the major cities. But he had sent a letter from Switzerland addressed to Baqir in his village. Somehow it got to him!

Baqir and Anwar had happily accepted a gift of a New Testament when they told us in Islamabad that they were going back to Afghanistan. Baqir had also shared with me that his father in Afghanistan had a New Testament that he read sometimes.

I walked some in the moonlight, then read some of *The Pursuit of God* before going to bed.

Thursday, November 21

Hassan came down from his post at *Zeek-o yuk* (so named because of the antiaircraft gun positioned there) and told me that he had been granted permission to take me home with him! After walking, singing, and praying, I sat down in the sun and went carefully through my clothes. I killed 39 lice. I realized that in the past I had not been looking for small lice. One flea escaped me!

I packed my bundle, and we took off after 9 a.m. It was a beautiful walk. We headed due south, a different direction from my former excursion with Muallim Hamid.

We arrived at Hassan's home by noon. After a *qurti* lunch I had time to rest alone. I again took off my clothes, and found 32 more lice, and one bed bug. I had a nap and then prayed for an inner joyous, victorious new life. I clung on to a verse from Psalm 141:

"Lord, place a guard at my mouth."

Hassan took me for a walk around the family farm. There were five **karezes**, horizontal wells, and five **nahoors**, irrigation ponds. Each one of these enabled a little more land to be cultivated. Hassan explained that the old family home had been in a huge walled fortress. At the time of his grandfather, people had lived in fear of invasions by the Pashtoons, so they had built strong defences. Now it was old and tenant farmers lived there.

THE UPPER HAND

Plus there had been land disputes. His father was an only son who didn't have brothers to support him.

Hassan showed me almond groves, *dolna* trees (these trees have a kind of small, red fruit), wheat fields, and carrot fields. On the rafters of the house, meat was hanging to dry for the winter.

We came back from our walk in time for dusk prayers. There was another guest for the night--Qariadar Salim, a man I came to respect and like. We had a long and interesting discussion. I pumped him with questions of history and local politics. He was interested to know what Christians believed and how we viewed Christ. As I explained these things I said, "How I wish you had a Bible you could read for yourself!"

"Is there such a thing in Farsi?" he asked.

I promised to send him one from Pakistan when I was freed.

A supper of delicious broth and meat came late. We listened to the BBC Pashtu broadcast until everyone became sleepy. I had a great sleep.

The Qariadar's Story

Here's a summary of what Qariadar Salim told me of the history of groups in the area. Iran took turns strengthening different Hazara groups. A relative of a man high up in the Iranian government became in charge of the office for help to Afghans. Later he was arrested and executed for being connected with the anti-government group, Mujahideen-i Khalq. He was probably a scapegoat.

Subsequent internal fighting among factions brought about the deaths of about 12,000 people in the Hazarajat. One party was driven out for being "American". Then another party was strengthened by outside sources to fight against a party labeled "Communists". Almost 2000 locals were killed and a unity party was formed.

Later the Hizb-i Wahdat party was formed. A powerful party in Jaghori didn't accept this new group. Disagreements resulted in an open attack in the summer of 1991. The opposition party captured the school and clinic in Sang-i Masha because they were supported by Wahdat.

The Soldier's Base

Qariadar Salim went on to explain how the HIA party rose to power in the area. The recognized leader of this party was now living in Quetta, as there had been a fallout between him and Akhund Salim. Then the Qariadar continued with some of the immediate causes for the two commanders to take Dr. Bill and me hostage. What a woeful story of ambition, intrigue, and bloodshed.

Friday, November 22

I exercised in a dry stream bed this morning.

Ibrahim, Hassan's brother-in-law was visiting. I wrote some letters. Then I walked out to a sunny spot in the rocks for a rest and quiet time. I read about 'indispensability' from *Daily with the King*. I prayed for the advance of God's kingdom, and that friends will follow on to know the Lord. Psalms 142 and 143 were an encouragement. The following verse became a frequent prayer and promise to God:

"Set me free from my distress;
then in the assembly of your people I will praise you
because of your goodness to me."

Hassan gave me a suit of his own so his mother could wash my clothes. I killed some more lice as I took my clothes off. The count was now up to 103.

I worked with Hassan on his English. I filled quite a few pages in a notebook of English words and sentences for him to learn. Then we both went outside to watch sheep. Hussain, one of Hassan's brothers, took me on a walk up a hill to the east, and we arrived home after dusk.

I retired after nine for a wonderful sleep.

Saturday, November 23

There were nine of us for a breakfast of fresh bread, dried mulberries, and tea. I wrote a letter to my family for Ibrahim to mail from Quetta. Outside I had a time of meditation on "*Crisis Discipleship*" from *Daily*

THE UPPER HAND

with the King. Crises are used to declare, strengthen, and purify a disciple. The wilderness experience was to prove what was in Israel's heart. I rejoiced that God is my wise, loving Father and I'm his chosen son.

Hassan's father asked if I would like to go along to get some firewood from the mountain. I was delighted. The family had a wood stove which they set in the middle of the guest room. Hard wood was best for this stove, and we could get this from Mt. Geru, not too far away.

We set off energetically. There was the father, his three sons, two donkeys, and me. It took us about one and a half hours to get to where we could start collecting wood. This was the side of Mt. Geru looking toward the lands occupied by *Augho*, Pashtuns. Twice we saw *kauk*, quail, fly away, but Hassan was not within shooting range with his gun. We gathered dry fuel and worked hard at a big, dead *khinjak* tree to saw and split it. The stump was hard to get out from among the rocks. I was amazed at Hassan's father's dexterity and stamina with the axe. We had several snacks of mulberries, bread, and walnuts. Finally we managed to get all the wood down to the donkeys below, load them up, and head for home. We arrived home around 4 p.m.

It was so good to get out! I told Hassan that today I didn't feel like a prisoner. I had enjoyed the huge rocks and the beautiful views. The father told how there used to be bears living in the rocks. As we returned home we passed bunkers and fortifications used in the war with the Pashtuns last year.

After some refreshing tea I went out to walk and pray alone. I thought of how God is His people's portion. Another delicious *shorwa* supper, then we listened to the radio until it seemed late. I went to sleep full of thanks.

Sunday, November 24

Hassan's father and the two younger boys left for another load of firewood. Hassan arranged hot water for baths in a place in the barn. I put my own clothes back on, and discovered that Hassan's mother had mended a place on my shirt and put a new rope belt in my pants. Thank you, Lord! Then I went out to a sunny place in the rocks for meditation. I thought of

174

The Soldier's Base

not knowing Christ through the flesh, but through the Holy Spirit in a way that transforms. I read some more psalms.

After lunch Hassan and I said good bye to Hassan's mother and headed for the base. We had only walked about half an hour when we met Hafiz (Atee Nadir's boy) who was also going to the base. Hassan put me in his charge for the return trip. Hassan didn't want to return right then because his father was busy making an arrangement for his marriage.

We had a good walk, arriving around 5 p.m. I visited some with the Chilbaghtu crowd in the office, and then had supper with Bostan. I read the second chapter of *The Pursuit of God* tonight before going to bed.

This is a wrap up of trying to see the trees in the midst of a dense forest of details. There are at least five different hostage negotiation processes under way that we know of.

1. The first suggestion is the most recent and the least credible. The carrier of Joel's most recent letter has stated, "Give me twenty thousand dollars (in Afghan currency) and I will bring Joel out immediately."
2. A letter arrived yesterday from a friend in Jaghori. He said he spoke with the HIA negotiators there the previous day. Their report: "Akhund Salim said Global Partners must promise to continue aid to Jaghori. That was his only condition for Joel to be freed."
3. The captor and Joel sent letters five weeks ago. The captor said Joel would be freed if GP promised to build a school.
4. The Hazara HIA commander in Quetta told his party boss that he would bring Joel out if he was given money, weapons, and the promise of regular support.
5. A team of HIA from Peshawar are in Jaghori at present negotiating with Akhund Salim for Joel.

Monday, November 25

My stomach was upset last night, but it didn't keep me from walking and singing after breakfast. I read from the devotional book how, by the

THE UPPER HAND

Holy Spirit, Christ's beauty gradually becomes ours and Christ rejoices in us. Then I read Psalms 146-150.

"Happy is the man who has the God of Jacob to help him."
"The Lord sets prisoners free."

I prayed for severance from things and for God's absolute lordship. I wrote some letters and picked out 15 lice from my clothes.

I spent some time in the afternoon walking and praying for my TEAM missionary family in Pakistan. God gave me great joy in being able to be involved through prayer.

Commander Ghulam Hussain of Baba had returned to the base and I gave him his notebook in which I had worked hard to write some English words and sentences. He was happy. I think he and others enjoyed the pictures that I drew for each vocabulary item--especially pictures of tools!

Muallim Hamid had returned. He brought an Iranian zip travel bag for me! I was thrilled. It was just what I needed. I didn't even mind that it had **"Death to America"** written on the side in small letters! Muallim Hamid also gave me an embroidered handkerchief that I used from then on to dry my face and blow my nose.

Lunch and supper were rice. I enjoyed my dessert of "cake". This is what I called the bread that Bostan made when I had it after a meal!

Tuesday, November 26

I stayed in the kitchen after breakfast to read. This morning's lesson was about claiming what we have in Christ. I thought of the song, *"Day by day"* and how I shouldn't worry for tomorrow.

"Day by day and with each passing moment,
Strength I find to meet my trials here.
Resting in my Father's wise bestowment,
I've no cause for worry or for fear..."

This morning I started a reading schedule that would take me up to my time of release. I read five psalms and one chapter of Proverbs each day.

176

The Soldier's Base

I walked to my office. It was cloudy, but it became warm, thank God. I prayed for myself and others that we would realize and claim the authority and ability that we have in Christ. I thought of a regular meeting in Islamabad tonight. Another reading schedule I started was one chapter of *The Pursuit of God* every morning after prayer. This book was deeply challenging and appropriate. Today, for instance, I read about "Apprehending God". We must know God personally with the senses of the soul. He is real.

Four lice today.

Back to the kitchen just in time for lunch.

I walked up to *Zeek-o yuk* and had a short visit with Arif and Muallim Hamid. I thanked them again for the bag. Arif talked to me about Mamur Ahmad and warned me of spies trying to help me to escape. Trusting them might worsen my chances for release, he said.

Tonight I enjoyed two chapters of *Hind's Feet on High Places*. Many themes and lessons from this book became a real help. Tonight I read about the path that looks impossible, but is not so difficult after all.

We had a radio contact at 11 a.m. with Afghanistan. Joel has been moved back to Chilbaghtu. He reportedly is to be freed in three or four days. Our UN contact is to remain in the area for three more days. He is willing to provide transport and logistical support for Joel. This UN contact is in the home of a prominent Hazara citizen where Mark had also stayed. This is a very encouraging development.

Engineer Kabir arrived in Quetta last night. He reports that Akhund Saleem does not want Joel to be handed over to Pashtun HIA people from Peshawar, because he wants Hazara people to get the glory for bringing Joel back.

All inside sources confirm that an agreement has been reached to free Joel.

Wednesday, November 27

After breakfast I began my "quiet time" in the kitchen--my new routine due to the colder weather. As I walked and sang, I prayed strongly for

deliverance from enemies. In my office I prayed about claiming new
ground--victory by God's provided power.

Nine lice.

As I started to write, two boys came to call me for lunch. I was pleased
that Rizayee came to my office later to visit. He shared encouraging words
about representatives who had come from Peshawar to "solve my problem".
On a later visit up to *Zeek-o yuk,* Muallim Hamid also told me of
representatives in the area, and of the end of fighting in areas of Jaghori.

At midnight there was some shooting and all of the soldiers ran out.
Apparently it was just a false alarm.

Thursday, November 28

My Bible reading this morning contained much comfort for those who
trust God. Men make fun of confidence in God, but God is over all. He
loves those who do good. He's the humble man's protection. I prayed
especially for love and the filling of the Holy Spirit for this day. In my
office I wrote thoughts down on Philippians1:6 about God's continuing
work in us.

I found many baby lice and two big ones.

After lunch I was at my office #2 as usual. (This was my office in
front of a big rock just above the soldier's room and kitchen.) The Akhund
called me to go along to a feast at Akram's in Kunagh. I scrambled to get
all my possessions. I had been primed to think that any call to go anywhere
might mean that I was being taken to freedom. So I wanted to take
everything. But when the Akhund saw me with all my stuff, he said, "What
do you need that for? You can leave that here."

I said that I wanted to take it since I never knew what I would be ordered
to do next.

After more assurances, however, I had Bostan lock my things up in the
ammunition store, and set off much lighter.

It was a long, enjoyable walk. As we went along I prayed for love for
my enemies, and I had my notebook in my hand and prayed through my
TEAM family.

The Soldier's Base

We arrived at Akram's at dusk. It was cold. It felt good to go into the room heated cozily warm by a tin wood stove in the corner. This stove, like many I saw, had a built-in water compartment on top of the stove to provide boiling water for tea and other purposes. Twenty-five or 30 men were sitting in the room. Since I knew most of them, I felt quite comfortable. Some of the Patu elders were there.

Delicious rice was served with *qorma*, stew, then apples, yogurt, and tea. We listened to BBC--an interview with Engineer Gulbuddin Hikmatyar--and then there was a lot of talk. I was really pleased when bed time came around, that I could go to Muallim Hamid's house to sleep. There were six of us in his small guestroom, but we enjoyed each other's company.

Friday, November 29

I woke to a half inch of fresh snow outside! It was still coming down. I managed to do some exercises, then we all went back to Akram's (Agha Nuri's) for breakfast. We had *chob josh,* fried and rolled bread, with regular bread, milk tea, and regular tea.

After breakfast the Akhund made a short speech to welcome Akram and his family into the Hizb-i Islami and express his hope for unity in the future.

Another topic for great discussion was the strength of the Hazaras. The Hazaras feel that, from the earliest history of Afghanistan, they have been denied their just rights and unfairly exploited. They feel they account for at least five million of Afghanistan's approximately 18 million population. "This makes them," one man told me, "the largest single people group in Afghanistan. Yet they have been repressed by the ruling Pashtuns -- and also other powerful groups like the Tajiks and Uzbeks."

A group of us headed back to the base while the Akhund and some others left for Nawa. I hoped their excursion had something to do with my release. The Kunagh valley was beautiful in a coat of new snow! I enjoyed the walk back.

As we walked, Muawin was much friendlier. He assured me that my problem would be solved, but wouldn't give me any details. We stopped for

THE UPPER HAND

tea and mulberries at Musa's. I was fascinated when he brought out an old British muzzle loader--along with the box of accessories for making bullets, etc. I could read some of the writing on the gun, but not the year. I was interested as they told about how these guns are still used. A kalashnikov, they said, cannot stop a tank. But the heavy lead slugs from this gun would mess up the tread of the tanks and cause them to stop! They had had experience when a Russian force of hundreds of tanks entered the Jaghori valley to try to subdue the area in the early years of the revolution.

As lunch didn't appear for some time, I grabbed the opportunity for rest and prayer. We kept waiting for the commander even after our *qurti* lunch, but he never showed. In the following minutes of waiting Musa's 15-year-old brother did something for me that was to be a deep and lasting lesson to me of God's love and care that reaches us everywhere.

I saw a pair of pliers and was eager for the chance to try to fix the zipper on my sweater with more sophisticated tools than stones and my knife! The connector hadn't been connecting the two sides of the zipper no matter how I tried to squeeze or re-shape it. Even now my efforts with the pliers proved futile.

Ali Reza said, "Let me try."

"Not much harm could be done," I thought, so I let him at it. In just a few seconds he had succeeded in breaking the connector. I felt like this was another blow to my spirits.

"Just a minute," he said and disappeared in another room. Soon he brought out a new metal connector that turned out to be exactly the right size! I couldn't believe it. I told him that I deeply appreciated this and considered it a miracle of God's love. God even cared about my zipper. I was to use that sweater for another month and five days.

I had another opportunity to send a note with a man leaving for Pakistan. This is what I wrote:

> Dear family,
> I'm returning from an overnight feast with my captor and a group of soldiers. Delicious food and a good night's sleep. Pray for me that I will really love my captor. And that I would have compassion for

> people instead of bitterness.
> (Then I related the story of Ali Reza fixing my zipper.) I told everyone this is just one more example of how God cares for us.
> My captor has gone to a town today to talk about my release. Some assure me that this time it will really work. *"My soul, wait upon the Lord only."*
> I love you all. Sent another note a couple of days ago. Nothing special to report--oh! Woke up this morning with a beautiful half-inch coating of snow! Gone by now.
>
> In His hands,
> Joel

We had another tea stop at a home along the way. Then, as we walked, Muawin asked some questions about the teachings of Jesus.

We arrived at the base around 4:30 p.m. A cold wind was blowing. I talked about Jesus with Musa and the guys. He told about movies he'd seen in Iran.

After a rice and *lobia* supper I read some from **Hind's Feet** and then wrote English for friends. Ali Reza had given me a notebook to fill up for him.

It was a cold night tonight.

Saturday, November 30

It was cold as I exercised this morning, but the skies were completely clear. I had breakfast in the *gulkho*, inside kitchen, and then read **Daily with the King** which talked about Jesus our kinsman redeemer. The words struck home as I read about being concerned for God's name rather than my own.

Then I wrote down Psalms 16:5 & 6

> *"You, LORD, are all I have*
> *And you give me all I need*

THE UPPER HAND

My future is in your hands
How wonderful are your gifts to me
How good they are."

I thought about these verses in my office as I prayed. When we have God, we have everything.

Lunch was **kauk**, quail, broth and bread. The afternoon passed with a nap, letters, three trips for water, and English writing. I was busy writing sentences and words for Ali Reza, Muawin, Juma, and Khan M. As others saw what I was doing, they wanted the material to learn for themselves. I said I would write for anyone on condition that they brought me paper or a notebook.

Before sleeping I read in **Hind's Feet** about the beautiful alpine meadows. I slept well, thanks to an extra blanket from Bostan. I thought long in my bed about the blessings I have here.

Sunday, December 1

It's a little warmer today.

I read Psalms 16-25, and jotted down parts of six verses. I got in the habit of going over the verses I wrote down as I walked back and forth after breakfast and reading time. In my office today I prayed that we might constantly gaze on the Lord. It was yesterday that I read Tozer's definition of faith as "the gaze of the soul".

I found many baby lice in my clothes, and didn't bother to count them!

When I went back to the kitchen for lunch, I noticed that some of the soldiers had returned.

My afternoon office was really cold, so I went into the soldier's room to do more English writing.

Supper was followed with story after story of war and fighting. I was tired of all the talk. Latif was going to Pakistan and had agreed to take a letter for me. So I wrote one. This letter never made it.

I was feeling down and alone. I spent a little time outside, and then slept late because of all the talk.

The Soldier's Base

Monday, December 2

As usual, I joined Bostan for breakfast in the *gulkho*, inside kitchen. From now on the outer kitchen was only used for baking bread in the *tanoor*, oven. We talked some about the Afghan wars before he went to knead the dough for bread, and I began my reading routine.

Many verses from Psalms 26 to 30 encouraged me.
"I avoid the wicked, hypocrites, and worthless people."
"One thing I have desired of the Lord..."
"I know that I will live to see the Lord's goodness in this present life."
"Tears may flow in the night, but joy comes in the morning."
"You have turned my mourning into dancing..."

I wrote in my new notebook about the difficulties of my present ordeal. Lovely, warm sunshine welcomed me in my office. I prayed that nights of weeping may soon end in mornings of joy.

Nine baby lice and one big one.

Read Tozer's *"Meekness and Rest"* as I worked on a suntan! Christ offers relief from the burdens of pride and pretense.

After lunch the *Zeek-o yuk* crowd moved back down to the base. I was busily writing in my office when some new faces appeared coming down from the saddle. Ayub and Commander Daud from Qarabagh came straight to me. They had come "for me", they said.

"Do you need any money?" Ayub said.

"No." I replied.

"Take some anyway," he replied, and gave me a wad of almost 15,000 Afghanis. I took it, but later on began thinking of possible obligations and difficulties. I returned the money. They told me that the Akhund would definitely release me, but wanted money. They said they'd take my letters, so I wrote to my family and Mark for them to take and mail. Neither of these letters made it.

183

THE UPPER HAND

I stayed up pretty late writing and reading after the soldiers had gone to bed. Though encouraged by the visit of the two new men, I have learned by now not to get my hopes up too much on individual reports.

The market rumor is that Joel should be free in three or four days.

A letter arrived from Joel after floating around Quetta for several days. Joel at that time was still very much unaware of the fact that our messenger had left Jaghori with his letters for Pakistan a month ago. It's clear that Joel is more than ready to come home.

Tuesday, December 3

I had breakfast in the soldier's room since Bostan was at home on break. Then I went to the inside kitchen for some warmth and privacy to read and make notes.

My meditations were interrupted by Ayub, who had come to talk business. We went outside on the hillside alone. Ayub explained that the Akhund just wanted money. Ayub wanted me to encourage my organization just to pay the money, and get the thing over with. I didn't agree. Ayub then explained the pressures on him. Aid was being cut to different areas of Afghanistan because I, a foreign worker, was being held hostage. He desperately wanted this aid in his region. He wanted me to write a letter for him to take stating that aid should continue to him because he was not in favor of my being held. I didn't agree to this, either.

Finally our talk ended and I went back to studying. Ayub and Commander Daud left soon after. I prayed for power to preach Christ boldly with love, and to demonstrate spiritual life. I felt encouraged that, if necessary, God would give me strength and I could stay here longer.

On return from my office, I was surprised with the presence of four new people. They were Latif, the brother of Najaf, and three boys from Pedgah. They had brought stuff for me! It was a three or four hour walk from their home to the base. A new black suit, a larger size of *kaloushes* (Russian felt-lined rubber shoes), a bottle of vitamins and pills for colds, bug powder (upon request!), pens, pads, envelopes, a glue stick, two books, tooth paste, tooth brush, soap, two small boxes of laundry detergent, a *Time* magazine, socks, and a cooked chicken! I was overwhelmed and deeply thankful.

I quickly surveyed the stuff Latif had brought, and then wrote quick letters to Mark and my family for him to take and send. I also sent some of the letters I had written before to friends in Pakistan. These letters reached Pakistan.

The messengers shared a quick lunch with us, then left. Since the Akhund was not at the base, Latif left a private note with me to deliver to him regarding some personal matter in which he wanted the Akhund's help.

I received letters from: Ed, Mark, Hillary, Juan, Rose, Donna, Olga and Dawn, Tim, Karli, Paul, and Julia, Mom and Dad, and the engineers. How encouraging to be reminded that people were praying for me! My brother Tim wrote, "Praying for you as the weather gets cooler...I pray for you when drinking a cup of coffee, taking hot showers, or things like that, knowing that God will provide what you need."

After writing some I walked until dark. The soldiers and I enjoyed a chicken dinner. Quite a change! After eating, the Mullah prayed for my release and reunion with my family. We had a good talk.

I started reading my new book, *The Last Raven*, a thriller about a British agent wandering around Central Asia, then back in California. I enjoyed reading this in the evenings.

Wednesday, December 4

Snow began falling as I finished my exercises. It was cloudy all day.

After breakfast in the soldier's room I went into the inner kitchen to study. I read the reading from *Daily with the King*, then Psalms 36-40 and Proverbs 8. The verses that stuck with me were Ps. 37:7 and 8. They spoke to me about my attitude at a time when I really needed it:

"Be patient and wait for the Lord to act..."

"Don't give in to worry or anger..."

In my office I prayed that God would deliver in many ways, and that we would testify in the assembly of the righteous and praise God.

On return to the kitchen for lunch I was pleased to see that Bostan was back. He had brought four eggs for me!

THE UPPER HAND

Tonight was unusual in that there were only five of us at the base! A shift of soldiers had left, and the others hadn't all come yet. No guard was posted. Only three of us were in the soldier's room! I listened to BBC news on a small radio. Then finished *Hind's Feet* tonight. It was very dark.

Thursday, December 5

After exercises today, I jogged back and forth along a part of my walking trail that was out of sight of the base. Though only a short distance, it felt good. I continued jogging most days when there wasn't snow.

After reading, I headed for my office and prayed for being patient with God and not giving in to worry or anger.

Five lice.

I decided to take notes on Tozer's *The Pursuit of God*. This helped me to imbed these truths, so well-expressed, into my mind.

There were a few extra people for lunch. We had *lobia* in sauce with bread. I carried a total of nine buckets of water from the spring, then I took a bath and put on my new, clean clothes. They even fit!

When more water had heated, I washed my clothes and hung them on the firewood behind the kitchen.

There were seven of us for supper tonight. Rasooli and Atee Nazir joined us. We discussed customs and religion. I read quite a lot before retiring.

Another messenger arrived in Quetta today. He said the HIA delegation went back to Peshawar with Akhund Salim's demands.

A phone call came from Quetta. A friend read the text of a letter from Engineer Kabir. The engineer wrote that many people in the area were saying that Joel had left Jaghori and was on his way to Pakistan.

The Soldier's Base

Friday, December 6

It was cloudy, but warmer this morning. It feels like rain.

The reading this morning from *Daily with the King* was meaningful. W.Glyn Evans wrote, "PEACE is the possession and realization of adequate resources." Christ has provided completely adequate resources. The work of the Holy Spirit is to make me realize them. The Holy Spirit is frustrated and grieved when I don't act on what Christ has done. There are two ways to not have peace: not knowing and not availing. PEACE comes by saturation in the Word. As we meditate on Christ's work, our faith is stimulated.

I went on to another reading. "Frustration is the result of unbelief and rebellion. Nothing in heaven or earth can stop or delay the blessing that God has reserved for me today!" If something is delayed, it isn't God's will at the moment. Why fret? Accept God's portion with joy!

I walked for a long time and prayed. I didn't go to my usual office because the Commander was there with his walkie talkie. Instead, I went to my exercise spot.

Three soldiers came at noon from points west. Rasooli left for Nawa. There was no one in the office, so I took my bag with me and went there for a nap. I wrote a few letters, then went out to carry water and to walk. I prayed through my letter list.

There were eight of us for supper tonight. Outside there was lightning in the west.

Saturday, December 7

I walked, sang, and prayed fervently over Psalms 46-55 this morning after breakfast.

"Save me. Set me free by your might."

"Leave your troubles with the Lord and He will defend you. He never lets honest men be defeated."

When I returned to the kitchen, the Akhund and Commander Khudadad had just arrived. The Akhund told me that he had just been to Moqor in

THE UPPER HAND

connection with my "problem". He said I would go home "very soon." He leaves for Baba after lunch.

I headed off towards my office, but was called to return. I prayed in my exercise spot for spiritual sensitivity and saturation in the Word.

Two lice.

I read the *Time* magazine after lunch, then went to rest and write in the sun. I was encouraged by the Akhund's words to me this morning.

I ate supper with Bostan in the kitchen, even though there were few men. Bostan said that Bayu hadn't wanted to eat with a foreigner.

I sent a message to Ed Rasmussen to ask him to consider helping us for the next few weeks. It has not been felt wise to ever have only one person bearing the responsibility for communicating, negotiating, and maintaining contact with scores of sources with widely varying sympathies to the hostage. In the past few weeks, there has not been a day in which no information has been received from at least one source. Frequently conflicting or mutually contradictory information is received the same day or concerning the same event. Letters two weeks old sometimes contain more accurate information than radio contacts purporting to have information only several hours old. Some letters by the hostages appear to have been written from the perspective of the captor.

The most frequent instances of contradictory information concern the demands, requests or conditions of the captor. Within the last week we have been told:

The captor wants no ransom.
The captor wants 250,000 Pakistani rupees
The captor will accept 125,000 rupees
The captor will let him go free for money and weapons
The captor will let him go with no conditions to a UN official
The captor has already released Joel to H... party
The captor has already released Joel to X... party
Joel is on his way to Peshawar right now
The captor will only release Joel to Mr. X...
The captor will only release Joel to Mr. Y...

The Soldier's Base

Within the last few days different people have told us that they are certain that Joel is being held in three different locations.

Deliberate disinformation is being disseminated concerning the entire situation. Making contingency plans for Joel's return based on constantly changing scenarios, none of which have yet proved accurate, generates great strain. Such stress leads to emotional highs and lows for everyone involved.

Our suggested role for Ed is to provide consultation, advice, interpretation, and back up support. He could both serve as the communication channel to the DeHart family, and monitor the stress level and strain that this crisis is producing in the Morris family. He could also provide pastoral support.

If Joel returns to Pakistan during this period, Ed could help with the hundreds of actions that will be necessary. Our hope is that Joel will return shortly eliminating the need for this assistance.

Sunday, December 8

In the kitchen, after tea and bread, I worked on my *Hazaragi* dictionary. Then I did my regular readings. I like the verse in Proverbs 10:24 *"The righteous get what they want, but the wicked get what they fear most."*

In my office I prayed that we wouldn't fear man for *"What can man do to me?"*, but walk in the righteous path.

Then I continued in Chuck Swindoll's *The Grace Awakening,* which I had begun a few days ago. This book was a great stimulation to thought and blessing.

In the afternoon I wrote notes on books and letters. Supper was *tafa,* broth made from onions or whatever else was available. I studied some English with Abdul Hassan before going for my walk outside, and then I went to bed.

THE UPPER HAND

Monday, December 9

Hassan joined Bostan and I for breakfast. Then we spent some time on English.

Psalms 61-65 contained several verses to which I had learned tunes.

"My soul, wait upon the Lord..."

"Hear my cry, O God..."

"Because Thy steadfast love..."

I walked, sang, prayed, and then went to my office. I thought of being an olive tree in God's house. What a satisfaction and sense of God's care!

As I walked and sang after lunch, I saw Mulla Ali Reza. I had sensed that he was more on my side, so I asked him about my situation. He said, *"Imkan dara,"* meaning "It's possible". Even this much of a positive response was encouraging.

Went to bed at 10 p.m. after reading and writing English lessons.

"Haji", a wealthy and elderly Hazara businessman agreed to help in the situation. He said, "Akhund Salim has told me that he will release Joel to no one else but me. I am the only one who can bring out the captive."

Historical note: this is the fifth person to have made the exact same statement--the second in less than a week.

Tuesday, December 10

The last two days were mostly sunny; but it was cloudy all day today. After breakfast I wrote down several songs that I had written with the music. The main one that God had used to encourage me was:

God has the upper hand
No matter what the plans of man
He rules and reigns above
And does His will.

190

The Soldier's Base

Just trust His sovereignty
Then you'll not discouraged be
But live each day with joy
And worship Him.

After some study time, I had a chance for another talk with Mulla Ali Reza. He told me that the Qarabagh commanders were going to get the cash that the Akhund wanted from the Hizb-i Islami in Peshawar. He also said that Abbasi had sent several letters from Quetta asking for my release. He finished with this encouragement that God is *"maslihat been"* or prudent and knowledgeable about the future.

I wrote letters today to my family and Mark to be sent by someone who was going to Pakistan. Actually they were notes added on to letters I had begun on Dec. 5. I wrote:

"After I write this letter I plan to take a bath and wash clothes. It's only been two weeks. I'll wash whether I need it or not!

The commander who came from Qarabagh three days ago didn't really raise my hopes--except to know that others are interested in my release. Apparently the price on my head is pretty high. They said maybe fifty grand in bucks would satisfy my host. Makes me ill to think of this. It's so evil. See Exodus 21:16. I pray for God to arise and save me in a way that people here will know there is a God. And that He is interested in justice and mercy.

If I'm here much longer, I have a request, Mom. Please type out Philippians 3 and 4 in the King James Version for me. I've finished memorizing chapters 1 and 2.

I'm fine--eager to see you. Interesting to compare Psalms 69:13 and 17. I pray both."

THE UPPER HAND

Dad and Mom received this letter on Feb. 11, 1992!

I walked and sang, but it was pretty late. Bostan and Khuda Dad accompanied me to my office. I prayed for an uncondemned heart, sensitive to sin.

We put all the blankets out in the fresh air (there wasn't much sun!). This helped to cut down on vermin, they said. Actually, since I had sprinkled some of the flea powder under the rug on which I slept, I had much fewer problems with lice. Bedbugs, however, seemed to have more advanced techniques. You could see them waiting in cracks in the walls. They would only advance when they felt their victim was asleep. They sometimes climbed up to the rafters and dropped on unsuspecting, sleeping victims!

After lunch it snowed some. I read and had an English lesson with A. Hassan. After supper we had a long talk about language learning, customs, and Christianity. I read and worked alone by lantern light, then went to sleep in my old spot, near the window.

Wednesday, December 11

A special breakfast treat featured sugar in the tea! Two spoons in each cup.

After studying, walking, and singing I was off to my office for a good time of rest and prayer. I prayed from Psalm 73--Lord, keep us from slipping. Give us faith in your goodness. Take our hand. Take us into your presence to see with the right perspective.

I wrote a restaurant dialogue in English for Hassan. Then he left. Thirteen donkeys arrived with loads of rice!

This afternoon there was no sun in my office. I kept myself busy writing notes and letters. Everyone had a scare when Qayum started shouting from the *jaba* above the camp that we were to surrender. It was quite a while before the men caught on that it was a joke! He had returned from being with the Akhund.

192

The Soldier's Base

The new group of soldiers had arrived by supper. There was lots of talk--the kind that was tiring and upsetting to me: war, guns, local politics. I was glad I had books and writing materials to keep me busy.

Thursday, December 12

It was cloudy today, but relatively warm. In the afternoon and evening we had a little rain!

My special prayer this morning came from *The Grace Awakening*. I prayed that my family and other friends would stand in the freedom of Christ and not criticize others.

Lunch was delicious *lobia* in juice over broken up bread. After my normal afternoon activities, I prayed for the friends on my list whose last names began with A to C.

We had about 13 for supper. I sat out in the kitchen, feet by the dying embers, as was my custom, until I got tired of my rock stool. Sometimes I would put a little firewood on the coals for a little extra heat. Then I would go down to the *karez* to brush my teeth, walk back slowly, and settle down for the night in the soldier's room. Nowadays Bostan and I kept our own bed rolls locked up in the ammunition room. We explained to the others that they were transients. We were permanent residents and, as such, we had special privileges!

We discussed a rumor with one local friend. He heard that some groups hostile to the Hazaras had ordered the kidnapping in order to stop any development in the Hazara areas.

Friday, December 13

I enjoyed breakfast with both Bostan and Atee M. Ali.

The reading in *Daily with the King* was really good this morning. These are the notes I took:

"Most of the time God leads us along an unknown path. We have no idea where we're going. If we understood everything God was doing to us, something would

THE UPPER HAND

be wrong. God doesn't explain His daily dealing. He
promises good, and asks us to trust. God is there,
beside me on the path. That's all I need for peace of
mind and heart. I need not see or feel Him. I believe
the path of the righteous shines brighter and brighter.
God, give me faith for dark days and twisted paths."

I walked, sang, and prayed for the Friday services in Islamabad and
Peshawar. Then I prayed through the verses I had noted from Psalms 81-85.
In my office I prayed for faith for dark days and twisted paths. "Surely He is
ready to save those who honor Him."

In my afternoon walk I prayed for those in my TEAM family. After
the usual rice supper, I finished reading *The Last Raven*. Then I
continued notes on *Hind's Feet*.

Saturday, December 14

As I walked, sang, and meditated this morning the soldiers were busy
doing target practice with the big guns. My prayer today was for staying in
the Bible for spiritual life. Lord, teach us how short our lives are.

Today I finished my notes on *The Pursuit of God*.

Before supper today, I walked up to the saddle and back four times.
After the rice supper, I decided to take notes on things I had learned from
Michener's *Space*. I wrote:

NGC-4565 ----   One of the most distant galaxies,
                invisible to most telescopes.
                It's 20 million light years away.
                What we see is 20 million years old!
                It's 117 billion billion miles from earth.
                It's traveling at three million miles per hour.

I am encouraged to think of how big my God is. Also I was
encouraged by my discussion with Bostan today. He told of a terrible film

he saw of prisoners in the time of Zahir Shah. He also said the snow has been delayed this year for my sake!

Sunday, December 15

This morning Bostan told me the rumor that Hizb-i Islami might take over Kabul soon. I fear for the future, but commit it to God.

Psalm 91 was the first new psalm I read this morning. What a comfort was the thought of safety under God's wings. I went on to read in Psalm 92 of the righteous who will be like palms and cedars--flourishing and strong, planted in God's house. Then, *"Whenever I am anxious and worried, you comfort me and make me glad."*

In my office this morning I prayed for living God's way--being gentle, and placing responsibility for my welfare on Him. Also I prayed for the churches I knew that would be worshipping today.

After lunch I had another bath and washed my clothes. Later Mulla Ali Reza came out to tell me, while I was walking, that a telegram had arrived saying that Hizb-i Islami-i Afghanistan (HIA) representatives were coming to try and sort out my "problem".

After our rice supper, I started another letter to my family. I wrote some English, then read some from *A Lift of Love* and *A Heart for God*.

Monday, December 16

There were some clouds today, but it was mostly sunny and windy.

I walked for an extra long time this morning after breakfast. I had read the wonderful praise psalms from 96 to 100. In my office I prayed for a fresh vision of God and sang songs of praise.

My other activities today were as usual. I have been writing so much of the same words and sentences in English for people that I decided to make an inclusive list of categories in one of my notebooks.

THE UPPER HAND

Mark is getting some much-needed diversion from the hostage crisis by beginning again to focus at least part of each day on some other tasks for Afghanistan. There is much work to be done.

Amazingly, our girls are exceptionally well, considering the indirect stress that must filter down to them from us. Cindy has worked hard at making it possible for them to maintain their normal activities and lifestyle.

Tuesday, December 17

It was cold, windy, and cloudy this morning. It made me think it might snow.

After breakfast and study time, I got into a lengthy chat with Atee M. Ali. He spoke of Doc's and my capture as a shame for his land. He told stories of working for the American company that built the road from Kabul to Kandahar. He remembered some English curses, unfortunately! He spoke of the Russians as "hungry", but the Americans as good workmen and good to the Shia people.

My journal page for today was almost filled with notes from the Scriptures I read. The reading from *Daily with the King* was excellent again. Here are my notes for it:

"Prayer is the most unpredictable and unexplain-
able of all my spiritual responsibilities. I must
dream of the unheard of and trust God for the incredible in prayer (Jer. 33:3). God doesn't promise to answer
MY way--only THE way. It is the mark of trust as well
as sense to leave the method of answering prayer
entirely in God's hands.

Do I need a command to pray? My tears, shrinking
strength, stricken land, sorrowing loved ones, hardened
neighbors, indifferent fellow-Christians and calloused
world should easily drive me to my knees."

196

The Soldier's Base

I gave notes for Zawar and Hafiz Naimi to Atee Salihee, who was going back to Chilbaghtu. I asked them to deliver Doc's notebooks to me, and to bring all my stuff from there.

In my office I prayed that we (my family, friends, and I) would trust God for His way of answering prayer. I thought of the fellowship in Islamabad and their cries for deliverance.

It was cold, so I went into the kitchen. There were some new folk around. Hussain Ali seemed to be a boy of 14. His father was Rais Nadir Ali, an elder of Patu and a man I had spoken to on some occasions. Hussain Ali was here to learn English from me--to be my disciple and student. I wasn't too comfortable with this idea at first. It made me mad as I thought about it one way. They were trying to take advantage of me. Why didn't they work for justice and my freedom? Did they expect me to return good for evil? Could I just refuse to teach the boy?

I slowly warmed up to the idea of having an English disciple. It was partly, I'm sure, an answer to my prayer for the mind of Christ. I didn't want a forced interruption in my established routine. But I began to see that I was free to set the time table. And I grew more enthusiastic as I saw that Hussain Ali really wanted to learn, and he would do the work I told him.

We began with one lesson this afternoon. I felt like I already had a curriculum established after teaching so many kids and writing notes for so many soldiers!

After supper I spent several hours writing out English for Qayum and Hafiz. Qayum spoke to me privately about some of the recent events concerning my case. He put himself forth as being on my side, and spoke of several others among the local commanders who were not in favor of my captivity.

Wednesday, December 18

It was beautifully clear, cool, and breezy all day.

After breakfast with Bostan and Atee M. Ali, I finished up the English I was writing for Qayum, since he was leaving for home.

My office time was later than usual this morning! There was great sunshine. I prayed for the people that I usually remember. I prayed that we

197

would all contribute to spiritual reversals where we are. The Gospel, after all, redoes, remakes, and renews.

Today was the changing of the guard. I sat with some of my friends from Kunagh. Mullah Ali Reza kindly offered to send mail with his son, who's going to Pakistan, so I prepared letters that I had for friends in Islamabad. I sent two packets. I think they never reached their destination.

I had an English lesson with Hamid Ali, then exercised by carrying water and climbing up the hill and back five times. I prayed especially for Columbia Bible College, where I had attended as an undergraduate.

After a *lobia* supper, I prepared letters to send to Engineer Salim Ali then read until it was pretty late.

Thursday, December 19

After breakfast, I wrote some letters to send with a man who will be leaving soon. Then I studied by the kitchen fireside.

In my office I prayed for freedom from the bonds and control of sin. The snow began falling before I got back to the kitchen. Bostan was getting ready to go home. The Akhund had come back. When he saw me, he told me that he had completed the work for my release. "In ten days, 100%, *inshallah*, you will be free," he said. (*Inshallah* means "God willing".) Apparently Bashi Habib, the HIA commander from Anguri, had gone to Quetta to sort things out.

I sat with Khadim and Hussain Ali of Chilbaghtu. They told me that both the Akhund's baby son and daughter had died. It was sad news for me since I had grown to love the family.

I brought some more water. The snow was still coming down. Then I had an English lesson with Hussain Ali.

I had rice with the guys, then tea alone in the *gulkho*. I wrote some notes, then English for Commander Qayum. Now people were saying, "Be sure you write English for me before you go!" I went to bed pretty late.

198

The Soldier's Base

I have had a flurry of excited calls from folks indicating that they or their friends had heard the broadcasts on both the VOA and BBC Persian services. One Afghan incorrectly reported that the broadcast said Joel was freed. Others indicated that the statement was that the captor had agreed to free Joel and that the release was imminent.

Friday, December 20

I woke up to cloudy skies and three inches of snow on the ground. I walked and exercised some, then joined the soldiers for breakfast.

I had a good time of study at the kitchen hearth. Psalms 116-120 brought to mind several songs. Light snow kept falling and accumulated to about five inches. I couldn't sit or lie down in my office because of the wet weather, so I kept walking back and forth on my trail. Soon the cold didn't bother me any more. My spirits were lifted to heaven. And I couldn't have been in a happier place! I must have walked back and forth for more than three hours. There was so much to think about, pray about, and thank God for. I remember singing, *"He's got the whole world in His hands."* I would substitute my family, friends, and organizations in place of "the whole world". How interesting after my release to find out that one group of believers would sing this song using my name!

The Akhund and his group left. My student, Hussain Ali, left after lunch. Commander Qayum, Ghulam Hussain, and Babai also left then.

I was called for an early *tafa*, broth and bread, lunch. I read some of *The Grace Awakening* by the hearth and then went to the commander's office to rest and be alone.

I helped with the rice supper. Arif and Mulla M. Akbar had arrived from Kunagh. We had supper together and an interesting conversation. The words of Mulla M.Akbar were a challenge to me. This is what he said:

"Don't be upset that you're here. Being sad won't help, but will ruin your health. You'll be free sometime. Your situation isn't that bad. Trust God."

At first words like this made me sort of mad inside. But now I realized the truth and wisdom of what he was saying--even if he was a mulla. Later in the discussion we got onto other topics. I remember the mulla saying,

THE UPPER HAND

"Christians are technically **kafirs**, infidels, because they don't accept the prophet, Muhammad. In Islam it's wrong to punish someone for someone else's sin, but no one lives by the book now."

I finished my notes on **Hind's Feet in High Places**. A beautiful full moon shone outside. I went to bed with a thankful heart.

Saturday, December 21

Musa woke us up extra early today. I went to the commander's office for my exercises and a time of prayer before breakfast. There was no one else in the office and snow outside. I remembered that the chief end of man is to glorify God and to enjoy Him forever. I prayed for revival in this area of Afghanistan.

I sat next to the kitchen hearth to study. I read from **Daily with the King**. If we want fruitfulness, we must expect tears--and maybe even blood. I was much encouraged by my readings in the Psalms. In Psalm 123 I read:

"As a servant depends on his master,
as a maid depends on her mistress,
so we will keep looking to you, O Lord, our God,
until you have mercy on us."

What a beautiful picture of dependence and trust! I want to look to God in this way for deliverance.

Just as I was finishing my study a group of five arrived at the base. They were chilled and soaking wet from their morning walk through the deep snow. They had spent the night at Mulla Ali Reza's in Balna Gum Qul.

I recognized Mamur Yaqub and one or two of his soldiers. I greeted them warmly. The other people were new. I found out later that Abdul Sabir was an HIA representative (from the Political Committee) from Peshawar. The other two men were soldiers from his home area near Ghazni. All three of them were **Pashtoons**. In a sense they had taken

200

their lives into their own hands by coming into Hazara territory to complete a mission which, I discovered later, was to make final negotiations for my release. It was interesting to hear the local soldiers talking about these newcomers. They called them "*Sunnis*", and I realized how deep the enmity was between the two sects in this area.

As the new arrivals were warming themselves in the soldiers room and drinking tea, I sat with them. A. Sabir spoke excellent English. He was in his thirties and had studied Islamic law. I grew to like his amiable personality, but I also recognized that he spoke with wisdom and authority.

I appreciated the educated company. And it also made me feel good to have these men so obviously on my side. They sympathized with me and seemed to sincerely feel for my plight.

After a rice lunch (not appreciated too much by our guests!), my student, Hussain Ali, arrived back. He had brought another keen English student with him--Amin.

I was touched by the kindness of Musa and Mulla Akbar. Each had been home. They each brought me dried mulberries and walnuts. Muallim Hamid arrived with my books from Chilbaghtu.

I spent time walking in the afternoon, then I had an English lesson with my new class. Over supper I had long and good talks with Sabir, Mamur Yaqub, and Muallim (one of Sabir's soldiers). They clearly told me that they hoped to be able to take me with them to Peshawar! They told of a renegade HIA commander in Kandahar who had taken two French IRC doctors captive for money last year. Sabir told how the commander had avoided meetings and was not willing to negotiate. Then the HIA had announced over the radio that this commander was no longer connected with the HIA. The next day he released the hostages. Sabir assured me that a threat from the central HIA office would carry a lot of weight with Akhund Salim. Perhaps I should have been more excited. However, I had determined not to let my hopes get up too high. I explained to Sabir my skepticism in this tactic--since the Akhund had held out so long for money. Sabir clearly recognized the difficulties of his assignment, but was still hopeful that with God's help, he would succeed. He assured me that it was against the HIA policy to support kidnapping, or to pay ransom.

THE UPPER HAND

The men tried to contact the Akhund over the walkie talkie to arrange a meeting, but they were unsuccessful.

The guests stayed in the office with Mulla Ali Reza. I spent time in the soldier's room writing and reading before bed.

> There was an article in a Pakistani newspaper today about Joel. The amount of errors was comical. Some parts are below:
>
> ### Mujahideen release ex-US diplomat
>
> An ex-American diplomat, who was made hostage by an Afghan commander in Afghanistan some three months back, has been released in Ghazni, sources said here on Friday.
>
> Hart De Joel was arrested in Ghazni and was accused of discriminatory "assistance" to the people in the liberated part of that province.
>
> Joel was one of those American diplomats who was kept hostage in the US embassy in Teheran soon after the emergence of revolution in Iran, led by Ayatullah Khomini. After his release along with other American diplomats he joined the British NGO working in Afghanistan for the rehabilitation of the Afghan people.
>
> The source said that his captor released him in Ghazni and he was on his way to Peshawar where he would be handed over to the US officials.

Sunday, December 22

It was clear as crystal this morning--and, indeed, all day. I exercised in the snow, had breakfast with the soldiers, and studied. *Daily with the King* had a good word on joy. This is what I noted:

"The Bible commands us to be joyful. Commands are
enablements. I can control my feelings more than I
think. I can't think of all that Christ has done for
me, is to me, and all that He has promised to do for me
without feeling joy. I am joyless only when my mind is
on circumstances or self. I must keep Christ alive in
my mind."

The Soldier's Base

Today's psalms were again encouraging. I read in Ps. 126:
"When the Lord brought us back to Jerusalem,
it was like a dream!
How we laughed, how we sang for joy!
Then the other nations said about us,
The Lord did great things for them."

I could feel the joy of being free again. I could imagine the praise that would go to God.

Then in Psalm 130:
"From the depths of my despair I call to you, Lord...
I wait for the Lord more eagerly than the watchmen
wait for the dawn."

Proverbs 24 gave me some good advice:
"Don't be glad when your enemy meets disaster or when
he stumbles."
"Don't let evil people worry you. They have no
future."
"Don't try to get even with people."

I sat with the guests for a while and then went for a long walk. There was too much snow for me to go to my office. Sabir and the others were on the roof of the base trying to soak up the sun. Some were burning *jirkina* bushes to get ashes to mix with tobacco for their *naswar*, snuff. People here generally grow a few tobacco plants near their homes to supply them with the main ingredient for *naswar*. Even some ladies in the area use *naswar*. Some have such a strong addiction that they have to use it several times during the night.

The men kept trying to contact the Akhund on the walkie talkie.

I climbed up the ladder to the room of the office to rest in the sun and pray. The sun was warm, but the air was cool. Soon I was delighted to hear a familiar voice. It was Nasrullah! He had arrived with some stuff for me! I went to the soldier's room to read mail and talk. My sister, Sarah, had sent me pictures of her family with the new baby, Philippa! And there was one

THE UPPER HAND

photo of my brother, Phil, and his family! All the soldiers were keenly interested in the news magazine that Nasrullah had brought for me.

Nasrullah brought two coats for me, cassette tapes and a player!, magazines, candy, sugar, batteries for my flashlight, and a large shortening can containing an iced chocolate Christmas cake and cookies! Nasrullah had a donkey and three accomplices to help him bring this stuff.

I received letters from Sarah, Hillary, Fiona, Pat, Dawn, Mark, Young Hee, the Daltons, Phil and Barb, Juan and Rose, and three from Mom.

Sabir and his group were tired of our rice so they sent a soldier down to the valley to buy a chicken for supper. This was to be a celebration in hopes of my soon release, they said.

I spent a lot of time talking with Nasrullah. He had brought a letter from Mark, authorizing him to act on Mark's behalf. He explained to me the efforts that were taking place for my release. However he didn't know what to do now that Sabir was here working towards the same goal from another angle. I encouraged Nasrullah to wait and see if Sabir was successful in his efforts. I felt that it would be a good, face-saving move if I were released by HIA. Nasrullah was agreeable.

Commander Qayum and Mulla Ali Reza arrived. The Commander seemed suspicious of my talking to Nasrullah.

I had a long English lesson with my students.

Supper of bread in chicken broth, followed by chicken meat, was delicious. I decided to make tonight our Christmas party since Sabir and the others were leaving the next day in search of the Akhund. I cut the chocolate cake, and passed it out with cookies and tea. Nasrullah took some pictures.

That evening I went to the office where the Pashtuns had settled themselves around the blazing wood stove. We visited and listened to the BBC news. They reassured me of their hopes of success.

I talked to Nasrullah some more in private, then wrote some English and went to bed.

A UN representative left the following message at Ed's hotel room at 4 p.m.: "We received good news today that Joel DeHart is to be handed over

204

tomorrow in Peshawar to the Americans." There is still no confirmation
that anyone has actually seen or spoken to Joel.

I was in Quetta chasing down the rumor that Joel had been released to
"Haji" and was on his way to Peshawar. There is a high level of
anticipation on all fronts. It's two days to Christmas.

Monday, December 23

It was cloudy. Fine snow was falling.

Breakfast was supplemented with left-over cookies. I wrote some quick
notes for Nasrullah to take. He had decided to leave with the other guests.
The warm red coat he had brought for me was too small. So he insisted that
I take his own beautiful down coat with a hood. This was also a little
small, but much more manageable. I was reluctant to take it--knowing that
Nasrullah had a lot more traveling to do. But Nasrullah was insistent.
Many times later I was extremely grateful to him and to God for this
necessary provision.

As I was saying good bye to the men, Sabir asked me to pray for his
success. I assured him that I would.

After the crowd left, I had a wonderful talk and time of fellowship with
the Commander and Mulla Ali Reza. I could see things more from their
eyes now. They were thinking, intelligent people. Pressures beyond their
control had forced them into the group they were in.

Now things were relaxed and I had time to study by the kitchen hearth.
Psalm 131 was a special blessing. As I walked back and forth later in the
light snow, I prayed for joy and rest. I prayed for humble trust. Like a
child in its mother's arms, I don't need to be concerned about subjects too
difficult for me.

"Lord, I have given up my pride
and turned away from my arrogance.
I am not concerned with great matters
or with subjects too difficult for me.
Instead, I am content and at peace.
As a child lies quietly in its mother's arms,

THE UPPER HAND

so my heart is quiet within me.
Israel, trust in the Lord now and forever!"

After a rice lunch, I read and walked. I saw Muallim Hamid briefly. I had a good nap in the office alone, then an English lesson with Hussain and Amin. Supper featured something new! A delicious carrot stew! I passed out my Russian candies to the soldiers to have with tea.

We contacted the DeHart family in Pakistan and informed them that there were strong rumors that Joel would be released in Islamabad the next day! The family decided to come. Joel's brother, Tim, and his sister, Sarah, and their families traveled overnight from Sahiwal, about 250 miles south of Islamabad.

Tuesday, December 24

It was clear as a bell again this morning. However, by mid afternoon it became cloudy.

Bostan had returned from home and had brought a special treat to share--**bosragh**, a kind of deep fried bread. It gave some welcome variety to the breakfast menu!

Studies today brought me up to Psalm 140 and Proverbs 26. As I was out walking in the path I had made through the snow, I saw Commander Qayum and Mulla Ali Reza trying to get through to someone on the walkie talkie. I paid no special attention, but when they got through they called me over. It was the first time I had talked on these instruments. Sabir was at the other end. His message thrilled my heart.

"We had a successful meeting with the Akhund. Sit tight. I expect to see you in a couple of days to take you to Pakistan. Don't tell anyone."

I thanked him, still not really thinking it could all be for real.

My stomach was upset. I lay on the roof of the soldier's room in the sun. A shawl underneath and one on top made me just warm enough to relax and think. I prayed for the hope and joy of Christmas and also for fruitfulness. I finished *The Grace Awakening* and I carried some water for exercise before lunch.

The Soldier's Base

Bostan did me the favor of giving me a haircut! I sat cross-legged on the ground as he wrapped an old sleeping bag around me and set to work. He did a great job, and the shorter hair made me feel a lot better, especially as this was all followed by a bath. I felt chilled after being outside and washing my clothes, too.

> Joel's parents traveled down the 85 miles from Qalandarabad to Islamabad today. The DeHart family gathered at the home of Pastor Ed Brown. "Where's Joel?" Mrs. DeHart said upon entering. Apparently they had been told that Joel would certainly be there. There was considerable disappointment. Tim DeHart left for Peshawar to assist in any negotiations.

Wednesday, December 25 -- MERRY CHRISTMAS!

It was clear as a bell all day.

I'm feeling better this morning. After exercises, I joined Bostan for breakfast of a *bosragh* that he had brought from home.

I decided to read through the accounts of the birth of Christ in the Bible. Then, as I walked for a long time, I sang through all the Christmas carols on my list.

It was cold, but the clear skies and sunshine made the roof of the soldier's room look very inviting. I went there, spread out one shawl under me and stretched the other on top, as was my custom. I thought of Christmas and the message of joy. The lunch call came as I was finishing my meditations.

Lunch was the usual rice. Then I went walking along my trail. This time I listened to a cassette that Mark had sent with the recorder. I enjoyed the songs. But I also realized, to my great inner satisfaction, that I didn't need to depend on gadgets. I had been communing with my Lord for months without any such things!

A new shift of soldiers arrived at the base. So, as I had my English class on the roof of the donkey's room, there was quite a big audience!

I walked for a long time--until dusk. I prayed through a list of friends. I sure was enjoying the down coat that Nasrullah had insisted I take. It was warm! As I walked, someone gave me letters from Uncle Ed Rasmussen and Mark. They were a few days old as they were written on December 14th.

Mark wrote:

"I am quickly sending this letter to you so that you will be aware of the current plans for your hand over. However, I hope that by the time you get this that you will be on your way home."

Mark went on to tell about a UN official sent to "participate in your hand over". It sounded almost like one of the efforts before that was bound to flop. But I was sensing that things were building up for a major change.

Today I made a careful list of all the things that had been taken from me personally, and some things that had been taken from the project supplies.

At dinner that evening, I was at my usual place--the hearth with Bostan. The Akhund came to talk. He was concerned with what I would say about him on my release.

"You won't say anything bad about me, will you?" he said. "The reason I took you was to deal a blow to those horrible Communists. I haven't treated you badly, have I? I assure you that we will be leaving soon."

That was an interesting exchange! And hopeful! But I didn't let myself think about it much. I read another chapter from *Heart for God*. It was about God's wisdom shown in Christ, and the part that Christ's suffering played. I finished praying through the list of friends. Tonight the room was full with the new soldiers in the Akhund's entourage!

D. Released   (Peshawar)

Dec. 26--Jan. 3

Thursday, December 26 -- The trip home begins!

It was cold this morning. At breakfast Bostan had noted the few clouds and a kind of redness in the sky. He said it would snow.

The reading today in **Daily with the King** was about confession for restoring fellowship and keeping sanity. What a joy that God can cleanse the subconscious! Then I read through Psalms 141 to 145 and made notes. Again I prayed these prayers for help and protection.

"I come to the Lord with all my problems. He knows what I should do."
"Lord, you are all I want in this life."
"Save me--my enemies are too strong. I will praise you."

As I was studying, the Akhund entered the kitchen. He had something to say and put it this way:

"I had wanted to leave today for Anguri. People there are waiting to take you to Pakistan. But you were concerned about your stuff that you left in Chilbaghtu. If I send someone to get that, it will take at least two more days. Should I do that, or should we leave today?"

I responded that it would be okay to leave today. He could send my stuff to Pakistan later. The Akhund nodded in agreement and left.

I made my usual walk, and then laid down on the roof of the soldier's room under cloudy skies for a time of prayer. I asked God to perform an

THE UPPER HAND

operation of love in my heart, and in the hearts of my family and friends. I had a joy and assurance that God could and would do this.

I obtained the key from Bostan and went back into the ammunition store room to sort and pack my things. Amazing what I had accumulated in my time at the base! Books, much dry fruit as gifts, some warm clothes that fit and some that didn't, a few medicines, extra stationary supplies, and, most precious of all, the letters and other things I had written. I divided everything I thought I didn't need or want among Bostan, Abdul Hassan, Muallim Hamid, and my two students.

I had determined not to set my hopes high, so I would not be disappointed if things didn't work out. I was sort of numb and skeptical as nothing had worked out yet. So, after the usual lunch of rice, I set to work on writing up English for various ones--especially my two students.

Snow started falling at noon. It continued steadily. I felt sure the Akhund would call off any proposed trip. But at two o'clock, he came and asked if I were ready to go. Two inches of fresh snow now covered the ground, rocks, and old snow.

Good-byes were touching. Bostan had brought a special hat, painstakingly embroidered by his sister, for me. He knew that I would appreciate it. I shook hands or hugged everyone warmly. I didn't know what the future held. There were changes, for sure. Probably my days at the base would later seem like a dream.

Bostan helped me to tie a sack of my possessions on my back. One of the soldiers kindly took my smaller bag of books. We set out climbing the path up to the saddle. I looked back and waved goodbye--taking a long look at Bostan. God had given me a good friend in him.

The pace was not fast, but I was glad I had been walking and exercising. As we descended to the "park" after the saddle, the snow was deep in some places. I was not as sure footed as the other men. There were nine of us, including Mulla Ali Reza. The steep way down from the "Number 2 base" trail to Balna Gum Qul was very slippery in places--especially where the path went through big boulders. It seems like we all slipped several times.

The song that stayed in my mind during this three-hour walk was:

Released

"You shall go out with joy, and be led forth with peace,
And the mountains and the hills shall break forth before you.
There will be shouts of joy and all the trees of the field
Shall clap, shall clap their hands!"

We arrived at Mulla Ali Reza's house around 5 p.m. It seemed that the others were colder than I. We sat around the tin wood stove that was in the center of the room. Soon the room was hot and I took off my shawl and down coat. The men told me to be careful. If I took my warm clothes off, the combination of the cold and sweat could make me sick.

After tea, we headed to the Qariadar's house nearby. He had a much bigger, fancier guest room. We waited under blankets for supper. Juma, the Qariadar's son, was an intelligent boy of about ten. He was studying in school and knew some English words. I wrote out some more English for him and gave him some stickers!

We had a delicious supper of rice, stew, and cooked apricots. Some time later the men tuned into BBC. It was interesting to catch part of a program about Christmas in Persian! It was culturally oriented, talking about customs in Sweden and Nigeria.

The room was cold, without a stove, but our bedding was more than ample. I had a wonderful night's sleep. It was still snowing lightly as I stepped outside for a rest stop before bedding down.

The DeHart family was VERY concerned and disappointed that there was no Christmas release. Joel's parents returned to Qalandarabad today, and the rest of the family returned to Sahiwal a few days later. Nevertheless, indications of an imminent release are flourishing. Again the information is contradictory.

Friday, December 27

It was a beautiful morning and there were clear skies all day. The snow had stopped sometime during the night--leaving about three more inches. I walked down the road to a small stream and I washed in its cold water.

THE UPPER HAND

Breakfast was bread and tea, of course. We each had an Iranian blanket to wrap around ourselves.

We soon set off. As we were leaving, who did I see but Hussain, my student and kind host from Uloom. He came up and greeted me warmly. I had heard that he had just been married, so I congratulated him. He expressed his joy that I was now on my way home.

We walked almost non-stop until noon. There were about ten of us. In the beginning my cold feet bothered me. We took some short cuts over ridges, as the road wound around a longer way. As we got closer to Sang-i Masha, we saw a few vehicles. By noon we had reached Sang-i Shanda, a town after the turn off going toward Anguri. We all padded up to Ali Jan's house. There we had a long wait and dinner.

One of their fierce dogs lunged at me as I was walking to the bathroom. I didn't even notice it until there was a commotion and I realized that I had narrowly missed a bite on the leg!

We took off our wet socks and hung them out in the sun.

Ali Jan was one of six brothers. One brother remembered me from the wedding in Sabz Chob the night before our capture. He remembered my camera from the wedding and told me that he had seen it for sale in Aslam's shop in Anguri for 120,000 Afghanis! Interestingly this family has relatives in Islamabad who operate a bakery! The family had a Mercedes truck outside which one of the brothers drove.

We hadn't completely finished lunch when a jeep arrived outside. It had been arranged previously that this driver would take us to Anguri, but when it snowed the day and night before, he wasn't sure he could meet his obligation. It was nice to pile into the jeep and take off at a fast pace. The Akhund, of course, sat next to the driver. The jeep had chains on the front right tire, and the back left one. It was only about an hour's drive. When we arrived in June, there had only been a little snow left on the mountains from the winter. Now fresh snow covered everything in sight. I had a sense of joy inside, as things seemed to be moving positively. I knew I was not in control of the situation, but kept reminding myself that God was. Perhaps this was the culmination of many prayers. Perhaps I would be free soon.

R e l e a s e d

We drove through the bazaar and took a right turn, heading for Mamur Yaqub's house. I hadn't seen a bazaar for six months! I began thinking of all the nice Christmas presents I could buy for my family and others. The only problem was that I didn't have any money! Plus, I could see that people were being very protective of me. They didn't want anything to happen to their investment--or their honor!

The Mamur had a house full! Still, he entertained us in the relaxed and easy manner that characterized him.

We had tea in the smaller guest room. This room had a wood stove that kept the air pleasantly warm.

The place was buzzing. I sensed that some wheeling and dealing was going on. This sense was later confirmed. Sabir and his group (eight others) were there with their two vehicles. I talked a little with Engineer Waris Muhammad from Paktia who, I gathered, was Sabir's assistant in this mission. He knew some English, and liked to use it!

A group from Chilbaghtu also arrived. It was nice to see these friends again. I could see how the Akhund would consider them his most loyal followers since they came from his home area.

I made a request to Sabir and Mamur Yaqub that my camera and some things be bought in the bazaar. But it was getting late.

We had supper together in the bigger room. We had chick pea and meat broth, followed by meat. Ten of us "Afghans" slept in that room. (Since I spoke Pashtu, I was grouped with the Pashtuns!) It was pretty tight, but now that didn't bother me at all! It was interesting to be using Pashtu again, after being away from it for six and a half months. There seemed to be fairly good relations between the HIA Shias and Sunnis (or Hazaras and Pashtuns). However, some differences couldn't help but surface. I noticed the Akhund didn't know Pashtu well, and did all of his dealings in Persian.

One nice thing about being nearer civilization was the variety of candies served with tea! I also admired the Mamur's cemented bathroom. It was the best I had seen in Jaghori.

We received news that Joel is definitely in Peshawar. The press conference to release Joel is set for Monday.

213

THE UPPER HAND

One soldier reports that he was in Peshawar when a commander showed up with Joel. He says he saw Joel in a HIA base in Peshawar. This is second hand, but the only sighting of Joel in Peshawar. We feel that Joel may be being sold from one commander to the next.

A Quetta source said today that the American is still in Patu, Jaghori.

Saturday, December 28

We woke up to a clear, but bitingly cold morning. People weren't paying too much attention to me. I was able to find a secluded place by a wall to do some exercises. Then I watched as the drivers lit fires under the diesel engines of their jeeps to get them started. Without this trick, these diesel engines wouldn't start! My feet and hands were really cold.

Matiullah of Ningrahar was driving the Toyota Land Cruiser Jeep that had come from Peshawar. The other Russian jeep was driven by a man from Qarabagh.

Our breakfast was *chob josh* with *nan* and tea. We prepared for departure. Then the Akhund called Sabir in for a meeting. I felt like the whole deal could fall through here. I steeled myself for a possible disappointment.

I was glad to have time to study while the men were meeting. I read Psalms 146 to 150 and took notes. Certain verses were meaningful:

"Don't put your trust in human leaders."
"Happy is the man who has the God of Jacob to help him, who depends on the Creator."
"God controls all nature for our good."
"God takes pleasure in those who honor Him."

The Akhund and Sabir came out of their meeting after 10 a.m. "Come on, let's go," the group of Pashtuns said. They must have arrived at an agreement. I said good bye to all my Hazara friends. I gave two soldiers souvenirs for the kids in Chilbaghtu. They also agreed to take letters to some people. I had written to Hafiz Naimi--asking again that he send Doc's notebooks. Then there were brief notes for several others. I gave the

214

R e l e a s e d

Akhund a letter asking him to send my possessions to Pakistan (he assured me he would) and to assist in getting Doc's notebooks.

The Akhund gave me a good bye hug. I felt great relief to be leaving him. The Russian jeep finally got started, and off we went. At Sabir's instruction, one of the soldiers took off the local red and black cap that I had been wearing for the last six months and positioned his turban on me. "Better to be safe," said Sabir.

As we were leaving town, we came to the HIA chain across the road. This checkpoint was under Mamur Yaqub's control and all the proceeds (money from taxes on all vehicles coming into the area) went to the upkeep of his base. We greeted the soldier on duty and sped through. There was a noticeable feeling of relief. The men announced that we were now in Pashtun territory. They assured me that we were now out of the control of the "low-down" Hazaras.

As the day went on, the weather changed from clear skies to haze. It became windy and very cold. Perhaps the change was due to our leaving the central mountainous region and coming east to the flat lands where the Kabul-Kandahar road lay.

I was recognizing things now along the way. There were many mud structures for drying grapes. There was the huge ditch that the Hazaras had unsuccessfully dug to try to keep Russian tanks out of their valley. Grape vines in vineyards had been covered with earth to protect them from the bitter cold.

My new friends pointed out a high hill where Russian garrisons had long withstood mujahideen attacks. Now a commander was using it as his base.

Finally, we arrived at the remains of the Kabul-Kandahar highway. We turned to head north. It was like riding a roller coaster. Huge pot holes filled the road. Tanks, mines, and fighting had been hard on the road surface! Many times we would gather speed on a smoother track off of the main road. Then we would return to bob up and down for a while on the patches of pavement.

We stopped at a roadside restaurant just south of Qarabagh at 1 p.m. "Let's just talk Pashtu or Persian," Sabir said. The food was welcome and

THE UPPER HAND

delicious. It was rice and sheep *qorma*. The people in the restaurant were speaking Pashtu. They didn't seem to pay much attention to us.

After we began again, the clutch in the Russian jeep went out. We took three more passengers in our jeep. And we headed off the main road to Qarabagh bazaar. The roads were rutted and muddy. We left the second jeep, the Russian one, there with the extra soldiers. On the way back to the main road we passed an area with many rocks which were painted red.

"What are those for?" I asked.

"They mark mine fields," the men replied. "All the mines haven't been defused, but the UN mine-clearing teams have been around marking the dangerous areas so people will hopefully stay away."

Back on the main road, we traveled for an hour on a section of the road that was in very good shape. I couldn't understand why this part hadn't been destroyed like the rest of the road. Matiullah stopped to take the chains off the tires. The freezing wind chilled us to the bone.

We made another stop in a small town to purchase diesel. There were perhaps 20 "gas stations" in the one bazaar. Each consisted of a group of 55 gallon drums. We stopped at several places and asked the price before buying. Russian diesel (more expensive than Pakistani or Irani diesel) was 10,000 Afghanis a tin. The dealers pumped diesel from the drums into empty vegetable oil cans (about five gallons) with hand pumps. Matiullah said he could judge the quality of the fuel by its smell and consistency. The Russian variety was more expensive because it wouldn't freeze.

After this smooth stretch of road, we headed east on a mud track. I discovered later that we were just south of Ghazni.

We got stuck once in the mud, but managed to work our way out. My admiration for Matiullah as a driver grew. It was dusk when we reached the local HIA base. This was under the benevolent leadership of Sabir's uncle. We had tea quickly in the soldier's room, but the men didn't want to stay long. We dropped off another soldier there.

The drive from that point on in the freezing darkness seemed to last forever. Probably it was only an hour and a half. Matiullah parked the jeep and all of us hopped out and headed across snowy fields to a settlement about half a mile away. The big, newly-built fortress belonged to Sabir and his uncle. What a relief it was to go in and rest in the guest room. The air

216

there was frigid at first, but a fire was lit to make our supper. Gradually the room warmed up as the chimney underneath the floor became hot.

We had eggs, milk and tea. Then we listened to the BBC news and talked. I had a good sleep under a thick quilt.

Sunday, December 29

I woke up to clear skies and extremely cold weather. As the others washed for prayer, I went outside and found a spot clear of snow near the massive wall where I could exercise.

Breakfast of delicious *halwa*, bread, and milk was served at 7:30. The commander, Sabir's uncle, arrived and we had a long and interesting talk. He seemed to be an educated and open-minded man, keenly interested in the development and well-being of his area. We discussed the projects in his area, and the security situation. There was peace there. There was a group of Norwegians living under his protection. They sometimes went on outings--like fishing trips to Lake Sardeh. One group was encouraging better ways of drying apricots. Another, Save the Children, encouraged local handwork. And VITA was doing road construction projects. The commander emphasized that leaders must work for the good of the people.

The Commander's white Toyota jeep was parked outside. It needed the engine rebuilt in Pakistan. He kept a beautiful horse and would use this for getting around--especially in the snow and mud.

I found some time when I could read alone, so I began reading the Psalms again--paying special attention to the Psalmist's cries for help. They spoke comfort to me.

We went outside to visit with the servants and children. The Pashtun culture had a very different flavor than the Hazara! We looked at the large barn. It had been constructed with mud domes, but these had been damaged in heavy rains. I passed around stickers to the kids.

Lunch was *shorwa*, broth, and meat. Sabir, Waris, Matiullah, and I took off for Mari bazaar. They needed to make some purchases for the trip the following day. And they wanted to fulfill my request to do some "Christmas shopping" before I left Afghanistan!

THE UPPER HAND

I suppose the drive was less than an hour. It was interesting to see the area in the light of day. We drove by the *Prozha*, and I could imagine how ten years ago it was a beautiful model of an agricultural farm, run by the Russians. Now it wasn't in operation. There were some abandoned armored vehicles lying around. And everything was in a general state of disrepair.

The roads had deep mud ruts. As we neared the bazaar, Matiullah dropped us off and went to make arrangements with the soldiers who would accompany us the next day. It was fun walking around there, because I almost felt free! Nobody seemed to notice that I was any different from anyone else. I borrowed money from Sabir to buy Russian candy, a Russian lock, and some Russian enamel bowls. We each bought a pair of gloves--which we would much appreciate in the next few days. I couldn't find any small *gilams,* woven wool rugs.

Waris and I went into a small hotel to get warm. We sat near the metal wood stove and ordered tea. I was enjoying the atmosphere immensely.

When we arrived back at the commander's house, I went for a short walk outside. I walked down dirt steps to the *karez*, underground water channel, flowing deep and fast about 15 feet below the surface. The water was warm! This was the water supply for the houses of Khana-i Baba.

In the evening, we had a real captain's dinner. There was *shorwa* and meat. And a vegetable dish made from dried spinach. Pudding was served for dessert. We visited and listened to the radio. Later I got into a religious discussion with Kabir, Sabir's cousin, who had been in prison for seven years. The others told me that his mind had been affected by the hardships he had endured in prison. For much of his imprisonment, he had been in one room with 200 other men. He had been well educated and knew some English. I also explained some common misunderstandings about the Christian faith to Engineer Waris.

Before bed, I went outside for a brief walk and a bathroom visit. I slept well next to the door.

After many meetings today, some information was confirmed by EVERY source:
1. Joel will be released
2. Joel is in the hands of the HIA

R e l e a s e d

> 3. Joel is definitely well, in good hands, and in no danger.
>
> My feeling now is that we must wait and see. We shouldn't push. The release will happen if nothing drastic occurs to dump the applecart.

Monday, December 30

The morning dawned cold and clear. The ordinary breakfast was supplemented with *halwa* and honey. Matiullah was outside tending a fire under the jeep. When the jeep started, we said our good-byes and set off. We stopped at one home to load two large sacks of raisins into the back of the jeep. Raisins were cheap there, but very expensive in Pakistan. Now the jeep was so full that we had to sit cross-legged on the seats, or put our legs up on top of the luggage! Matiullah, Sabir, and Waris sat in front. Abdullah and Hashim, with their kalashnikovs, were in the back with me.

At the bazaar outside the *Prozha*, we picked up a shovel. Then we drove for half an hour to Muhammad Khel, where we stopped for diesel and mulberries. This is where we joined up with two Russian jeeps heading in the same direction as we were. The road was terrible in places. Matiullah always had to choose from several tracks the one where he thought the ruts would be the least deep.

Soon we passed the Sardeh dam and drove around the lake. As many other places along the way, there was a small contingent of soldiers from one of the parties to control traffic. We had no problems because this was Sabir's home territory. There was lots of mist around the lake.

My feet were freezing. We munched on mulberries, walnuts, and raisins. There was no place and no time along the way to stop for lunch. The Russian jeeps left the traveled track and set off on a new way through virgin snow. I guess they knew a short cut. We met up again later and then we came to a place where they were having difficulty navigating. After repeated tries neither of the Russian jeeps could get up a slippery hill. We decided to put our chains on the jeep's tires. They were a great help.

Finally, all three vehicles made it up this incline. But this was just the beginning of our adventure! We got stuck in many other places. The two Russian jeeps were full of paying passengers. It always amazed me how,

THE UPPER HAND

when the vehicle got stuck, everyone would give his piece of advice. Only a few would half-heartedly push. And nothing was done in complete unity! We were stuck in the worst place for about an hour. It wasn't long before sunset. I think everyone was concerned that we should leave before darkness fell. I was glad that I didn't know enough to worry about where to spend the night or what would happen. Wasn't God going before me to do His wonderful will, anyway?

The leading jeep was stuck in a deep pool of water. The thick ice had broken. The young driver kept gunning his engine and trying to go forward, then backward. Nothing worked. Pushing didn't help. The other Russian jeep tried to pull from behind. Then it somehow made it around the stuck one and tried to pull it from ahead. Shovels, rocking, roaring starts... nothing was working! This difficulty helped all of us in the three jeeps to get to know each other to some extent. Some of those in the other jeeps were a group of mujahideen apparently going to Pakistan for rest and supplies. They spoke Farsi among themselves, but seemed to be free in Pashtu, also. They were from Paghman, they later told us. They had several rocket launchers with them.

Finally a cheer went up! We saw a huge Russian tractor heading towards us. We had passed it perhaps an hour ago. Yes, the driver would help us. He effortlessly drove around the disabled jeep and positioned himself to pull the jeep out. The next thing we knew, the tractor was stuck in a deep rut. It was 20 minutes before he was finally free! Ironically, the stuck jeep had managed to drive out of the pool of water in the meantime! I was glad that we didn't leave at that time. We all stayed until the tractor was out of the ditch.

Matiullah was a little frustrated with having to go at the slower pace of the Russian jeeps. We took off in the lead. The sun had set before we looked back and noticed that the jeeps weren't following us. We waited. Then we turned around and headed back to where one jeep had gotten stuck in one of the many stream crossings. (The roads were basically dirt tracks that followed the stream beds. They crisscrossed the stream many times to get to the side that was easiest to drive on.) We pulled him out without much difficulty.

R e l e a s e d

About an hour after sunset we pulled into a small bazaar. It looked like nothing was open. I couldn't see any lights. "Char Baran", I was told. That means "Four Rains".

Matiullah parked the jeep and we bundled out. One of the men opened a plastic and cardboard-covered door. What a welcome sight--or welcome feeling! It was toasty warm inside! It was a wayside inn. A good supply of wood kept the tin stove in the middle of the cooking area well stoked. A tin pipe carried the smoke out of the roof. Typically the fire was under a large metal sheet. On this hot surface were many small teapots along with pots filled with food that had been cooked earlier. At the end of the fire was a large, tin *samovar* with a spigot for keeping boiling water for tea, and anything else for which it was needed.

The room was pretty full, but we new arrivals managed to get places near the cooking fire. Oh! How good it felt! We took our shoes off at the door and climbed up on to the raised mud platform that was covered with old rugs.

What was for supper? There wasn't much. In fact, they said they were out of bread until the morning. Still, we did get a little potato curry and some bread--supplemented by more bread from a kind fellow traveler. There was plenty of hot tea.

After the meal the activity died down a little. Sabir and I were accorded the best place to sleep. We each used small sleeping bags that Sabir had brought with him. It was sufficient because of the warm mud platform under us and the stove nearby. Before we settled down to sleep, a four-wheel drive Russian truck pulled up with a crew of loud-talking Wazirs. They too were glad for the warmth of the inn.

"What's there to eat?" they asked the inn keeper and his ten-year old assistant.

"Nothing," was the reply.

There was a lot of complaining and discussing. Finally, the boy went out and brought back some eggs and dough. Another half an hour and they were eating voraciously and continuing the loud talk. At last they decided to get some sleep and thereby gave the rest of us some peace and quiet!

Poor Matiullah didn't get much sleep as every hour or two he would get up and go out to start the jeep and run it a while. I had given him and

THE UPPER HAND

Waris my shawls, as I had ample bedding. There were about 30 of us in the long hotel room.

Tuesday, December 31

Things came to life in the hotel about 5:30 in the morning. I had slept off and on, and was really grateful for the rest. It was still a little dark when I made my way out and walked in the snow for quite a way. The skies were clear, and it was COLD! Again I thanked God for the snug down coat from Nasrullah.

All of our trip yesterday, I had enjoyed the beauty of the thick snow and trees. Char Baran was especially beautiful this morning. There was a special kind of pine trees around on the hills. And the bazaar was nestled in some flat area near a running stream. During our trip today I kept thinking of a "winter wonderland"--especially as we made our way through wooded mountains, up stream beds, and through groves of monkey nut trees. (These trees supply the long nuts that are so popular in Pakistan in the winter.). Many places along our trip would be great vacation spots--that is, if there were peace in the area.

Breakfast was tea, bread, and mulberries. Then there was a lot of time to sit around. One of the Russian jeeps couldn't get started. Sabir discussed with the others whether we could go on ahead alone. It was wild country, and he felt we would be much safer in the company of others--especially since the mujahideen group was armed. We would wait for them. Sabir told me to keep talking Pashtu or Persian so the others wouldn't get an idea of who I was. He didn't really trust the armed men.

Our men put the other chain on the jeep's front tire. I kept walking around as the men tried everything to start the one stubborn jeep. The morning was wearing away. All the passengers got out of the hotel and began pushing the jeep. Nothing happened! Our jeep began towing it. About a half mile from the inn it finally started.

It was good to be going again. However, a short distance later, one of the Russian jeeps got stuck again. We waited and helped them out. But this was the last straw. We consulted together and decided to go it alone.

222

Released

It was a beautiful trip! We had no major stops. All of the passengers
got out for one steep haul over a pass. Then we descended on to the
beautiful, white Sarobi plains. What an enchanting sight! We passed
several settlements, then seemed to cut back the wrong way. Then, after
driving through a dense monkey nut pine forest, we came out to a
well-traveled track that took us a short while later to some shops and, most
especially, a restaurant!

It was after 12 noon when the restaurant helper lit the wood stove in the
middle of the room and we all sat around it. The ***hotali***, man in charge of
the "hotel", brought us ***qorma*** and ***dal***. There was so much we couldn't
finish it all! Sabir really enjoyed some home-made corn bread that they had
there.

Soon we were on our way again. Now we drove through mile after
mile of pine trees and mountains. We met occasional trucks coming the
other way. I asked Sabir to stop so I could get some of the pine cones as
mementos. Waris explained to me how his people had the hillsides of these
trees divided. They would gather the pine cones from their area and beat
them until the monkey nuts came out. It was the big cash crop for them.

As we kept heading east, the road got more muddy and less covered with
snow. We had then arrived in the area of the Kharoti and Wazir tribes. We
pulled up in front of a large and fancily decorated restaurant at Kharoti Ada.
There wasn't time for tea, but we took the chains off the tires. It was in
this area that Waris could really help us. Being from Paktia, just to the
north, he knew the people and the dialect well. And Sabir was concerned
about this next section. The Wazirs and Kharotis were rather independent
and could pretty much do as they liked with the traffic coming through their
territory. We were alone now, too.

The roads improved some and Matiullah was really driving fast. I was
amazed at his stamina. We passed more and more home forts until we
finally reached Angur Ada, the town just on the Afghan side of the Pakistan
border. The men told me of the Russian bombs that had been dropped on a
mosque here several years ago during the height of the war with the
Communists. This spot had always held importance as a launching place
for different mujahideen groups going back into Afghanistan with fresh arms
and supplies.

THE UPPER HAND

We filled up with diesel and the men said their evening prayers. We drove for half hour further to the HIA mujahideen launching base named Jundullah. We drove straight up to the cement and stone command base at the top of a hill. The men had been there on their way into Afghanistan for this "mission of mercy".

I knew where we were and I felt disheartened. What would HIA do with me now? I certainly would rather have stayed in a hotel in the bazaar than in the military base. Contrary to my fears, the men were warm and friendly. They spared nothing in being hospitable to us. First, we had tea in a warm guest room. Then we had *qorma* for supper. There was lots of joking.

As the talking continued, I got my bag of books out of the jeep and began writing in my diary. I was relieved that they didn't put new restrictions on my movements.

I reminded Sabir again that I wanted to telephone my family as soon as possible. Now we were in Pakistani territory, and telephones were available. Sabir put me off. "Maybe tomorrow from Wana. We'll do our best."

All of us guests stayed in one room. I soon fell into a sound sleep and I know the others slept well, too. Especially Matiullah!

> We continue adapting a press statement for Joel's eventual release. Reports of Joel being sighted are not substantial. We are still getting signals that Joel might be in Jaghori, even today.

Wednesday, January 1, 1992 -- New Year's Day!

I rose early for exercise in a place behind a cedar tree where there was no snow. It was cloudy this morning, and for most of the day.

Matiullah started the jeep before breakfast. This was a reassuring sound to me. Maybe they wouldn't leave me here. Maybe I was really going home!

We had delicious, hot *nan* for breakfast along with honey we had brought from Sabir's home. We sat briefly. I had time to read Proverbs 29 and 30 carefully. *"If you trust the Lord, you are safe."* The reading from *Daily with the King* was entitled: "Owning nothing--enjoying

224

everything." I was challenged by the call to resign all rights to myself--my reputation, place of service, possessions, demands, privacy, and other needs. I read:

> "Most of the time I'm touchy, irritable or peevish, it's because I've reclaimed what I thought I had surrendered to Jesus."

We picked up two boxes of dates, then hit the road by 8:30 a.m. We were in Wana, the capital of South Waziristan, by 11:30 a.m. It had been a bumpy, dirt road most of the way. Now we had left the snow, mountains, and trees behind.

In Wana, we made our way to the Zarai Noor refugee camp where a wealthy HIA leader lived. He was Haji Palwan (the name, *palwan*, means "wrestler"). Among the scattered mud dwellings, Haji's home and guest house was quite kingly in its decor. It had an attached bathroom with water supply, a large wood stove in the middle of the room, rich Persian carpets covering the floor, numerous fat pillows, and plenty of spittoons and kerosene lanterns.

We had tea, of course. Sabir and the others left for the bazaar and work there. Sabir would contact the HIA office in Peshawar and tell them of his progress, I was sure of that. Waris and I remained with Anwar, Haji Palwan's son. We ate lunch together. Then I helped Anwar with some English. He was studying in a local Pakistani private school, and doing very well.

I spent some time resting and praying. I re-surrendered my life to God and His lordship.

Waris, in spite of his deformed leg, agreed to go out on a walk. Anwar was our guide. We walked north, soon getting out of the inhabited area and coming to rocky plains. There were many interesting rocks, and I collected some small ones for Julia, my niece. Waris, Anwar, and I enjoyed talking to each other. I found out a lot about Wana and this huge refugee camp.

When we returned to the house at dusk, Sabir and the Toyota had returned. There were other guests, too. Haji Palwan was giving a special dinner to some tribal brothers who had recently returned from Dubai. It was truly a wonderful meal. There was rice, french fries, *shorwa* with potatoes and turnips, *qorma*, salad, cooked apricots, pudding, and oranges. We

THE UPPER HAND

listened to the news, and then I had some time to write in my diary. There were nine others sleeping in the guest room.

Thursday, January 2

Sabir planned an early departure. It was interesting for me to watch how he firmly, yet courteously, took immediate leave in spite of Haji Palwan's forceful insistence that we have tea there before we left! I did some exercises out in the courtyard under the stars.

We left around 6:30 a.m. (I still didn't have a watch or any money!). Sabir, Waris, a Wazir driver and his assistant were riding in a new Toyota double cab pickup. It was so comfortable! It even had a heater! When Sabir had mentioned the night before that he was getting another vehicle to take me to Peshawar comfortably, I told him not to do it for me. "I'm just as happy in the Toyota jeep," I said. He replied that he was just following instructions that he had received from Peshawar. "Plus, we'll make better time," he added.

The driver drove all the way to Peshawar as if he were trying to escape for his life! I was interested in the scenery because it was all new for me until we came on to the Zhob-Dera Ismail Khan road. The road was good all the way. There were many old block houses from days of the British Empire on the surrounding hills. We went through many check posts marked by chains across the road. We didn't have tea until 10 a.m., when we arrived in Tank, the largest city in the southern part of the North West Frontier Province.

The driver had his Pashtu music on much of the time. One tape of jokes was interesting. I remember this one:

> One Pathan went to visit his friend. This friend had shaved off his beard from just half of his face.
> "What's gotten into you, friend? Why have you shaved just half of your face?"
> "I have two wives, you see. One of them likes a beard, and the other one doesn't!"

Released

When I got tired of their music, I decided to make use of my own! I got out the cassette player Mark had sent and put it in my pocket. I listened to two good sermons by Steve Brown, **Communion** music, and **The Final Word**, by Michael Card.

After Bannu, we stopped for lunch at a roadside restaurant. I had delicious meat curry. Matiullah and his jeep wasn't far behind us. They joined us for lunch.

Soon after this, the police stopped us at a check point. "What's all this stuff? Where are you going? Do you have a permit for this?" Their questioning stopped when Sabir gave them each a generous portion of big, red Ghazni raisins. My bags were also searched, but there was no objection. Matiullah didn't fare so well. Later he told us that they had to pay a bribe of several hundred rupees.

Several things impressed me about coming back into this familiar part of Pakistan. The masses of people, the lush fields, and the *chai*! Afghanistan and the border areas were populated so sparsely, and they had seemingly unending barren, rocky and snow-covered mountains. I was so happy to be back where I could enjoy Pakistani *chai*, my favorite milk tea!

We were in Peshawar by 4 p.m. We followed the canal road until we got to Shamshatu, the HIA headquarters area just east of the city. We went straight to a guest house that was now occupied by the Jamiat-ul Ulema. There I was left under the care of Waris. We had tea and apples. I had time to stretch out and pray. We tried to heat water with an immersion heater for baths.

Waris and I went out for a walk, then we had rice and kabobs at one of the many hotels which catered to the large refugee community there. It was so nice to get out and feel free! We returned to the guest house for tea made by the attendant there. Then we listened to the radio. While Waris bathed, I wrote up some of the things I had learned from my experience, and some points I thought I might be asked about if there were an interview the next day.

The electricity went off, but my bucket of water was hot, so I enjoyed a bath.

THE UPPER HAND

> We made another trip to Peshawar today. A time frame of one or two days for release was given by the HIA political advisor. A strong overall message is: "Wait for a couple more days. Don't spoil the process now as it is close to resolution. DON'T DO ANYTHING."

Friday, January 3

I woke up in the dark after an excellent sleep. I walked around and around the perimeter of the beautiful rose garden. It was cloudy, and much warmer than the places I had come from. I prayed for a change in lives and for joy and unity. I thought especially about the churches meeting in Islamabad and Peshawar. I had asked Sabir to be able to go to church this morning. I said it was important to me. He responded by saying he would talk to his superiors. Later he told me it wouldn't be possible.

Waris and I had tea with *nan* and Peshawar's famous morning cream.

Then I read Proverbs 31 and *Daily with the King*. This morning's selection on "No formulas for God" was so good. I can't manage or fathom God. His dealings with me are strictly personal. "God's timely deliverance for me today will not necessarily be His deliverance tomorrow."

Sabir came around 9 a.m. to visit and see how things were going. Later two other officials from the HIA political committee appeared. Interestingly, both of these men had spent some years in America and spoke excellent English. Around 10:30 a.m. Engineer Fakhruddin Halim, the chief of HIA's Political Committee (the equivalent to a minister of foreign affairs for HIA), came to visit. He was the boss that Sabir had mentioned. He asked how I had been treated. We discussed the reason for my capture. He told about his education in Poona, India. Then he spoke of his four years of work for the Afghan government, seven months in prison, and then work with the HIA. He went on to talk about how they had heard of my plight and how they planned to help me. He was glad that we had reached Pakistan safely. Engineer Halim explained that they had moved slowly and deliberately so as not to put my life in danger. They would give no quarter to kidnappers. Kidnapping and committing crimes were not a part of the HIA policy. Akhund Salim was told that either he would obey higher authorities and release me, or be rejected by the party.

228

Released

Engineer Halim had sent Sabir to the bazaar to buy me some things which had been taken from me. Waris ordered lunch for the five of us to share at the guest house. There was a good atmosphere of friendship. My heart felt a little more at rest after meeting these important men and hearing their sympathy and apparent intention to release me.

One of the officials related a story from his time in the States that was refreshingly down to earth compared to the political discussion we had been having. In some western state he was driving around a city and noticed a police car following him. He was careful to do everything according to the law. But the car kept following him. Finally, the policeman stopped him and asked to see his papers. The official didn't have them, and didn't make any excuses. The officer wrote him a ticket, and then asked,

"By the way, where are you from?"

"What difference does it make? I know I deserve the ticket."

"Just for interest."

"I'm from Afghanistan."

The officer's face broke into a large smile. "Good for you! Keep up the good work against the Russians! And I won't give you this ticket. I thought you were an Iranian."

Engineer Halim had to leave, but the others stayed a little longer. We parted warmly.

Sabir came back with a bag full of his purchases. I was astounded. He had brought me two new suits of clothes, socks, dress shoes, a warm jacket, a diary, a Parker pen, a towel, a large traveling bag, a Chitrali hat, and a gold Seiko watch. Later he gave me 5000 Rupees to cover the cost of the camera I had lost! I was humbled and grateful.

They assured me that they would call the American consular officer today and also call my family and Mark to let them know of my hand over tomorrow.

I spent more time in the afternoon walking around the rose garden--thinking and praying. Even with the prospect of six months of captivity being over tomorrow, I didn't seem to be too emotional. It seemed easy to trust my life with my Lord.

THE UPPER HAND

Waris and I went out for another walk at dusk. Then we had supper together back at the guest house.

Saturday, January 4 -- Release!

Again I was up early to walk around the rose garden. I committed anything that might happen today to my Lord--praying through all the thoughts I had. God gave me peace and a good time of intercession for others.

After breakfast, Engineer Halim appeared in his new, double cab, four-wheel drive pickup with his armed driver. He approved of Sabir's purchases for me. Soon I was in his pickup and we were heading off towards University Town. He made a call on his car phone, speaking Pashtu. We had an interesting conversation. He told of one of his children who had some kind of health problem. Some Christian ladies had been helpful to his child. He spoke of visiting a church on one trip to Germany. He seemed very personable.

We pulled into the parking lot of the HIA Political Committee office and Waris and I went into a waiting room. I noticed the headlines on the most recent HIA newspaper. Engineer Gulbuddin Hikmatyar claimed that just as the Soviet Union had crumbled, the United States would soon divide into 52 parts (many Afghans and Pakistanis have been taught that the USA has 52 states!).

After about 45 minutes I was called into Engineer Halim's office. "Someone has arrived to see you," I was informed. There was the US Consul, Gerald Fierstein! We greeted warmly. He seemed very concerned and genuinely happy to see me. We exchanged a few words, and then began to interact with the group. Mr. Fierstein did an excellent job of answering each question in a well-informed and kind way. The discussion continued for about 20 minutes before the next guest entered.

It was Mark!! He was smiling and gave me a bear hug! How good it was to see him. My confidence was growing that this was not just a dream or a ruse. I really was going to be free. Mark handed me a manila envelope with some instructions, and a copy of that morning's paper. There was a caution to speak carefully so that my words or attitude would not endanger others or my future here. There was information on who should be thanked. There were ideas on what to do in the immediate future.

Soon, we received a call that lunch was ready. We took our shoes off outside the door to the committee room. A beautiful catered meal was ready on a long table. I was ushered to a seat across from Mark. There were several reporters and other HIA officials.

When everyone was finished eating, things were set up for a "meet the press" type of meeting. Engineer Halim, Mr. Fierstein and I sat behind a table. Some cameras were pointed at us.

Engineer Halim spoke first. He said how glad HIA was to deliver me to the US consul. He stressed that HIA was against actions like kidnapping and added that Akhund Salim had performed the action of taking me hostage entirely on his own initiative. I had been released, he stated, because HIA had used its influence with the local commander.

The reporters asked some pointed questions. One said that HIA was considered a terrorist group. How could Engineer Halim show that they were not so? There was some talk in Persian and Pashtu which I understood. I made some comment and one reporter asked me to say something in Persian, which I did. Then I made a statement in English about how I had been treated well and deeply appreciated the people in HIA (I named Sabir and Waris) who had gone to so much trouble to effect my release.

After this part was over, I was hustled outside. There were a few pictures. One reporter gave me his card to contact him later. A reporter from the BBC asked if I would be willing to do an interview in Persian. I responded that I didn't know where I would be, but we could get in touch later. I said good bye to Sabir and Waris and others, then got in the car with Mr. Fierstein. As we headed out the gate, the Pakistani driver called to the consulate that we were on our way.

This is when the sense of relief became complete. I knew it was for real! Mark went in another vehicle. When we got to the consulate, I was delighted to see Uncle Ed Rasmussen. He gave me a big hug. Mark was documenting everything with pictures!

"What would you like to eat most, now that you're free?" Mr. Fierstein asked.

THE UPPER HAND

"Some *gajar halwa*, carrot dessert," I replied.

Inside we waited for news that the US embassy plane from Islamabad was ready for a return trip. Mark was on the phone.

"Do you want to talk to your family?" he asked.

I sure did! What a joy to speak to each one assembled in Islamabad, waiting for my arrival.

Mrs. Fierstein shared some chocolate chip cookies. Then we were off to the airport. It was amazing to walk out on the tarmac and climb up into the little plane with Uncle Ed and Mark. There was the pilot and two other men in addition to the three of us. One of the men wanted to ask questions, so we talked most of the trip to Islamabad. Another of the men gave me a soft drink in a can and a bag of chocolate coated peanuts!

Mark was taking pictures again as we got off the plane in Islamabad and went to the special waiting room. There were Mom, Dad, Tim, Karli, Paul, Sarah, Philippa (whom I was seeing for the first time), as well as Auntie Barb Rasmussen, and a representative from the US Embassy. There were tears in Sarah's and Mom's eyes. I held four-month-old Pip (Philippa).

The first stop was the US Embassy for a visit to the Embassy doctor. He did a checkup and found nothing particularly wrong. He suggested stool tests for parasites and a TB skin test.

Then we went to Mark's for a family celebration--some delicious food and a time of praise to God.

I stopped by my house briefly and then we were off in the family VW micro bus to Qalandarabad, the village where Dad and Mom work in a small mission hospital. The trip provided a good time to talk and share in between Pippa's crying!

We arrived about 10 p.m. The Cutherell boys heard us pull in and came out to give a warm welcome. Their family lived next to us. A welcome sign from the Condie's was on the door. The Condies were some other neighbors.

I was home again, just like I had dreamed so many times in Afghanistan! Now life often seems so normal that my six months in Afghanistan seem like a mere imagination. Was it time wasted? Six months of intense work for Mark and his collegues, fervent prayers of many friends, and my eager longing. No, it was not wasted time. God, who has

R e l e a s e d

the upper hand, was working out His good plan. Some of His good
purposes are even evident now, as the following pages show.

A letter from Joel's brother, Phil:
"We hear that you are to be released in about three hours from now!!
That is so incredible yet such an appropriate answer to all of our prayers!
We are trying desperately not to get too excited, knowing that even now
things can go wrong. Yet we are praying fervently that the Lord will be
merciful and bring you to us. And we know that his program is the best
and most perfect."

Mark and Cindy wrote to co-workers:
"We are extremely grateful to God that He has enabled our friend, Joel,
to be freed today after six months of captivity in Afghanistan. *KhudA
mehrabAn As*! (God is merciful!) TO GOD BE THE GLORY!
Joel has many new friends in the area. He is healthy, in great spirits,
and is now visiting with his family in Pakistan. This is a day of rejoicing
for all.

"...from the Lord comes deliverance." Psalms 3:1-8

The last six months of 1991 were, without a doubt, the most trying,
challenging, exhausting, and frustrating half year of our lives as we worked
daily on efforts to monitor Joel's and Dr. Lewis' whereabouts, and to obtain
their release. We saw multiple efforts to free our friends come close to
success, only to be thwarted by some last-minute glitch.
Throughout this situation God has preserved and greatly strengthened
Dr. Lewis and Joel and their families. He has also done the same for our
family. We have been humbled at the whole-hearted and self-sacrificing
support we have received from the entire organization. The efficiency has
also been amazing.
At an extremely low moment two nights ago, I told Cindy that I did
not think I could bear another day of living constantly with this crisis.
(That was not the first time I had come to such a conclusion.) But in His
greatness, He preserved us all.

233

THE UPPER HAND

Certainly all of us involved in the crisis have been tempered through the flames of 1991. But faithfully the Lord has not allowed us to be tempted beyond what we could bear. He has provided a way to escape, that we might be able to bear it."

2. EPILOGUE

After my release, I spent about a week at home in Qalandarabad. Then I went to Islamabad to begin work on regularizing my official papers. During my stay in Afghanistan, my residential permit had expired.

Friends at the US embassy kindly helped me to explain my extenuating circumstances to the concerned Pakistani officials. And I encountered no real difficulties--except that the whole process took longer than I had hoped! I finally got a visa to leave and re-enter Pakistan on February 12. The next day I bought my ticket, and the following day, I flew out of Islamabad for Philadelphia!

Before leaving for the States, I had many opportunities to tell of God's goodness to me. Special thanksgiving services were held in Qalandarabad, Peshawar, and Islamabad. Opportunities like this continued during my time in the US, and even since my return to Pakistan in May, 1992. I was able to keep the promise I made to God in Afghanistan. In the words of the Psalmist, I had told God:

> *"How much longer, Lord, will you just look on?*
> *Rescue me from their attacks;*
> *save my life from these lions!*
>
> *Then I will thank you in the assembly of your people;*
> *I will praise you before them all."* (Psalms 35:17-18)

I was glad to spend time with several of the US embassy people who had been involved in working for my release. It was special to visit

THE UPPER HAND

Ambassador Nicholas Platt, and thank him for his concern and work. Mark and I also visited some of the key helpers from different agencies in Peshawar.

I was amazed and humbled as I began to realize how many people had been working and praying for my freedom. Mark's thick "hostage log" detailed the story of each day's efforts--meetings, phone calls, reports, visits, trips, etc. Many friends, and many people I didn't know sent expressions of joy at my freedom. Praise belongs to God for His gracious answers to prayer and His wonderful ways.

Here are some updates on people who were involved in Afghanistan:

Doc Bill Lewis

I visited Doc at his home in Texas in March, 1992, where I also met his wife and three of his children. We had a lot of catching up to do! I got the story of Doc's release and trip out of Afghanistan. There is a closeness between us that we can't explain.

Doc was healthy. He was not bitter at all. He wrote recently, "I think about you and Afghanistan (the people there) so much...I, too, want to go back but probably won't live long enough...I can visualize my mountain home and the inhabitants. Praise God for His glory and goodness in all things!!!"

Engineer Kabir

He was selected by Global Partners as the coordinator for the Animal Health Project. In June, 1992, Mark and I visited Quetta. There we had a de-briefing time with Engineer Kabir. He left for Afghanistan soon after our meeting . Now he manages a business in his home town. We still keep in touch.

Muallim Hamid

He was the soldier who took me to his home in Kunagh for one night. He came out of Afghanistan in December, 1992, and is now working in Quetta. He reported that the base where I was kept was totally destroyed in an attack by Hizb-i Wahdat in 1993. Five or six were killed.

Epilogue

Mullah Ali Reza

This leader under the Akhund had been kind and helpful to me. He is one of the ones who was killed in the fighting in 1993.

Abdul Hassan

He was the soldier who studied English with me, and later invited me to his home. He was killed in a motorcycle accident shortly after I left Patu. He had only been married a matter of days when this happened.

Bostan Ali

He was my close friend, the cook at the base. I heard that he is working as a farmer. He has a son now. I have sent him letters.

Akhund Salim

He was my captor. He was defeated and forced out of Jaghori along with Commander Wasim in the early part of 1993. Now Hizb-i Wahdat maintains sole, though not quite comprehensive, control of Jaghori.

I have kept in touch with others I met in Afghanistan at this time. A number of them have come to visit in Islamabad. One is a student now at the ESL Centre where I teach English!

Results of the hostage experience? Foreign aid organizations still find this area difficult to work in because of the security situation. Thankfully, neither my health, nor my ability to continue work in Pakistan was adversely affected because of my time in Afghanistan. I have no anger in my heart for the people of Jaghori. I would dearly like to return some day to visit friends, but the situation there, like most of rural Afghanistan, is still unstable because of the lack of a strong, just central government. I know God loves the people of Afghanistan. His heart is touched with their grief. I pray that His kingdom will come and His will be done among them. I believe this is happening, and the momentum is increasing. Yes, we can see God's hand in our lives. But how much more His upper hand is evident in the events of history.

3. APPENDIX

WRITINGS FROM PATU

I wrote all of the things in this section while I was in the soldier's base in Patu, Jaghori, Afghanistan.

A. Our Troubles Seem Grievous at the Moment

When I'm free again, my months of captivity will seem like a dream. They will seem to have gone by quickly and easily. It may be easy for me to be proud of my experience and to think that I have great strength.

But, LORD, let me not forget the weakness I feel now. The helplessness. How often I've cried to you for deliverance. How often I've been at the end of my rope. How weak I am--so much controlled by emotions, rather than by confidence in you. One moment I'm up and the next I'm down.

How often bitterness has overwhelmed me. "How can they be so evil and not care for God or principles?" How often I've felt that everyone's against me. I can't really trust anyone. None of them really care about injustice.

Then how often I've been humbled by kindnesses or God's special touch. A gift. Good food. An outing. An encouraging word. A

THE UPPER HAND

sympathetic ear. God has made a truth, a verse, or a line of a song meaningful. I've grabbed on to it.

How often I've been totally wrapped up in my difficulties. Then God has let me see that I have it better than many. There are other forms of imprisonment and torture. Others don't know God's fatherly presence. I have a hope in God that I will be released some time. I have family and friends.

I've known release and joy by praising God, by looking to Him, by praying for friends, by praying for this land and those in deep trouble. My perspective has been re-adjusted. My confidence renewed that God is in charge and that He is good!

What have been the difficult parts of this ordeal?

One great pain in my heart is the EVIL of my situation. How can anyone kidnap a person for money? And everyone seems to go along with it! It's all done by a religious leader who says his prayers, is a "hospitable" Afghan, claims to be part of the Islamic revolution, and has an Islamic party. It's inhumane. And it was perpetrated in a cowardly, deceitful way. We were taken by force of weapons--without prior discussion. Soon after our capture, the leader met us and outright asked for money--threatening us with physical persecution, surrender to Kabul, long imprisonment, and even death. Then, hypocritically, he keeps asking about my welfare. Whenever he's around, the wounds become raw again. I prefer being away from him and I have to ask God for love for him, a right attitude, and a guard before my mouth. Discussion or reasoning with him is useless. Once he said that, according to the Jafari school of Islamic law, he will get merit for taking me captive. He has accused me of being a spy, helping atheists (local "Communists"), not caring for the poor, not having permission to enter the country, etc. But I know these accusations are all just a smoke screen. He's really just after wealth and power. I just happen to be a convenient means to this end.

One of the hardest things has been WAITING in uncertainty. Hope springs eternal in the mortal breast. From day one we thought the next day might bring release. "Hope deferred makes the heart sick." Hopes kept being built and kept being dashed. Day followed monotonous day. Some changes seemed to be for the worse. Some for the better.

APPENDIX -- *Our Troubles Seem Grevious*

Everyday--and many times during the day--I have cried to God for deliverance. Thankfully some days have passed so pleasantly that I had hardly a pain in my heart from being a captive. How many times have I cried, "LORD, how can I last another day?!'"? Especially after a new change and disruption, or after one attempt for release brought my hopes crashing down.

Being CONFINED has been hard. I've always been free and loved being alone and outside. Being locked up in a room was a great psychological blow. Having to bang on the door to go to the bathroom--sometimes when no one was outside--was humiliating. Having kids lock me in, and tell me where I could and couldn't go was offensive to my pride. I often felt like a caged tiger pacing back and forth. Anger would well up inside of me.

Then, when I got used to being outside, these words were hard to hear: "There are no men around today, so we'll have to lock you up." One day Dilkha went away visiting. She took with her the only key to the lock of my room. Confined in this way, boredom was a real problem. The days seem to stretch on and on.

I have often felt LONELY. Doc and I were together for 18 days. When I saw that we were being separated, my heart sank. After that there was no one to speak English with, to share with, or to pray with. Sometimes I felt like everyone was against me and I could trust no one. There was no one to encourage me in the Lord. I especially feel lonely when the Akhund is around and all the others are playing up to him. Or when a group of new soldiers is here. Or when everyone is speaking about war or topics I'm not interested in. And I can't escape this or go outside. At first I found it hard to sleep among the soldiers.

Minor difficulties in life included parasites. I've had stomach trouble five or six times. Fleas, bed bugs, ticks, lice, and flies all seemed to be in abundance at different times. It was hard not having toilet paper and being far from water when I had to use the bathroom. In the second day, or so, of captivity, it was a treat to receive a toothbrush along with toothpaste and soap. At the base, food is very simple. Sometimes not much to look forward to! Also sleeping facilities for a long time were uncertain and covering was sparse. Not being able to bathe or wash clothes often was hard. Also, not having my own room or space was hard at times.

241

B. BLESSINGS

My ordeal here has been agonizing, yes, but not without blessings. When I think of these, I'm overwhelmed.

I am a student of languages and cultures of this area. Afghanistan has long held a fascination for me, and now I have had a chance to live here for over five months! I have always been interested in the life of the common people, and this is what I have been able to observe closely now. My time here has allowed me to observe the language and culture closely. I've made a dictionary and taken cultural notes.

When I think of my busy life in Islamabad, this has been a break! No phone calls, door bells, lists of things to do, and running around. A break from the constant giving in discipleship and a chance to be renewed myself! I've spent much time in prayer, praise, reflection, and memorization of scripture. I've gained a new perspective, new insights, and new experiences which, I trust, God will use for the rest of my days. I'll look back on this, maybe, like I look back on the things I learned from my hepatitis experience.

I remember back to the time I had hepatitis in 1983. Some aspects are similar to my present situation. I didn't know when it would end. I had a tendency to depression. I kept crying to the Lord. Yet God used this to deliver me from my struggle of doubt and unbelief. He enabled me to work for a year, be discipled, and be guided to my next place of service. I trust the ordeal I face now will have pleasant fruits. Maybe God will use it to guide me. This shake-up in my life may be God's way of delivering me from the ordinary and leading me on to the next place.

I've gone to bed early almost every night and risen every morning at the first light of dawn. Could this set a good precedent for my daily schedule from here on? I've had plenty of good, simple food. I've missed the fancies and sweets, but maybe they haven't missed me!

THE UPPER HAND

The weather has been unbelievable. Clear almost every day with nice, cool temperatures. And the surroundings are strikingly beautiful. I couldn't have asked for a more beautiful prison.

God has blessed me with overall excellent health. I have had occasional stomach trouble. And I need to see the dentist soon after I'm freed. However, for the most part, I've been physically up to every challenge, test, and opportunity--even long mountain walks.

With God's help, I've been able to adjust to the different schedules, settings, and demands. I've always been able to carve out a prayer time. Always been able to exercise. And I've been able to walk and sing at each place.

I've not experienced physical abuse, torture, hunger, or sleeplessness. The closest thing to torture was the time when Doc and I were cooped up in one room for six days--only going out to use the bathroom.

Most people have been very kind and sympathetic to me. This feeling of their sympathy has often lifted my spirits. Gifts, invitations, and activities seemed to come at just the right times to keep me from depression or self-occupation.

I can think of ways God has prepared me for this ordeal. He has given me a love for this land and people. I've worked with refugees for the past eight years. I'm used to a simple life and simple food (I usually slept on the floor in Islamabad). I'm somewhat of a loner, so I don't miss companionship in an extreme way. I'm "laid back", so I'm not as emotional or prone to ups and downs as I could be. My solid family and my wealth of spiritual teaching has helped me to stand and witness. And my past experiences have taught me a little of waiting on the Lord.

Furthermore, kids have been a great distraction and blessing. They've brought cheer to many hours. They've been my language teachers, sympathizers, and students.

I have been fortunate to get letters and packages from Engineer Kabir and from home. Since August, I have received letters from Pakistan about once a month! I've had several visits from friends who were trying to help with my release.

I know that I have had fewer temptations in some areas. I've had less stimulus to evil thoughts and less chances to over eat.

244

APPENDIX -- Blessings

Lastly, I've had the opportunity and motivation to do some writing, studying, and reading.

D. LESSONS

Sometimes lessons learned from experience are not describable, or not even realized. As I have thought over my time in Afghanistan, I wrote down these 10 things that were evident to me.

1.   I understand refugees and prisoners better. I learned more of the value and joy of freedom. I experienced being in a situation for a long time when I just wanted to escape! I will treat refugees in this light--always seeking their best interests and understanding their frustration at not being able to go home and waiting for something better. I didn't appreciate offers of staying on here to teach as a captive. Probably my refugee friends in Pakistan don't appreciate me planning too much for them in Pakistan when they have their hearts set on escape. I don't want to act like I'm holding them back selfishly from going west. I need to have higher, purer motives.

2.   I learned a lot about waiting in uncertainty. If I let God supply grace and strength, and take one day at a time, I found that I can go on in good spirits. Too often I look to the future and get upset. How can I go on? I need to expect good things from God. Each move and each new place (in fact, each day!) had many good and unexpected things.

3.   I was forced to learn something about dealing with unscrupulous and evil people. I struggled with my attitude. I knew that I must hate sin but love the sinner. I knew I shouldn't give a foothold to bitterness, malice, and depression. I saw the value of continued prayer for God's blessing and guidance for my enemies. However, like the psalmist, I continually prayed for God's justice and intervention by salvation.

4.   I learned about my weaknesses. How weak my faith was in spite of my upbringing, my Bible studies, and my prior spiritual experience. I would go

247

so quickly from a spiritual high to a low. I struggled to conquer depression and bad attitudes. It was difficult to be alone.

5. I learned how to make a routine, and how that helps to pass time. I sometimes wake up with nothing to look forward to, but the routine helps. These are some of the activities I do or have done regularly: Exercises before breakfast. Quiet time after breakfast to think about God's Word and pray. Walking, singing, reading, studying, writing letters, working on farm activities, teaching English, taking a nap, carrying water, playing with kids, going to the spring, and working on language.

6. I learned of the problems of Afghanistan's poor. I saw the harsh economic and social realities close-up. As a result, I am closer to the Afghan people.

7. I learned about the value of singing and praise. I received continuous encouragement as I focused on God and the truths of His Word. I found that my attention was diverted from present problems.

8. In the same way, I learned the value of praying for others. I was encouraged as I thought of and prayed for others. I realized in a small way that there was a special ministry of intercession. I could use extra time to impact situations far away.

9. I was often impressed that God's love reaches us EVERYWHERE. God sends encouragement at the right time, usually in unanticipated ways. My zipper, my buttons, a new belt, gifts, letters, kindnesses, etc. God encouraged me so many times by helping me see He was there and He cared.

10. I learned about the importance of living DAY TO DAY. Wherever I am, I can choose to make the best of my circumstances. I shouldn't always be wishing for something else, or worrying about the future. I noted all the lines from songs and verses from the Bible that spoke of God's daily sufficiency. I thought of Elijah and the crows, manna in the wilderness,

APPENDIX -- *Lessons*

"*Give us this day our daily bread*", "*As thy days, thy strength shall be in measure*", and so on. God proved His ability to supply my daily needs.

E.

IN HIS TIME

God's Sovereignty in Time

We know that God is sovereign--that He controls everything in the universe. Not only does He control what comes into our lives and how it comes, but He also controls the "when". We as creatures will never know all the timings of the Creator. Often our ideas of time are in conflict with God's.

For example, in my present ordeal I pray at least several times each day for deliverance and freedom. Has God not heard me? For a week or 10 days before this date, I felt like I should pray for freedom by November 15 because I thought it would give me time to be involved in Christmas activities in Islamabad. That date came and went. I'm learning about God's timetable!

I have thought much on two examples in the Bible of God's deliverance. These are Joseph in prison and the Israelites in Egypt. Joseph's words to his brothers are precious to many of us, I think. "You meant it for evil, but God meant it for good." Time had taught Joseph a lesson of God's goodness and sovereignty.

Joseph encountered a chain of injustices which people around us would call "bad luck". His brothers sold him to traders going to Egypt. He was falsely accused in Potiphar's house and ended up in prison. He was forgotten there by the cup bearer whom he had helped.

THE UPPER HAND

What a sad and tragic story! But this wasn't all. The Bible records that God was with Joseph both in Potiphar's house and in prison. Why didn't God deliver Joseph sooner? Imagine Joseph waiting for help from the cup bearer after he was freed. Two years went by. Probably, like me, Joseph prayed several times daily to the God of his fathers for deliverance.

God had a timetable. At the right time His good purpose was seen. His goodness and justice were vindicated. The good that resulted--Joseph's exaltation to the prime ministership of Egypt and the deliverance of God's chosen people from death in a famine--was far greater than the human mind could have imagined.

We would describe Joseph's time in prison as "wasted". Yet in God's eyes this was necessary preparation time for what lay ahead. We see Joseph making the best of each situation. Sure, there were depressing times. But we get the impression that Joseph didn't mope around in deep despondence. He had faith in God which gave him energy and hope. Not only did Joseph take advantage of opportunities, but he managed to escape from these negative situations without bitterness. We see no evidence of malice toward Egypt or the Egyptians. And we read of his tears, forgiveness, and deep affection for the brothers who had so wronged him.

The next example of deliverance in God's time comes from Exodus--the Children of Israel in Egypt. Remember the verse where God, speaking to Moses, said that He had heard the cries of His people from bondage and that He now had come to deliver them? Our God hears, cares and acts in response to our cries! But did He do it in a lightning flash? No! He had His time and His way. Things got worse before they got better. No straw for bricks. Anger at Moses and Aaron. Why the 10 plagues? Why the hardening of Pharaoh's heart? Why did Pharaoh's army pursue the Israelites after they left?

The answers to these questions only become clear later. Israel was forced to turn to the God of their fathers. All other apparent sources of help had dried up. God wanted to turn an impossible situation into a dynamic and unforgettable demonstration of His power, sovereignty, and saving character. This demonstration worked beyond any possible human speculation. Israel would always remember this miraculous victory. The nations heard and trembled. God received great glory.

In this example, however, we learn lessons from the human failures of our subject, Israel. Time and again, we see unbelief. We see their conflict of time and method with God's. "Why did you come to make our work harsher?" "Why have you led us to death?" "It was better back in Egypt!" Here we see God's sovereign love. He saved His people in spite of their disbelief. He received glory anyway.

The Old Testament has some more examples of God's sovereignty in the frame of time. Job's patience and faith were severely tried--and, in the end, broken. But God mercifully answered and restored. God showed His goodness in time, but not all of His purpose.

Abraham waited for God's promise of a son and heir. Often he lapsed into unbelief: Hagar, laughing, Egypt. Yet ultimately we remember him for his faith. He is the father of all who believe in God. At a hundred years of age, he received God's promise, and later obeyed God's command to offer Isaac as a sacrifice, believing that God could raise him to life later. God's timing for Abraham was hard, yet so good.

In Judges we see the cycle of oppression, deliverance, and then return to sin. It's God's nature and covenant responsibility to save His people. But the time and way are His alone to decide. The jawbone of an ass. Three hundred men. A lefty. A woman. And all in the right time.

Samuel was late. And Saul couldn't wait. So he went ahead and did the sacrifice himself. When Samuel came, he told Saul that the kingdom would be given to another. To obey is better than sacrifice.

David was anointed by Samuel to be the king of all Israel. He didn't try to rush God, remember? He wouldn't lay his hands on God's anointed. And

THE UPPER HAND

he waited for 11 years, as the king of Judah, before all of Israel came under his reign. He wrote from experience, "My soul, wait upon the LORD only". "I waited patiently for the LORD, and He inclined His ear to me". "They that wait upon the LORD shall renew their strength".

God reminded David in Psalm 73 not to fret at the prosperity of the wicked. Why? Because there is justice in the end. In God's time. David had come to appreciate God's sovereign timing. He was a man after God's heart.

Solomon wrote of a time for everything. In Esther, we read of God's arrangements to save his people again from annihilation. Mordecai exhorted Esther that she had been made queen "for such a time as this". In spite of Jonah's original disobedience, Ninevah repented in time and escaped God's wrath. Habakkuk testifies of his learning to trust God's goodness and timing in spite of situations that didn't seem to make good sense. In the end, he rejoiced in the God of his salvation in all circumstances. Why? Because God would perform His good purpose in His good time.

God promised a savior to Adam. This promise became clearer and clearer as it was reiterated to the patriarchs and prophets. But all God's people in Old Testament days waited for the deliverer--not knowing when He would come. Even Daniel, who predicted the exact time of his coming, didn't understand exactly what was revealed to him. Throughout centuries believers kept longing, expecting, and agonizing.

Then, "*when the fullness of time had come, God sent His son.*" Everyone was surprised at God's way and time. But in retrospect, we can see how good it was. The Roman Empire, the census, the destruction of Jerusalem in 70 A.D., the star, and the wise men.

Jesus' whole life and ministry was marked with an understanding and realization of God's sovereign timetable. There was no conflict. "*Not a blast of hurry*" is seen in the gospel accounts. Many a time Jesus said, "*My time has not yet come*". Then, in the events surrounding his death, he said,

254

APPENDIX -- *In His Time*

"The hour has come", and He calmly faced the cross with its untellable agonies.

Jesus taught his followers not to worry for tomorrow. Trust in the God who takes such good care of lilies and sparrows, he taught. He slept in the boat during the storm until His students, frantic in their desperation, woke Him. *"Teacher, don't you care that we're perishing?"* He rebuked their unbelief and their misunderstanding of God's program. Then He sovereignly demonstrated His power over nature. Jesus told a story of a persistent widow and a judge--the lesson being that men ought always to pray and not to faint.

After His resurrection, Jesus told His followers to wait in Jerusalem for the Holy Spirit. When asked about His return, He said, *"No man knows the day or the hour."* And so we wait for God's perfect time for Christ's return and the end of the age.

Our waiting, however, is not illogical or vain, contrary to the current thought around us. Peter encourages us. *"One day with the LORD is as a thousand years, and a thousand years as a day"*. God is not slow about fulfilling His promise--as we have seen before in Joseph's freedom, Israel's deliverance, and the coming of the Savior.

Paul speaks of patience as one of the fruits of the Spirit. We must be like farmers, patiently waiting for the harvest. *"Be not weary in well doing for in due season you will reap, if you don't faint."* Paul himself waited for years in different prisons. He kept himself busy writing, praying, witnessing, and planning. He had a deep conviction that God's time and plan were best.

Jesus is the Alpha and Omega, the beginning and the end. He is the Lord of all time. His return will mark the end of time and the continuation of eternity. God is above and outside of our time frame. The eternal God is our refuge.

THE UPPER HAND

So, in a world where the common sense is that "waiting is worse than death" and where human reason demands preeminent control, the child of God must stand against the tide and proclaim a sovereign God whose purposes, ways, and times are higher than our reason and better than our furthest imaginations. Let us constantly abide in the vine that our desires, acts and thoughts might be more like God's; and that our view of time would grow more and more to synchronize with His sovereign and good timetable.

Some lessons condensed:

1. God is always good--whether it seems so at the moment or not.
2. God has promised to deliver his people, but the manner and time are His alone to control.
3. God works according to His overall plan of the ages. This plan is governed by His love and character for the highest good of all men.
4. God's plan is beyond the confines of human reason and may, at times, go against our logic.
5. Difficulties and trials will surely come.
6. In difficulties, we are called on to:
   a. Be active and make the best of each situation--not just wishing for a way out.
   b. Wait on God and develop patience.
   c. Pray without growing weary for our deliverance, but, beyond this, for God's greater glory and the furtherance of His good plan.
   d. Guard against the root of bitterness, complaining, self-pity, self-preoccupation, self-reliance, and envy-- which all stem from unbelief.
7. We must constantly reevaluate our concepts of "time-well-spent" and "time wasted" in the light of God's Word.
8. Judgment comes to the wicked and reward to the righteous in God's time.

APPENDIX -- *In His Time*

After finishing the first page of this essay, I headed back from my rocky "office" to the kitchen of the military base for lunch. I glanced up and noticed two men coming down the path from a saddle going to the next valley. I paid no attention. Soldiers are always coming and going.

When they reached the kitchen at exactly the same time as I did, I recognized them. They brought me eight books, 22 letters, a sewing kit, and a shawl. One of the books was a BIBLE, which I hadn't been able to read for four and a half months. That morning I had just thought that I'd have to borrow a needle and thread to mend my shirt. Not only did the little kit have a needle and thread, it even had a button that I needed!

The news these friends brought and their consultation with my captor, who "happened" to be there, were like the first ray of light at the end of a tunnel. Hope was born in a new way--in God's good time.

November 18, 1991
Patu Base, Jaghori
Ghazni, Afghanistan

God Has the Upper Hand

Joel DeHart, 1991

God has the upper hand, no matter what the plans of man.
He rules and reigns above, and does His will.
Just trust His sovereignty, and you'll not discouraged be,
But live each day with joy, and worship Him.

Glossary

aghil -- a small settlement, village
ahoor -- an irrigation pond
akhund -- a Muslim religious leader
chadar -- a men's warm shawl
chai -- tea
chob josh -- a kind of fried, crisp bread
gilam -- a woven wool rug
gulkho -- the kitchen hearth area
halwa -- a sweet dessert made from wheat, etc.
Hazaragi -- the Persian dialect of the Hazara people
jaba -- a rocky knoll, outcropping
karez -- a horizontal tunnel to a water source
kinar aoo -- bathroom
lobia -- kidney beans
minbar -- a Shia mosque
nan -- local bread
nan boota -- a dish of hard bread soaked in buttermilk and butter
naswar -- ground tobacco put between the lip and gum, snuff
qurti -- a dish of regular bread soaked in buttermilk and butter
Sayyid -- one claiming to be a decendent of the Arabian prophet
sheer brinj -- rice cooked in milk
shola -- Chinese Communist
shorwa -- meat broth in which bread is broken up
toot -- mulberry
zeek-o yuk -- a Chinese antiaircraft gun

Rural Jaghori

Rural Afghanistan is full of rustic charm,
but it's not an easy life.

Colorful, hard-working and friendly,
*the **Hazara** people live in the central part of Afghanistan.*

Aoo spee, buttermilk, is a wonderful thirst quencher!
The people share what they have so generously.

Karezes
*or underground channels
make life and farming possible
in this land
where there is so little rainfall.
It's some of the best water
anywhere.*

*The caretaker of the local **minbar**, mosque,
collects brush from the mountainside
to burn during the long, snowy winter.*

Animal Health Project

Doc examines a sheep on the way into Afghanistan and watches a team of vaaccinators.

The Commander's House

*In the commander's house with his son, Reza,
who had meningitis, and some of my other best friends!
The walls are painted mud plaster.*

This is the kind, educated Khan and his wife from Mastak.
Their ancient fortress was visible from my windows
at the commander's house.

The Soldier's Base

My office #2, where I'm sitting below,
can be seen in the circle above.
Also the soldier's room (A), the commander's office (B),
and my walking trail(C).

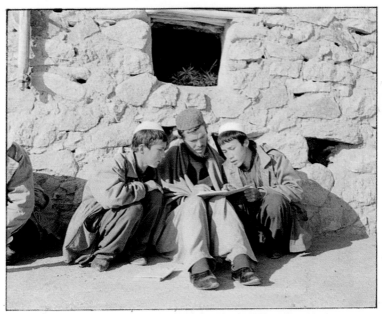

On the roof with my two keen English disciples.

*Some of the soldiers celebrating Christmas three days early
with the Christmas cake Engineer Kabir sent!
Notice the orange and red **gilim**.*

Free!
January 4, 1992
with my parents and Mark Morris in Islamabad.

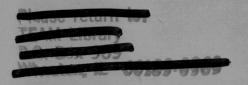